King of Algonquin Park

Joseph Emmett Chartrand

(Photo by Nelson Lindsay)

King of Algonquin Park

Paton Lodge Lindsay

GSPH

GENERAL STORE PUBLISHING HOUSE INC.

499 O'Brien Road, Renfrew, Ontario, Canada K7V 3Z3
Telephone 1.613.432.7697 or 1.800.465.6072

http://www.gsph.com

ISBN 978-1-77123-035-3

Copyright © Paton Lodge Lindsay 2013

Cover photo: Nelson Lindsay
Cover painting: Paton Lodge Lindsay
Cover art, design: Magdalene Carson

Printed by Image Digital Printing Ltd.
dba The IDP Group, Renfrew, Ontario
Printed and bound in Canada

Cataloguing data available at Library and Archives Canada

This book is dedicated to
Joseph Emmett Chartrand
December 5, 1914–September 14, 2000

The Last Voyageur . . .
The King of the Long Runners . . .
The King of Algonquin Park

Joseph Emmett Chartrand.
(Photo by Paton Lodge Lindsay)

It is in listening to the stories of the old people that we learn
to appreciate our past, our ancestors, and our history.
To know the paths they chose to blaze in the past
will help us understand the paths we choose to blaze
in the future as we endeavour to preserve our heritage.

*What went ye out
into the wilderness to see?*
(St. Matthew 11:7)

Contents

Preface

The story *King of Algonquin Park* is based on actual happenings in the life of Joseph Emmett Chartrand as he personally related them to me over the years; and others as we experienced them together. To the best of my knowledge, his stories are true, based on his most excellent memory and that of my own now aging recollections. I have chosen to make use of some literary licence in the completion of the story.

This story was written purely to share the history and the life and times of an absolutely extraordinary wilderness man, and the struggles and hardships he suffered and endured merely to survive. It is very sad to realize he might well be the last of his kind to know real wilderness survival skills first-hand. Joseph Emmett Chartrand had a tremendous impact upon the lives of most of the people with whom he came in contact. It has been said by men that he was "an icon of what a real man was and should be."

I have made every attempt to credit my sources and to acquire permission in writing where required, for the materials used herein. In the cases where after several attempts no response appeared to be forthcoming, I used the material and credited the source.

Thank you to all my friends who saved the letters from the wilderness and suggested these experiences be saved between two covers for the enjoyment of others in the future. I thank my husband, Keith, who sat by my side night after night and burned the midnight oil into the wee hours of the morning for months. I don't know what I did to deserve him but I'm certainly very glad I did it; to my sister Suzanne, whose excitement and energy has always spurred me on through the tough times in life; to my brother Roderick whose so many successes in life made me strive to reach my goal; to my parents, Kathleen D. Scarlett and W/C Harry Arthur Lodge Lindsay, who taught me to strive, to persevere, and to never be satisfied with anything less than my best effort; and to the many friends who shared my life with the King of Algonquin Park.

I don't really know how to thank the staff of General Store Publishing House: Tim Gordon, publisher; Jane Karchmar, senior editor; and Mag Carson, art director, for their encouragement, assistance, expertise, and professionalism. Tim, I truly thank you for giving me the opportunity to reach up and grab hold of the bottom rung of a very long ladder and hopefully climb to become one of the "new, fresh authors to join the formidable roster" of General Store Publishing House.

I extend thanks to the *North Shore Sentinel* for previously publishing some of these short stories, and the Ontario Arts Council for their validation and financial support to complete the project. A very special recognition is due my cousin, Nelson Lindsay, for capturing the wonderful portrait of "The King" selected for use on the cover of *King of Algonquin Park*.

Most important, I thank the King himself, Joseph Emmett Chartrand, for the love he shared with me and for the knowledge he imparted. He taught me to observe and to listen; to see, to hear, to smell, to feel, and to CARE about my environment and to be aware that I was but one of many reciprocal partners living within my surroundings. He made me recognize that none of the things that were really important in Life could be bought; they had to be earned. Among the myriad of wonderful thoughts gleaned from his most magnificent mind I learned that, "Not taking chances in life is like being born dead and waiting a lifetime to be buried." Emmett, I thank you.

Paton Lodge Lindsay

Prologue

The King of Algonquin Park . . . who was he? Let us begin at the beginning, with the beginning of Nouvelle France and with the beginning of the French fur trade. In the sixteenth century, the explorers of many countries were out to claim new lands and the riches and resources to be found there. These resources were for the most part fisheries, forests, and furs.

During the period 1589 to 1610, we find Henry IV sitting on the throne as King of France. He was without doubt one of the most advanced and popular of the French kings, showing considerable concern for his subjects and an unusual religious tolerance for the times. He guaranteed religious liberties to Protestants, offered enlightenment, education, and the arts to all people of every class; built the Palace Royale, and returned the capital city of France to true greatness. The vision of King Henry extended far beyond the shores of France. He financed several of the expeditions of Pierre Du Gua and Samuel de Champlain in their explorations of the new world as they sought the riches to be found in natural resources and new lands to colonize.

In 1603, Henry IV granted to Pierre Du Gua exclusive rights to all colonial lands in North America between forty degrees and sixty degrees north latitude. That was approximately all lands from Philadelphia on the south to Ungava Bay and central Hudson Bay on the north. The King also gave to Pierre Du Gua a monopoly of the furs on these lands and named him Lieutenant General of Acadia and New France. In exchange for these grants, Pierre Du Gua had to bring at least sixty French immigrants annually to populate the new French colony.

Samuel de Champlain suggested to the king that Trois–Rivières would be an excellent location to develop a new French colony. The following spring, Pierre Du Gua organized an expedition of some seventy-four settlers and left France with the royal cartographer, Samuel de Champlain, on board. As autumn approached, they formed a small settlement on Ile St. Croix in the Bay of Fundy; but ill-prepared for the very harsh winter, many of the settlers died of disease and the hardships of the severe weather. In the spring of 1605, the twenty-eight surviving settlers were moved to Port Royale, where they established a new colony.

There, the colonists were set upon by members of the Dutch West India Company, who ransacked the colony and pillaged their ships of ammunition, supplies, and furs. Following another extreme winter of frigid temperatures, deep snows, and the loss of their supplies, by spring only eight of the seventy-four original settlers had survived.

Pierre Du Gua then turned his colonization interests to Nouvelle France on the St. Lawrence River. He returned to France, but his cartographer, Samuel de Champlain, in 1608 started a new French colony at Quebec, thus establishing what is believed by many historians to be the first permanent French colony in North America.

In the spring of 1627, the king of France sent Michel Leneuf, a young provincial nobleman born in Caen, Normandy, France, in 1601, to investigate and to negotiate a trade alliance with the Aboriginals. He was in Canada at the same time as Jean Godefroy, who served as an interpreter for Samuel de Champlain. Michel Leneuf returned to France and suggested that the king establish a new colony at the site that would become known as Trois–Rivières. Although his heart was not in colonization, Leneuf did return to Canada. The Company of New France, also known as the Company of One Hundred Associates, by their charter had to settle Nouvelle France by bringing over 300 settlers per year. In 1634, the Company started to grant large tracts of land known as "seigneuries" to wealthy gentry and nobles in France on condition they bring settlers to populate the French colony. During the next several years, members of the French nobility and gentry, including Michel Leneuf, obtained large grants of land to colonize with French settlers. In 1667, there were only four noble, aristocratic families from France who had settled in Nouvelle France: de Tilly, de Repentigny, D'Ailleboust, and the Leneuf family.

The story of the King of Algonquin Park actually begins on a hot summer's day in the early afternoon of July 11, 1636, with the

Map of Nouvelle France.

(Courtesy of GNU Free Documentation, Licence Version 1.2)

creaking of pulleys and chains as the large, plank gangway was lowered from the side of a ship to the dock at Quebec. A crowd of excited immigrants from France waited on the deck to disembark. They waited in hopeful anticipation of a better life in a new world—one that would prove to be very different from the world they had left behind.

Among the many immigrants standing on the deck waiting to disembark that July day was the widow Jeanne Leneuf. She was the daughter of Lieutenant Gervais La Marchand, Sieur de Celloniere et La Rogue in France—reportedly carrying the very genes of Charlemagne in his veins—and his wife, Stevennote St. Germain. In December 1599, at Thury–Havort, Caen, Normandy, France, the young Jeanne La Marchand had married Mathieu Leneuf, Sieur du Hérisson. Now, thirty-six years later, she faced life as a widow in a new world; but she would not face that new life alone.

Her eldest son, Michel Leneuf, Sieur du Hérisson, had previously come to Nouvelle France on behalf of the king to negotiate a trade alliance with the Natives. Now, nine years later, and himself widowed, he had returned and stood on the deck of the ship with his mother at his side and his only daughter, Anne, then but four years old, in his arms. These new French colonists could never in their dreams have anticipated the hardships, horrors, and fears that awaited them.

Arriving in Nouvelle France that same day were Michel's sister Marie Leneuf, who later married Jean Godefroy, the interpreter for Samuel de Champlain; and Michel's younger brother Jacques Leneuf de la Poterie and his wife, Marguerite La Gardeur, the daughter of Rene La Gardeur, Sieur de Repentigny, and their two daughters, Anne and Marie Leneuf. Jacques Leneuf de la Poterie and Marguerite La Gardeur had a son, Michel Leneuf de Valleriere de Beaubassin, who was the captain, commandant, and Royal governor of Acadia.

Michel Leneuf du Hérisson, the father of young Anne, became one of the wealthiest landowners in Nouvelle France, at one point holding the deeds to over 800,000 acres of land. The Leneuf family and their Repentigny in-laws were the most illustrious family in Nouvelle France. Michel's four-year-old daughter, Anne Leneuf, grew up, and on November 24, 1649, she married Antoine Desrosiers at Trois–Rivières.

These earliest of French immigrants to Nouvelle France are entwined among the family roots of the paternal ancestors of the King of Algonquin Park. They were the founders of Nouvelle France and the founders of the fur trade in Canada. The French came to Canada for beaver. The king's family had trapped the beaver for nearly 400 years. There were beaver to be had and, according to the King of Algonquin Park, they were his by right of the king of France. This is some of his story — the story of The King of Algonquin Park.

This year of 2013, we celebrate the epic journey Samuel de Champlain made in 1613 up the Outaouais (Ottawa) River and his first contact with the Algonquin Anishinabeg Nation.

1

Morning

King of Algonqin Park.
(Painting by Paton Lodge Lindsay)

This is my Father's world
I rest me in the thought
Of rocks and trees.
Of skies and seas,
His hand these wonders wrought.[1]

From some distant time sector, a lonely, plaintive cry filtered through the depths of sleep to announce the dawn of a new day. My eyelids struggled against an unknown force that dared to hold them shut. I stretched the full length of the cot until cold nibbled at my toes. Quickly they recoiled to my warm body and in protest

I threw the folds of the arctic sleeping bag back around my shoulders. Once more, my eyes gave way to that involuntary force, and I sighed, "Just ten minutes more." Again, that eerie call from afar lured me from the peaceful depths. Nature surely seemed to be laughing at my comfort. She beckoned again and again. If you listened, She seemed to be calling, "Come-on-get-up; come-on-get-up." From mist-enshrouded ponds she laughed, ushering in the dawn of a new morn.

Mother Nature, too, must have heard the call as morning flickered a golden light up over the eastern hills. Along the shore, conifer damsels in their long green robes waltzed to and fro to the music of the spheres. A whispered breeze escorted the milky veil mantling this mural painted by the great architect of the universe. As Mother Nature exhaled, the mists lifted, and this masterpiece unveiled quiet black waters, mirrored lacy tamarack and hemlock, fluorescent poplar and birch, and maples hot with fire from a sun dripping flames to the waking earth. All of nature seemed to rise to the call. "Come-on-get-up, come-on-get-up."

A solitary sentinel paraded into each bay; in plumage of black and white, this primitive goddess rose to fan iridescent wings to the morn and become a lone ballerina on a stage of shining gold. Behold the beauty of the forest. Feel the presence of God. "God reveals His presence, Let us now adore Him, and with awe appear before Him."[2] Through silent lips slip the words,

> This is my Father's world,
> And to my listening ears,
> All Nature sings, and round me rings
> The music of the spheres.[3]

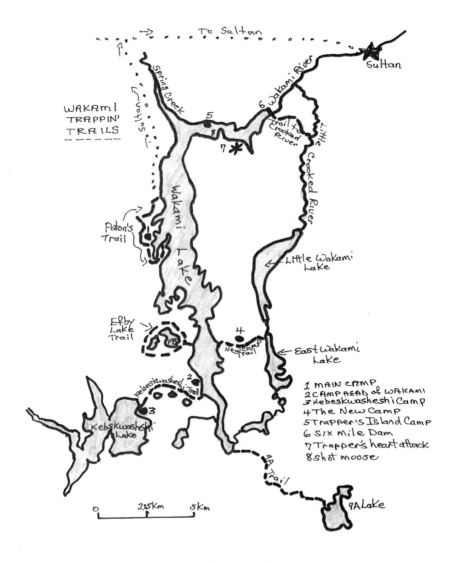

The Land Baron

2

Map of Wakami Lake.

He stood quietly looking out the small, four-pane window by the cabin door. Like an old land baron, he surveyed his kingdom. Decades of brilliant sunshine flashing on dancing waters and reflecting off windblown snows had chiselled crow's feet about the outer corners of his eyes.

"It's goin' to be a good day today."

"How can you tell?"

"It's not hard once you know the habits of the animals. You can learn a lot from them, you know, if you listen to them and you watch."

"I *have* learned a lot from the animals, but I wasn't aware they were experts in the field of meteorology."

"It's not only city-educated people who know things, you know." He tapped a gnarled index finger to his head, "I may be rough but I use this ole noggin for more than hanging my hat on. Get up. The stove is lit. I'll go and fetch some water."

Rising from beneath the warm down sleeping bag, I threw it aside and sat up on the edge of the cot. As my bare feet touched the old, hewn pine boards of the floor, cold stung my toes and tingled up my thighs. In mere seconds, I resembled a plucked duck. The cold continued to nibble its way up through my spine until I cringed and threw the down sleeping bag back about my shoulders once more in an effort to ward off this invader of the morning. The floor seemed to gnaw at my toes and virtually chew at my feet with each step as I tiptoed across the cabin floor. My teeth persisted in carrying on a somewhat singular conversation with themselves.

Finally, cold bit right into my kidneys. I was stranded. I didn't dare move. The muscles in my thighs tightened and my feet curled to avoid contact with the pine plank floor. In desperation, I slid already semi-frozen feet into a pair of oversized rubber boots and flew out the door to the wilderness relief station out back. So urgent was my plight that even the raspberry canes that grasped and tugged at my granny gown couldn't detain my flight. In a last desperate lunge, I plunged into the wee outhouse only to slide across the seat as bare butt hit the rough sawn boards covered in frost. I had made it. My entire self relaxed, and I sat alone in total quiet.

Thought pushed aside all preoccupation of the cold. He was my father's very best friend. We always just called him "Trapper." Somehow, in the wondrous puzzle of this universe, Life had seen fit to bring them together from the opposite ends of the earth. My father was born of an aristocratic Scottish family whose lineage was documented from Joshue, the Rama Theo, better known as Joseph of Arimathea, as well as from Julia, the sister of Julius Caesar. From Joshue there is a direct descent of nineteen generations to The Swan Knight, Lohengrin, and Supreme Knight of the Holy Grail. From Lohengrin's daughter Gwenalarch it directly descends through 1,500 years to my father. In my direct paternal line I was the first female child born in 1,000 years. My father spent the younger years of his life in the best boys' boarding schools in England and Australia, and travelling about the world. He was the first in many generations not to choose medicine but rather enrolled at the California Institute of Technology to study aeronautical engineering. He was six years old when his Lodge cousin Charles Lindbergh flew across the Atlantic. That was when Father knew that he, too, would be a pilot.

Trapper, it is rumoured, was born in a canoe in a snowstorm somewhere in the remote wilderness of Northern Ontario. He would be a true Canadienne, being a somewhat effusive fusion of Aboriginal, French, and Irish blood. Dad always said, "What a mixture, a keg of dynamite, a fuse, and a match."

Trapper's family had for many generations eked out sustenance from the wealth of furs and timber in the northern forests. Trapper had no formal education whatsoever. He often joked about having gone to school for three days but the teacher wasn't there. The unexpected death of his mother at an early age had forced him to work in the logging camps when a mere child of eight back in the 1920s. He said he soon learned that "one could fill a long pocket more quickly by trapping beaver at thirty-five dollars a pelt than by helping about the logging camp for six dollars a month." At the age of ten, Trapper had caught his first beaver. Some sixty years later, he was still at it and still living off the land and, to say the least, he was a man recognized as being exceptional in his field.

Trapper is a man of the last frontier. He is rough and rugged—something like a modern-day Jim Bridger. He is a man who lives in the wilderness side by side with the animals. His life depends on whether he outwits the animals or is outwitted by them. For Trapper, too, the law of the land is survival of the fittest. I have to wonder if he is the next species of the forest to be forced to give way to Time, to Progress, and to the whims of the public.

My morning ablutions completed, I returned down the narrow footpath to the camp, to find a sizzling griddle awaiting bush scones. Trapper never used a bowl to mix his dough. I mean, what trapper ever carries a mixing bowl through the bush? He had washed a pair of old jeans and cut one leg off at the knee and sewn it together along the bottom. Then he ran an old bootlace through the top of it, making a bag, into which he put flour, powdered milk, salt, baking powder, and, if affluent, a little sugar. Whenever he wanted to make scones, he simply opened the bag, made a well in the flour, and poured in some water retrieved from a nearby stream or lake. He then stirred up the flour mixture with a wooden paddle he had specially whittled for the purpose. All of the flour mixture that was moistened with the water would form into a ball that was then lifted from the bag. The remaining mixture stayed dry and was stored for future use. This method of carrying flour in the bush proved to be most advantageous, as when the bag became dampened by the weather, the inner flour become safely encased in a plaster cast, which preserved it for a lengthy time.

As Trapper picked some choice red pine knots from the woodpile and placed them into the wood stove, I dressed in long woollen underwear, three pairs of woollen knee socks, heavy Melton pants, and a checked doeskin shirt. Not in the least feminine, but as Trapper would say, "The squirrels don't give a damn how you look, so best you feel good."

Breakfast this morning was to consist of hot oatmeal, bush scones, and clear tea. While I finished dressing, Trapper quickly threw together the two cots so as to make room to sit down. We had to do things turn about because there wasn't any excess room in this small twelve-by-fourteen-foot log cabin. He often joked, "You damn near have to go outside to change your mind."

The little log trapper's cabin was built on the northeast shore of Wakami Lake in Chapleau country. It offered only the necessities of life: shelter and warmth. It had been built of Jack pine logs, chinked with sphagnum moss, and plastered with mud from a nearby swamp. As it was entirely constructed by hand, the timbers were short, and due to its size, there wasn't enough room to swing a pack onto your back. On each of the long walls was a small cot. Between them on a side wall was an improvised wash-stand with a metal bucket of cold lake water, an old chipped enamel washbasin, and a sardine tin for a soap dish. The soap had been recently chiselled about its edges by mice. On the opposite wall was a small pine table encircled by four hewn pine stumps, which together served as the dining area.

A great old cast-iron drive stove from an old logging camp served to furnish both heat and cooking facilities. Behind the wood stove was a dishevelled heap of boots, rubbers, and muk-luks. Above them, hung upon a row of spikes driven into the wall, was an array of well-worn and tattered old coats, some caps that had seen many a hard day, and a variety of woollen, leather, and fur mitts. Surrounding the boots on the floor were traps of all sizes: number two jump traps, number three coil spring, and number four-and-a-half long spring traps. A pile of one-fourteens, and Conibears in three sizes: 120s, 220s, and 330s. A bunch of bear traps hung from the ridgepole. Among ropes, chains, cables, wire, and snares hung about the walls, one also found axes, snowshoes, rifles, and an old Swede saw. Since we had just arrived the night before after travelling thirteen hours by truck and then a few miles by boat and canoe, everything was just stashed into any little nook or hook that would accommodate it.

The wood stove glowed red and crackled within. The water in the one-gallon coffee pot rolled about vigorously beneath curls of escaping steam. Very impolite and effusive sounds burped in the porridge pot. Breakfast was ready.

Trapper sat on a pine stool so that he could eye things out through the small, four-pane window that faced the lake. He pulled a rusty, old, fifty-pound lard tin up to the table and tapped on the lid. Without need of further invitation, Tracker jumped up and awaited his share of the upcoming vittles. Tracker was an abandoned pup left behind by hunters at the end of the hunt a few years back. He and Trapper had met along the trail one cold and stormy night when dark had come early. The two of them, tired, cold, and hungry, curled up together beneath a single blanket, the dog snuggling in close to Trapper, gaining warmth from his body heat. Together, they spent the night by a flickering fire and warded off hunger, frostbite, and possibly death. In the early hours of the morning, Tracker returned to the fire with a rabbit, which he laid at Trapper's feet. From then on, Trapper and Tracker would share everything equally.

"How can you tell about the weather, Trapper?"

"What?"

"The weather," I repeated. "You said earlier you could tell the weather by the animals. How do you do that?"

"Oh, that! That's not hard. You just watch the animals and see what they do. If the ducks and geese and water birds are all out in the open water, you know there is going to be good weather. When a blow comes, they all go back into the bays or little lakes until the storm blows out. Did you hear those owls calling last night? They are a good sign of the weather. If they are up on the hilltops calling, that is a sign of good weather. When an ill wind blows, they get hidden down in the swamps and hang tight until the storm blows out. Those loons this morning, they are like the ducks and geese. When you see loons out in the open water, it is a sign of good weather. When you find them all bunched up in the bays, you know you're in for bad blow. They'll soon be headin' outta here flyin' backwards."

"Flying backwards? I thought the hummingbird was the only bird that could fly backwards."

"You city folks all think you know so much. Shows you how much you don't know. Loons always fly backwards in the winter."

"Really? Not many people know that. Why do they fly backwards in the winter?"

"It keeps the snow outta their eyes!" He laughed, and with that, he drew the sleeve of his shirt across his mouth and moustache and pushed back off the stool onto the cot. He rooted about in a back pocket to remove an old trucker's wallet that was attached to his belt by a long brass chain. He set the wallet onto the corner of the table. The wallet was leather and tooled with deer and bear, moose and beaver. On the reverse was an otter, a mink, and a marten, and in bold letters, his name, Emmett Joseph

Chartrand. I commented on the beauty of the wallet. It must have been custom made. I had seen wallets with initials on them, but his name was spelled out in full.

"Who made that wallet for you, Trapper?" I asked.

"An old friend made it for me a long, long time ago."

"Why do you have your whole name on it?"

"I told you before, I never went to school. I don't write much and I read only a little. I tried to learn how to read when I was a kid, but my father would beat me for wasting my time. The old man said a working man didn't need to read; a working man didn't have *time* to read. So now if someone asks me how to spell my name, I just show him my wallet."

Let it be known that over time there was not a Louis L'amour or a Zane Grey Western he had not read. Trapper became an insatiable reader; and, as for his self-learned ability with numbers, there was not a fur buyer alive who could cheat him out of a miniscule dollar. If one tried, I guarantee you he would wish he weren't alive, and they all knew it.

Trapper leafed through the papers and cards and licences to finally remove a well-worn map, the fold lines actually cut from use, and he laid it out on the floor at his feet. It was a topographical map of the area and showed all the lakes and ponds, rivers and creeks, hills and gullies, swamps and marshes. We sat on the floor cross-legged, one on each side of the map. I watched and listened intently as he spoke of and pointed out places on Wakami Lake, the Little Crooked River, and Mink Creek.

This was a lifestyle far different from my own. Why, I'd never been to the remote wilderness before and not anywhere alone with a man. My intentions had been to further my education at university with four years of biology, a fish and wildlife major, or perhaps possibly swing into a lengthier stint in veterinary medicine. Medicine had over the past six generations been the profession of choice in our family. But somehow I found the four-footed patients more amicable to work with. I believe generally animals are more co-operative, affectionate, and appreciative than people. Besides, should I ever find myself in a malpractice suit, my patients might settle for a box of Milk Bone or a case of Puss 'N Boots!

Among my injured animal friends, I had tended a great variety of birds, the odd frog, a skunk, dozens of rabbits, both tame and wild, several raccoons, a few squirrels, a couple of red foxes, and even a lizard. Our neighbours would seek my advice regarding cats and dogs, hamsters, guinea pigs, and mice. It reached the point that before descending to the family room, my family would question me as to their safety or what they might expect to find. As a kid, I used to bring home all the roadkills I'd come upon and dissect them to check out the organs and how things were put together and worked. My father never knew what he would find pinned out on boards in his workshop. My live four-footed patients didn't always understand my good intentions and consequently on more than one occasion they made a patient of me. I have several scars to attest to their good taste.

However, the best-laid plans of mice and men . . . I now found myself many hundreds of miles away from home *and* in the company of a near-stranger to me. Why? Because all the world was up in arms about a savage luxury carried on in our northern forests by a breed of supposedly cruel and bloodthirsty men. Were the stories I had heard true? Were the media articles I had read and seen honest?

"Don't accept verbatim everything you hear," my father would say.

"Never criticize a man until you have walked a mile in his footsteps," my mother would say.

Well, there was only one way to find out. I would go out into the wilderness and seek the truth. I would walk that mile in his footsteps.

I fully intended to ask some questions. I fully intended to walk that mile. I would walk that trail and I would get some answers. So, there we sat on the floor of the cabin looking at the map and discussing his lifestyle. I asked endless questions. He offered endless answers. We did indeed have our differences.

"What is that red line on the map, Trapper?"

"That's the boundary of my trapline, 263 square miles, as close as I can figure it: some fifty lakes and ponds; miles and miles of marshes, creeks, and rivers. It is the best of trapping country. Not touched by modern man. It's the real thing."

I asked: "When you set a trap how do you know where to set it? Do you just set it out anywhere and hope for the best?"

"Hell, no. If you want to be good at it, you have to know what you're doing. It takes a long time to learn how to live off the land. I've been living off the land all my life and I'm still learning. I've been learning for over sixty years now. No matter how good you think you are, there is always someone who can come along and show you an easy tip, or a different way. Living off the land isn't only catching animals, you know. You have to know when to catch them, where to catch them, how to catch them, how many to catch, when the little ones are all set for the winter. You want to take older ones and always leave the younger ones to carry on and reproduce. It's no good just taking young ones and leaving the old ones. Then you don't get a healthy new population. Part of living off the land is knowing how and when to do all that."

"But how do you find the different animals? How do you know how and where to find them?"

Speaking very slowly and deliberately and carefully choosing his words, he proceeded to explain, "You have to know the habits of the animals; what they eat, where they live, how they make their home, which animals are their enemies, and so on. Then you look at the type of country you are in and you have a pretty good chance of figuring out just what kind of animals are likely to be there. By checking the terrain, you can figure out where they are likely to travel and then you start to set out a plan depending on what you need to do."

"Oh," I said. "You make an impromptu environmental study of the area. The population and species of animals is controlled by the environment of the immediate area. Animals require certain food, shelter, protection, availability of water, etc. It's called 'habitat.'"

"You city people can call it whatever you want. I told you I don't have book learning. I only know what I've seen and that's how I do it. I'm not city educated. I can't read a book and claim to know all about the forest and the environment. Up here we call people who do that 'citiots.' I only know what I know from seeing it and actually doing it." He stretched out his legs and slid back to lean against the stove.

Continuing, he said, "There are other things, too, though, that help you to figure out what animals you can see and watch. Some animals run all over the bush and just keep on roaming. They hole up in a hollow tree or log or stump for a night and go on running the next day. Other animals have a definite home and stay close to the den or lodge all the time. Others have certain routes or runways and they travel these same trails every three or four days or every week and keep circling on them."

"It would be a good idea to sit on or near a runway, then, wouldn't it? You'd be sure of seeing something there every few days. You could hunt or trap that way."

"Good thinking."

He rose and picked up his Number 1 Wood's Special packsack. Reaching to the wall, he took down his Winchester model 94 lever action rifle. Both of these he laid on the cot. A handful of .22 magnum cartridges from the windowsill went into his hip pocket. Taking a pouch of pipe tobacco from his shirt pocket, he placed a small amount of tobacco in the palm of his hand. After replacing the pouch, he ground up the tobacco and placed it onto a sheet of cigarette paper. With the skill acquired from years of repetition, he rolled a cigarette with one hand, licked the edge of the onion paper, and slid his little finger along the edge to seal it. Tapping the end of the cigarette three times on the back of a lightly haired hand, he then put it to his lips. He took a match from his chest pocket and placed it against the zipper on the front of his pants. He snapped it in a quick upward jerk on the zipper, and the match flamed a brilliant orange. With a twinkle in his eye, he looked for the expression on my face. "With my greying hair, you think I'm an old man, eh? Well, when there's smoke up above, there's fire down below." He winked, and raised the flaming match to his face, where it illuminated the crow's feet and the narrow twitching lips that were holding back laughter. In cupped hands he lighted the cigarette. He inhaled in a long, deep breath and held the smoke captive for a while before exhaling through flared nostrils. Releasing the smoke, he rather resembled a fire-breathing dragon.

"Trapper, how come you smoke?"

"What?"

"How come you smoke? It's dangerous to your health you know. It can cause cancer. Just read the label, you'll see it says right on the package."

"Told you, I don't read."

"Give it to me. I'll read it for you."

In a sudden rage of anger—presumably at my daring to question his habits—he roared back at me, "Well, I've smoked a hell of a long time, thirty years before you were ever thought of, and no one has buried me yet. You worry about smoking a cigarette? With all that shit you eat in them newfangled foods these days? They put fertilizer on the ground to make stuff grow faster, and shoot drugs into it to make it grow bigger, or grow with thin skins, or grow with no seeds . . . God, these days they even change the genes, then they dowse it with bug spray to de-lice it, and finally they add the essence of pure shit to improve the flavour. After all that, they piss preservatives all over it so they can store it for several months or years and then they ship it to the market, where they have three prices for it,[4] you pay for it, take it home, cook it in a no-stick pan you sprayed with God knows what so there is fewer calories and no cholesterol, and then you put it on a fancy, shiny plate all glazed with lead, and you eat it and you think it's just great. You do that day after day after day and you worry about a cigarette?"

"There's nothing wrong with it, Trapper. It's all government inspected and it tastes good. We can't all live off the land like you do. Over 90 percent of this country relies on commercially pre-pared foodstuffs, you know."

With a hearty laugh, he retorted, "If 90 percent of the country is eating that stuff, it's no wonder over half the country has gone plumb crazy. Jeez, they're all eatin' glucosamine for breakfast and Ritalin for lunch and Viagra for dinner."

"Trapper, you really infuriate me sometimes. Everybody is crazy but you. Is that what you think?"

"Never mind, I've got to get a move on."

"Close the barn door, then!" I quipped.

"What?"

"Zip it up." I gestured to the front of his pants. The wry grin curled the corners of that sexy mouth again.

"Don't worry, if the old stallion can't get up, he can't get out!"

He took one more look at the map to decide just where he would start the fall beaver count. Dressed in a long, fringed, buckskin coat, beaver cap, and one-fingered leather gauntlet gloves, he hoisted pack and rifle to his shoulder, ducked through the door, and in long, purposeful strides made his way to the shore of Wakami Lake. He was a man from a different time, a different era. Somehow it was as though he had stepped right out of the pages of a history book. History, in fact, was in his very genes. His earliest ancestor had reached these shores more than 350 years ago.

The first Chartrand to immigrate to Nouvelle France was Thomas Chartrand, born in 1641 to Louis (Cherten) Chartrand and Hermine Queval of d'Ectot–les–Boons, Rouen, France. Thomas Chartrand disembarked at Nouvelle France in 1655 and on January 6, 1669, at Montreal, he married Thecele Hunault (Hunaut), the daughter of Toussaint Hunault. In historical and genealogical records, one finds that the Hunault (Hunaut) family were related to the famed Medard Chouart des Groseilliers and Pierre Esprit Raddison. Pierre d'Esprit Raddison Sr., born in France in 1590, had married Madeleine Hunaut, the widow of Sebastien Hayet. By her first marriage to Sebastien Hayet, Madeleine Hunaut had a daughter Marguerite, who married Medard Chouart des Groseilliers. Through her second marriage to Pierre d'Esprit Radisson Sr., Madeleine Hunaut had a son, Pierre Esprit Raddison, the famous voyageur, explorer, and fur trader. Perhaps this could explain why Trapper always had to know what was around the next bend on the trail; what was on the other side of the hill.

Settlement was extremely important to the development of Nouvelle France. Many young men signed up to immigrate to Nouvelle France. Young girls, called *filles* in French, were transported by ship to the new settlements where they could find suitable husbands among the settlers and soldiers, then marry and raise a family to help populate the new colony.

One such woman was Francoise Capelle, born about 1627 in Normandie, France. It is said she arrived in Nouvelle France among the *filles à marier* ("marriageable girls") with Jeanne Mance on September 8, 1650. The following April 25, a Monsieur Leneuf of Trois–Rivières drew up a marriage contract between Francoise Capelle and Jean Turcot, born in 1625 to Francois Turcot and Josephe

Puinandeau of Fontenay–le–Comte, Poitou, France. Jean was the first Turcot to immigrate to Nouvelle France, having arrived in 1647.

These young colonists soon learned the horrors of life in their new world. Trois–Rivières in the 1650s was not a very large or very safe place in which to live. The Jesuit priests were among the first Europeans to arrive in Nouvelle France. They kept journals of daily activities, detailing their travels and happenings. It is said that in the Jesuit journals, Father Pierre Francois Charlevoix penned the words, "The Iroquois came like foxes, fought like lions, and fled like birds." In August 1652, the Iroquois raided the village of Trois–Rivières, killing several settlers. Jean Turcot was captured, never to be seen again. A few weeks after this horrifying incident, Francoise Capelle Turcot gave birth to a son, Jacques Turcot, who would be the only child of Jean Turcot to carry on the line of Turcot. Antoine Desrosiers had been captured with two of his companions and yet another had been tortured and burned to death. Nothing had been heard of Antoine in several months. His wife, young Anne Leneuf, must surely have thought he, too, had been tortured to death. Some years later, the families of Francoise Capelle and Antoine Desrosiers would be united when their children, Jacques Turcot and Marie Anne Desrosiers, would wed on April 4, 1674, in Trois–Rivières.

La Marchand, Leneuf, Desrosiers, Capelle, Turcot, and Chartrand . . . These early settlers to Nouvelle France came in search of a new life and to make their fortunes. They learned to live with horror and hardship. They fought and died for the right to build new settlements, to till the soil, and to trap furs. Their sons and grandsons would become the explorers and voyageurs who would explore and travel from the Atlantic to the Pacific, trap furs for the major fur companies, and open up the route to the west. These were the founding immigrant settlers of Canada.

During the French colonization period, the fur trade was the major economic source to sustain the colony. The fur trade was a very organized and specialized organization of procurers and businessmen. At the top, the CEO—chief executive officer—of the time would be a French merchant who lived in France. He purchased the supplies such as tea, sugar, tobacco, dyes, firearms and ammunition, and food that were required to supply an expedition.

North West Company voyageur's canoe.
(Photo by Paton Lodge Lindsay)

This CEO in turn had an agent, a French "*merchant-equipeur,*" or outfitter, who lived in Nouvelle France and was responsible for the purchase of equipment and supplies needed to travel into the back country, as well as the hiring of the crew for these expeditions.

The leader of the backcountry expedition was the "*merchant-voyageur,*" or travelling salesman, a licensed trader with a permit who did the actual buying and negotiating with Native trappers. Next in line were the "*engages,*" or canoe paddlers, the porters or portagers, and the general labourers, all of whom came to be known as "*voyageurs.*" Also, as part of this expedition, there were always included an interpreter to assist the merchant and the Natives to communicate; and a clerk to record all business activities and transactions on the expedition. At the bottom of the line were the "*coureurs-de-bois,*" who, without a permit from the governor of Nouvelle France, traded furs illegally with the Natives. Many integrated into Native communities and took Native wives.

In the journals of the voyageurs, one finds the direct ancestors of the King of Algonquin Park. Between the years of 1735 and the 1850s, we find the Chartrand voyageurs. "The King" descends in three lines from Thomas Chartrand (1641–1708), his sixth great-grandfather through two of his sons, Thomas and Pierre, both being fifth great-grandfathers. His sixth great-uncles—Charles, Joseph, Francois, Pierre, Charles, Jean, Benjamin, and Augustin—made many canoe trips from Montreal to Pontchartrain (Detroit), La Poste Illinois, the Mississippi, Missouri Territory, and to La Baye (Wisconsin). They paddled from Montreal to Fort St. Joseph and Fort Michilimackinac; to Penetanguishene and Michipicoten; they crossed La Grand Portage to Pays de l'Ouest and to La Portage de la Montagne.

To travel from Montreal to La Baye, they would paddle and portage their canoes up the St. Lawrence River, the Ottawa River, through Mattawa and Lake Nipissing, down the French River into Georgian Bay, through the islands, and down to the southernmost point of Lake Michigan, thence up the Chicago River, and portage all their goods several leagues and thence down the Illinois River into the headwaters of the Mississippi River. The bundles to be portaged weighed about ninety pounds each. These trips

Voyageurs trapping beaver.
(Photo by Paton Lodge Lindsay)

often covered over a thousand leagues, and the men were away from home for several years. An unknown voyageur penned in his journal, ". . . to the Pays du Nord Ouest or La Grand Portage the difficulty is so great as almost to amount to impossibility. The distance is above 1000 leagues and from the west end of Lake Superior nothing but small Indian canoes can be carried into the Mississippi near its sources. Whoever attempts to pass that way must run the risk of perishing by famine or the depredation of numerous tribes of fierce Indians."

The Chartrand voyageurs were known by the major companies. They were in the service of McTavish and Frobisher; McGillivray; Parker, Gerrard, and Ogilvie; Alexander McKenzie and the Hudson's Bay Company. The Chartrand voyageurs were not merely hired as *engages*, or porters, or the general labourers who were paid eighty to 250 livres annually. The Chartrand voyageurs were found among the elite; many known as winterers paddled from Montreal to La Pays de l'Ouest, spent the winter in the west, and returned to Fort William for the rendezvous in July, and then back to Montreal.

Augustin Chartrand was a guide and interpreter. Joseph Chartrand was on more than one occasion working as the *"gouvernail"* or director in charge of several expeditions. He was *gouvernail* of the king's men. They were trapping furs by royal right and they were granted the rights to hunt and fish whenever necessary. Joseph Chartrand was in such high demand he could negotiate his terms of contract and was known in 1802 to have signed a five-year contract as *gouvernail* with Alexander McKenzie and negotiated 1,000 livres annually for the first two years and 1,200 livres annually[5] for the last three years, obviously payment commensurate with his great knowledge and expertise. The King of Algonquin Park was raised on the stories of his voyageur ancestors. All three lines of descent from Thomas Chartrand merge in his very own grandfather, Michel Chartrand, who is listed as a voyageur on his marriage registration to Elizabeth Felicitas Turcotte on July 7, 1879, at Pembroke, Ontario.

The Indian Wars, the Seven Years War, and General James Wolfe's victory on the Plains of Abraham brought an end to Nouvelle France and the French control in North America but it did not bring an end to the fur trade. The Chartrand family trapped furs in the forests for over 350 years. They operated out of Montreal for a century and a half, with Jean residing at Ile Jesus, in the Parish of St. Francois–de–Sales, and Joseph, the Grand Voyageur, residing at Rivière-des-Prairies and St. Vincent de Paul. Now, some three hundred years later, standing right before my eyes, I watched this Joseph Chartrand as he stood at the shore of the river ready to put paddle to water just as his voyageur ancestor had done so many hundreds of years ago. He would never give up trapping the beaver that he felt were his sovereign right. It was as though he was the voyageur ancestor reincarnated, returned 300 years later to the sacred wilderness. It was as though he was resurrected from the past and "beamed-up" to the present. He was the last voyageur . . . the king of the wilderness.

"Where are you going, Trapper? You should never head out into the bush without someone knowing where you are going."

"W-h-a-t?" he said as he turned to stare at me.

"I just wondered where you were going, in case you get lost or something. A matter of in case you don't come back or something."

"L-o-s-t or something." He drew out the words and in disbelief shouted, "Lost? Is that what I heard you say? Lost?"

"Or something," I timidly repeated.

"Downstream, I guess," he said. "I'll start there."

"That really doesn't tell me which way you are going, does it?"

"Missy, that tells you exactly which way I am going." Irately he advised me that there was indeed a head and a foot to every body of water. When you travel toward the head of that body of water, you travel against the current. That is travelling upstream. When you travel toward the foot of that body of water, you travel with the current. That is travelling downstream. "Now you know precisely where I am going, don't you?"

"Yes, sir, I sure do know where you intend to go, and I know where you can go, too."

He smiled, winked, and said, "I'll be back about noon. Now, don't you go splitting any firewood while I'm gone. It's a hundred-and-fifty-mile trip outta here to the nearest surgeon. Timmins or the Sault. Understand that?"

He was a good walker and a good paddler. I wondered just how many bush miles he must have put on in the past sixty years. He had been known to travel 700 miles by canoe in many a summer and do his work besides. Fall and winter travel by canoe, on foot, and on snowshoe would certainly amount to that much. If we estimate an average of 1,500 miles per year over some sixty years, we are talking about a human being who has spent literally thousands of nights in the bush alone beside a campfire, from buggy summer nights of ninety degrees above zero to bitter, frosty nights at fifty below zero and totalled up a possible one hundred thousand miles by foot and paddle.

Slipping a foot beneath the gunwale of the twelve-foot cedar and canvas canoe, he flipped it upright. He slipped the canoe into the water until the bow just kissed the shore. The pack was placed up ahead and jammed between the stern and the seat. He jacked a shell into the rifle and laid it carefully in the bottom with the butt toward him. Tracker jumped into the centre. Trapper lifted the canoe free of the shore and, stepping in, took up a position on the bow seat facing the stern. Taking paddle in hand, he stood erect and paddled slowly, almost motionlessly, across the bay, around the point, and out of sight.

3

Water Woes

Tracker

(Photo by Paton Lodge Lindsay)

"Men, now don't you go splitting any firewood while I'm gone," I mimicked.

I looked about the camp. Where to begin? That was a good question. The dishes, I guessed. Get them out of the way and wash down the old lumber shelves and then sort and pack the supplies away. There was sufficient water in the big old pot to do the dishes and then wash down the shelves. By the time I got everything straightened about and the shelves stocked, the camp resembled the proverbial quartermaster's store. There were powdered milk, coffee, tea, brown sugar, salt, buckwheat honey, molasses, flour, rice, some macaroni, beans, shortening, baking powder, a jug of maple syrup, a couple of three-pound tins of jam, a huge jar of peanut butter, some cans of ham and bully beef, and a square tin of wooden matches. On the beam above hung a couple of old cast-iron frying pans, some old, dinted boiling pots, a few cooking spoons, egg turners, and a ladle. A variety of knives were stuck into a log. Below the bottom shelf were two large, covered metal buckets filled with water. A large metal ladle hung on a nail beside them.

Taking advantage of the sunny morning that had emerged as forecast by our woodland friends, I decided to rinse out the few soiled clothes from the trip up. As all washing would have to be done by hand, it would be important not to let it accumulate. The lake water proved to be very soft. No matter how often I rinsed the articles, more and more suds foamed out over the rim of the enamel basin and stretched like a river of pearls to the floor. Before the battle was done, my water supply had become exhausted. With buckets in hand, I took to the water and waded out to a depth nearly to my boot tops so that I might scoop up clear, pure water without disturbing the intricate particle picture that had formed on the sandy bottom. I tipped the first bucket on its side and slowly lowered it into the water. The water swirled about in a whirl and filled the bucket to the brim. That bucket I set on the shore in exchange for the second.

I noticed a school of tiny diving ducks frolicking off the island in the bay. They would glide along the surface with their heads bobbing back and forth like a child's windup toy. Suddenly, they would upend in a maze of bubbles and flying water to disappear below the surface. Scanning the water, I made a game of trying to predict where they would emerge. They never ceased to amaze me by popping up in the most unexpected places. They would puncture the watery reflection and look directly at me. They seemed to take as great an interest in my activities as I did in theirs. After several minutes, they took to the water on foot and in an urgent upheaval, like a team of miniature sprinters on a hurdle track, they raced along the water, rose into the air, circled about once, and were gone. What had disturbed them?

A great fear welled up in my heart as I realized I was hundreds of miles away from home, at least forty miles from the nearest civilization, and all alone in the bush. I sensed that something behind me was separating me from the safety of the cabin. Motionlessly, I listened intently. I heard the moaning of the wind in the Jack pines, the sucking of water in the flood wood of dead trees and roots that had collected along the shore, the groaning of tree trunks rubbing on one another as they swayed in the wind, and the rustling of long, dried grasses in the open area about the camp. Intently, I tried to hear what was behind me, but my ears were deaf to any sound from there. It was there, though. I could sense it. I could feel its stare cutting into my back, feel the tension in its limbs as in mine. In terror, I was frozen to the ground, afraid even to breathe. Perhaps if I gathered together all of my courage and energy, I could surprise it and move quickly enough to make a dash for the cabin. I could feel it stalking closer and closer. My fear was growing to panic. A big wind seemed to surge through my innards just as it surges through the big pines, making them rock and teeter, even though they are welded to the ground. The various wild animals came to mind: deer, moose, fox . . . wolf?

Trapper had said you needn't fear the wild animals in the bush. They were more afraid of you than you need be of them—all but the bear . . . bear, b-e-a-r? My heart stopped. I felt it fluttering like the wings of a butterfly. Oh, my God, it couldn't be a bear. My mouth filled with saliva, and my ears tingled to hear some sound. There was nothing—yet, I knew it was there. I pictured its nose extended to the air, nostrils flaring as it tried to get my scent. I pictured it rising on great hind legs, forepaws extended, stretching to enwrap me. In fear, my legs turned to rubber, a cold sweat trickled down my face, down my neck, between my breasts; and suddenly, I felt a wet, very warm sensation flowing down about my knees. Oh, my God.

Anticipating the sudden onslaught building behind me, I slowly reached for the other bucket of water. On the silent count of three, I turned in blind terror and, emitting as thunderous a roar as my vocal cords would permit, I flung the two buckets of water ahead of myself and charged like a mad bull through the flying ice water and tearing brambles for the door of the camp. My temples pounded, my tongue swelled in my mouth, and my lungs gasped for air. In tears, I collapsed on the floor of the cabin without even sufficient strength to close the door.

To my horror, as I looked toward the lake, I wondered: How could it be? There was nothing there—nothing at all. Had anything ever been there? How could something imaginary seem so real? How could I have been so afraid, so mortally in terror of something that didn't even exist?

In time, my breathing returned to normal, the paralyzing fear was replaced with anger, and the anger was eventually replaced with humiliation. I sat defeated on the front step of the camp and eyed the two buckets resting on the ground some twenty feet from one another. I still had no water.

Counting Beavers and the Depression Years

Paton paddling to count beaver houses.
(Photo by Keith Harlen Hoback)

As I sat in the cabin doorway and looked out across Wakami Lake to the far pine shores, a sense of pride welled up in my heart. THIS was MY Canada. The wind wafted a whispered song to my ears,

> My paddle's keen and bright
> Flashing with silver,
> Follow the wild goose flight,
> Dip, dip and swing.

I quietly sang back to him,

> Dip, dip and swing her back,
> Flashing with silver,
> Swift as the wild goose flies,
> Dip, dip and swing.[6]

To my left, the sun did flash silver from a wet paddle blade announcing the return of Trapper and Tracker. As they approached, Trapper lifted the paddle blade in the old voyageur salute and waved to me. Within a few feet of the shore, with one stroke he swung the canoe at right angles and with a second stroke he drew the canoe sideways into the shore and stepped out onto a rock. Tracker followed, and the two made their way together to the camp. Trapper stepped into the camp, stooping so as not to hit his head on the low door frame, and dropped his pack to the floor. He stood his rifle by the door. In a silent, circular glance, he surveyed all the camp.

"Been busy, haven't you?"

"Yup, I washed up the dishes, washed down the shelves, and stowed away all the supplies. Then I washed up some soiled clothes, sorted out all your gear and put it under your cot and shoved all our clothes and packs under my cot. I even hung up the rifles."

He was appreciative in his own way, eyeing up the supply of newly split firewood stacked in the woodbox, but refrained from comment.

"I even baked you some scone—some good scone, city scone." We sat on the hewn pine blocks, one at either end of the table. Lunch, though primitive, was tasty and filling.

"Oh, I brought you back four partridge. Just wait till you sink your teeth into those."

"I'm not eating those. I'm not touching those. If you want them, you eat them."

"Well, Jesus Christ. They aren't dirty, you know—a damn sight better than those foul fowl things you call chickens down south."

"We won't get into that again. You quite obviously have no toleration for anything but what you know and what you do."

"I found eleven live beaver houses this morning. That's eleven beaver so far on this year's quota."

"Trapper, what do you mean by a 'live' beaver house?"

Once more chewing and spitting about his improvised toothpick, he sat down to explain.

"When you trap beaver, you trap on a quota. We don't want to clean the whole damn country out, despite what those educated animal lovers think. No, we have to live off the land and the animals, yet preserve them for the future, too. I need to be able to make a withdrawal next year and the year after that.

"The beaver quota is set each year by the Ministry of Natural Resources. Each district sets a quota based on their beaver population. In districts where they are overrun with beaver, they may have an open quota, and people can catch as many as they want. Sometimes on private land, beaver are a real nuisance and very destructive, and the landowner wants all the beaver taken out. Some places, they have a quota of one-and-a-half beaver per house. Here in the Chapleau District, the quota is one beaver per house. Each trapper cruises his trapline every fall and counts the number of live beaver houses he has and then gets a quota based on the annual count. Here, in Wakami country, the quota is set at one beaver for every live house."

"But Trapper, what is a 'live house'?"

"It is a house with beaver living in it."

"Well, how can you tell if beaver are living there or not?"

Lighting up yet another cigarette he proceeded to explain.

"At this time of year, beaver begin to prepare for winter. They have travelled about after the spring flood and found a good spot to have a pond or house. In the fall, they build a new house or fix up an old one. Beaver prepare for the long sleep, only they don't sleep all winter. They mud up their houses by getting mud from the bottom of the pond and holding it in their paws and against their chests. Then they portage it to their houses where they literally plaster the house with mud to make it weathertight. They plaster the dam, too, so that it is watertight. Some people say they use their tails to flatten and smooth out the mud, but that's just a bunch of bullshit and you know what they use that for!"

"What?"

"They use it down south to put on fields to make things grow."

"Well, maybe someone did see a beaver doing that sometime."

"Maybe they did. But you know what? If they did see a beaver doing that, their trappin' partners were Johnny Walker and Jack Daniels, or maybe it was one of them new young, highly educated horny-ologists the government's got."

"What is a 'horny-ologist'?"

"You know, those young university dudes dressed in skin-tight blue jeans with red braces and shiny, new fifteen-inch leather work-boots laced tight right to the knees and a hundred-dollar Tilley hat. They always got a pair of binoculars and a packsack full of books and they drive about the back bush roads lookin' for bugs and slugs and stuff. Yup, you can tell them every time. Red braces, a can of fly dope, a book and binoculars in hand, and gold-rimmed testicles!"

"What?" I asked, not sure of what I thought I had heard. "Gold-rimmed t-e-s-t-i-c-l-e-s?"

"Gold-rimmed testicles. Didn't you hear the story 'bout them southern folk talking downtown? One fella says, 'Hey Amos, did juh see the new rectum down at the church this afternoon? And Amos, he answers, 'Yas siree, I sure 'nough did. He da tall fella with da gold-rimmed testicles!'"

"That's what I'm going to be."

"You're going to be a rectum with gold-rimmed testicles?"

"No."

"Oh, you say you're going to be a certified horny-ologist?"

"No, Trapper. I'm going to be a government biologist!"

"Well, you'll never have to worry about wearin' the knees outta your pants 'cause you'll wear the ass outta them first. What with readin' books, and sittin' behind the wheel of a truck or in front of one of those idiot boxes watchin' those pixel pictures from satellites."

"And what might I suppose that to be?"

"You know, one of them desktop TVs where the machine does all the thinkin' for you."

"It's called a computer, Trapper."

He leaned forward, placing his elbow on his knee and resting his chin on a closed fist, he continued, "In the fall, the beaver spend all of their time cutting trees in the bush and dragging the tops back to their houses for feed. They dive to the bottom of the pond with the branch in their mouth and ram it into the mud so the branches remain under water and later are under the ice and available for winter feed. When you see a beaver house that has been freshly mudded, has new white sticks on top, and a fresh feed bed in front, then you know somebody is at home—eh, Tracker?"

"How come the beaver travel in the summer, Trapper?"

"Don't ask questions before you think. You can figure that out for yourself. A beaver isn't a fish, you know. He can't stay under water indefinitely. He dives down into the water to get into the trench; then once he is in the house, he lives high and dry. In the spring, when the heavy floods come and the waters rise, the beaver are flooded out of their houses so they usually move downstream with the flood, feeding on their way. They follow rivers and small creeks until they come to a spot where they can build a dam and back up the water to build a pond and take up housekeeping again."

"Do they always build a new house every year?"

"No. Sometimes they don't even have to move. They might stay several years in the one place until they eat themselves outta house and home, or till the fleas drive them out. Other times they will find an empty house and they'll patch it up and stay there. The beaver relies on the dam, though, to regulate water. You've seen a beaver dam in the summer. They are made mostly from mud, stones, and sticks, are always built bowed upstream so the water pressure of floods can't wash them out easily. These dams back up the water to make a beaver pond so the water doesn't dry up in summer.

"But the beaver relies on that dam to regulate water in the winter, too. It gives the beaver a place to store feed in the winter so that it can get at it. Some beaver are under the ice for eight and nine months of the year. Once the big freeze-up has come, they cut a couple of sluices in the dam and lower the water level a few inches. Then they can swim around anywhere just like in the summer, only they don't have access to land until the spring thaw when the current and the sun open up some holes along the shore or at the dam. It is only for a few nights that beaver in a pond rely on the air in the house."

"You mean beaver actually do that? Sure you weren't trappin' with Harvey Wallbanger?"

"Don't get smart. I wouldn't be tellin' you if I hadn't seen it often with my own eyes. We're just talking, here. Wait till the ice is on and then you'll see for yourself."

"When they say the beaver are nature's engineers, they aren't kidding, are they?"

"Well, we can't sit around the camp all day. Get off your butt if you're coming with me. The beaver won't come into the camp to find us. Better get a hitch in your git-a-long!"

Tracker was already at the canoe and waiting when we reached the shore. I took my black cherry paddle that Trapper had handcrafted for me with only an axe and a knife. He had taken a nail heated in a hot fire and burned a timber wolf on the face of the blade for me with a bear on the reverse. They were my two favourite wild animals. My face grew hot and red as I looked at the bear and recalled the incident of that morning. I slipped that memory into the water and pulled on the paddle. We paddled into a small bay just to the south of the camp. Trapper pointed to some white sticks floating along the shoreline. As we paddled along, we found other white sticks caught up in flood wood along the shore, and beaver trails where they'd cut down timber in the bush and were skidding the tops out to the water.

"Beaver close here somewhere," he commented. "A whole family here."

"How can you tell?" I asked.

"Simple! Look at the tracks there in the runway. There are big tracks and little tracks there on the sandbar. So, there is a family here."

We paddled on, ever watchful for signs of wildlife, for signs of the beavers he would trap.

"Trapping is a business," he would say. "It's renewable, a type of farming; a type of animal control, it's 'GREEN,' and it is my livelihood. Thousands of families rely on trapping for their livelihood. It prevents diseases like rabies and tularemia from spreading. Trapping is important."

"I realize that, Trapper. It is just that we read so many awful things about it. We see terrible pictures and movies about it. In the Bible, Matthew asks, "What went ye out into the wilderness to see?" That is why I wanted to come out here on the trapline and see first-hand for myself what goes on. Then I'll know the truth and the facts from experience. They say you are the king."

"That's what they called me—The King of the Long Runners."

"What is a 'long runner,' Trapper?"

"Oh, years back, through the wars, and the Depression, when there was no work, you tried to make a dollar any way you could. In the big cities, you could make a buck as a delivery boy for a grocery store, if you owned a bike. You could sell newspapers on the corner or maybe sell vacuum cleaners or sweep the streets with a broom or pick garbage. A telegrapher could make fifteen dollars a week. In the cities or towns you could see children laughing and playing in the streets but in the bush settlements, you never saw children playing. Everyone worked. In the bush, there were no jobs like in the city, but there was always lots of work. There was always work in the logging camps or cutting and selling firewood; making maple syrup; working on the depot farm; or you'd jump a train and ride the rails out West to help harvest the crops. You could feed your family on venison or moose; birds or fish. You could eat beaver meat and you could also get a dollar for the pelt—a really good dollar. One good winter, beaver pelt could bring you a month's wages. When you had a family to feed, you got that dollar any way you could.

"Today they think recycling is new. Back then, we saved and re-used everything. Sugar came in large cloth bags. The women would wash them and cut down one side and across the bottom and open them up flat. They were used for towels or sewn together to make sheets or shirts or even some beautiful quilts. It was always the fronts of pants that got worn out, so the women would cut the backs out of the old pants and then cut them up into squares and they would make heavy quilts or blankets with them or sew pants for the little ones with them. You didn't throw out a sock or mitt when you got a hole in it. The more they were darned, the warmer they were. You didn't waste anything. Used to be the three R's was Readin', Ritin', and Rithmatic. Now the three R's are Reduce, Reuse, and Recycle. Reuse and Recycle, there is nothing new about that. And as for Reduce, we had so little, you didn't have anything to reduce."

5

King of the Long Runners – Taking Count

Beaver house with fresh feed bed in front.
(Photo by Paton Lodge Lindsay)

Trapping and timber were the two resources that sustained most families in the early colonization periods. When Wolfe conquered Quebec on the Plains of Abraham in 1756, a lot of French families—including the Chartrand family—began to move about. Some eventually left Quebec and moved westward and even crossed the Ottawa River into the Ottawa Valley to find work in the square timber camps and to trap furs, as some felt was their right. The king of England meant little to them. They were French and they were still the king's men. By this time several small trading posts had been built at Ottawa, at the mouth of the Petawawa River. Trappers would paddle up the Oxtongue River, through

Smoke Lake, Big Porcupine, Harness, down the Madawaska River to the Ottawa, or paddle via Canoe Lake, Ottertail, Burntroot, Cedar Lake, and then down the Petawawa River to the Ottawa River, and sell their furs. Trapper's paternal grandfather gave up his life as a voyageur and moved to the Ottawa Valley. Several generations of Chartrands logged and trapped furs and reaped a living from the pine forests of the valley.

The 1830s saw logging and settlement move into the valley. A settlement road known as the Opeongo Line was started in 1854 and ran from the Ottawa River to Madawaska. Then in the 1890s, the railroad was put through the wilderness. A new enemy presented itself in the wilderness: The logger, the farmer, and then the tourist invaded their kingdom.

In 1892, the National Parks Act set aside an area for preservation. Rangers were hired to patrol the area and prevent poaching. The French trappers, the old voyageurs, had been here for hundreds of years. They were ousted by Wolfe in 1756, and now, in 1893, they were to be ousted once again by the English government. Some trappers did move to other lands outside of the park boundaries and trap elsewhere; others took on the job as patrol rangers; and still others refused to give up their RIGHT to trap.

Trapper had been raised on the stories about his ancestors and the tales of the old voyageurs. Remember, his very own grandfather, Michel Chartrand, was listed as a "voyageur" on his marriage licence. The beaver and the rights to hunt and fish as necessary had been given to his family by the king nearly 400 years ago. The British had invaded his kingdom of Nouvelle France and now they thought they would invade his kingdom of Algonquin Park? As the "King" said many times in his own words, "When the Lord made the world he didn't make Algonquin Park first." There were lots of beavers to be had; they were his by right of the king and he'd make damn sure he got his share.

Trapping in the park wasn't easy work, but it was a guaranteed dollar, if you didn't get caught. Men crossed the park boundary by the dozens to poach beaver. Most trappers would sneak into the park, grab a few beavers, then turn and get the hell out for fear of being caught. A very few trappers would tramp the wilderness wetlands and swamps, where beavers were to be found from Highway 60 and the Opeongo River all the way across the east side, across the Petawawa River and across the Ottawa River, and sell their pelts in Quebec. These very few men who travelled on foot and made the 300-mile return trip across Algonquin Park were called "the long runners."

"It is true I made so many runs across the park and never got caught, they called me 'the King of the Long Runners.' Oh, I had some near runs a few times, but I never got caught. It wasn't an easy way to live. It was real hard work. You were just lucky not to freeze to death or go through the ice and drown, or starve or get killed by a bear when you were carrying all the raw pelts on your back in spring. You were darn lucky not to have a ranger get his damn hands on you and throw you in the clink for doing exactly what they were doing themselves. Those damn old bastards would run the heart right out of you and they shot wolves and loons and deer and beaver in the park themselves. Some of them would catch a trapper poaching in the park and seize his furs and then sell them themselves. They trapped and poached, too.

"The old rangers were good bushmen. They'd run us through the park until we'd nearly die. Some of them nearly died, too. Some of them *did* die. One lost a leg to frostbite. Old Jack Billings and Joe Stringer were found burned to death in their ranger cabin. Rumour was they had been murdered and then burned in the cabin to cover up the crime. Times were tough back then. You were fighting for the right to live. I trapped that goddamned park all my life. I know every last inch of that park as well as I know the back of my hand. I walked or paddled it all: Big Eddie, the Half Mile, the Petawawa, Crooked Chutes, the Rollaway, the Natch, Schooner Rapids, and the Five Mile. I spent my whole life in the park. You'd trap furs or cut down the pine in the winter; run the river drive and then do maple syrup in the spring; guide fishermen all summer; pick the princess pine and pick cones in late summer; get your venison in for the winter; and then it was back to trappin'—that was life.

"You could always go to the bush and make a dollar. I trapped and hunted the park all through the war years; I guided out of all the big lodges and all the kids' camps. I guided in Algonquin Park from right after the war until 1968. By then, the guiding was done. The park was done. It was just full of city people and their kids and dogs and million-dollar toys. I had lived the life of my heroes. When I was a kid, my heroes were Zane Grey and Joe Mufferaw; Grey Owl and Joe Two Rivers. His real name was Joe La Valley. He was the most famous guide in the park, Joe and his wolf. An Englishman wrote a book about him, *The Indian and the Paleface*. Those were the heroes of a kid livin' alone back in the bush them times.

"We lived some hard times, but there were some good times, too. Oh, yes, and then the war came, and they put a military base by the park. We couldn't hunt there, but the government could bomb the hell out of it. I put my time in at the base, too, but not as you might think. Now there's another story."

We continued paddling and keeping an ever-watchful eye on the water and the shoreline for signs of wildlife. Trapper went on, "There is good and bad in everything. It sometimes happens in trapping just as it does in everyday living. When people go out for a nice Sunday drive or to the cottage for the weekend, they don't intend to become involved in an accident. They don't intend to be killed or to kill someone else. Sometimes no matter how careful you are, the unpredictable happens. Today, with proper equipment and proper trapper training, the object is to try and set a trap that when triggered it goes off and immediately renders an animal unconscious or dead. That is said to be a humane set."

He talked on, and I knew he was right. I remembered back one time when I was cutting the grass for the first time in the spring. In the long grass and heaped up leaves from fall I ran the power mower into a nest of baby rabbits. There were leaves and twigs flying all over the place, and blood and chunks of fur stuck on my pant legs. They were so tiny and fluffy and the power mower just chopped them into pieces. Some were cut in half, others had a leg or a head cut off but were still alive and struggling to pull their little half-bodies about on the grass. There was blood and fur all over the place. To this very day, I can hear their squeals of pain and see the terror in their wee, shiny, black eyes looking up at me. Oh, God forgive me. That was an accident that shall stay with me the rest of my life.

There was one wee rabbit that had the fur slashed about its middle. It seemed to be a flesh wound that reached across the back and down both sides to the abdomen. Just the fur and the skin seemed to be cut. It wasn't bleeding at all. With wee casualty in hand, I raced off to a neighbour of the medical profession, and shortly thereafter the three of us headed out for the local general hospital, where he was a surgeon on staff. For reasons soon to be understood, the name of the doctor and the hospital shall remain unknown. My doctor friend swiftly darted about, taking care of our furry casualty as though it were of major importance to save this tiny life; and it was. Twice he stitched the wound, but that tender baby skin refused to hold the stitches. It was just like onion skin. Finally, in a last heroic attempt, my faithful physician absconded with some of the synthetic thread used in corneal implants and stitched the baby rabbit up with that.

The surgery seemed to have been successful. After a day or two in the doctor's care, the bunny was returned to me with the express instructions to keep it quiet and not let it jump about. Did you ever try to keep a growing wild rabbit from jumping about? It was impossible. As Fate would have it, that wound did again open up. In my determination to save this wee creature, I decided that surely if it were kept clean that wound would grow in with scar tissue. My rabbit had two daily showers with a disinfectant solution, and after several weeks, the wound did heal over. My rabbit resembled a Dutch Belt Rabbit. It was furred in front and back with a leather belt about the middle. She became known as "Vikki," named after Vic Seddon, a great friend of mine who was the head of Conservation Education for the Ontario Department of Lands and Forests at Queen's Park, and she, the rabbit, remained a faithful companion for over five years. I still question if my actions to save her were humane, or would it have been more humane to have killed her? But I couldn't do that.

"Look!" I shouted. "Look over there," I pointed.

"Sh-h-h-h, you have to be quiet in the bush if you hope to see anything."

"It's a beaver. Did you see it, Trapper? He's got a poplar branch in his mouth."

"Just sit quiet and watch it. It'll go to the house and dive with that branch and store it in the feed bed."

We sat motionlessly and in silence in the canoe and watched the beaver swim along the shore until it came to a hemlock branch hanging out over the water. I motioned to Trapper to paddle closer. He propelled the canoe forward, never removing the paddle from the water and not making so much as a ripple or a drip to stir the air. I sat spellbound and watched the bottom as it raised to within vision. It was a sandy bottom, covered with sticks and bark and needles. Long, leafed weeds grew in clumps here and there among the deadheads and sunken logs that were a tangle beneath us. As we approached, a shot cracked through the air. I jumped with a start from my underwater fantasy world. The beaver had slapped its tail upon the water, and the long, yellow poplar branch slipped beneath the surface of the water.

The beaver house was built against the side of the bank and supported by the trunk of a long fallen hemlock. The house was massively constructed of sticks all cleaned of their bark and well packed in layer after layer of mud. The current layer of mud was not yet complete, and a trail was visible up each side of the house where the beaver had been busily transporting this new layer of plaster. In front of the house was the beginning of the new feed bed. Poplar and birch branches pierced the surface of the water. The wilted leaves twisting and turning in the breeze reminded me of cocoons. As they twirled about and the sunlight glistened from their underside they resembled the shiny glass ornaments that adorn the family Christmas tree.

The afternoon sun danced on the rippling waters, and the aroma of pine permeated the air. Quiet ruled supreme. You could in fact *hear* the quiet, something I had never heard before. As we drifted in the canoe with paddles across the gunwales, Trapper took out his map and marked an "X" where the live beaver house was located. He raised his paddle and it flashed silver in the sunlight. A splash of water jumped ahead of us and a shiny sleek shape slipped beneath the canoe.

"Did you see that, Trapper? Was it a little beaver?"

"No. That was a muskrat. They sometimes live in the house with the beaver. Some people say the beavers use them as slaves.

If the beaver sense that there is danger they may send the muskrat out to investigate. If the muskrat returns, then all is okay. If the rat doesn't return, then the beaver stay safely in the house."

"Is that really true, Trapper?"

"A lot of people believe that. Lots of times you do see a beaver go into the house and then you will see a muskrat come out and swim around looking about."

We paddled outward from the shoreline and continued searching the rocky ledges and hanging banks and circling the islands for further signs of beavers. By nightfall, we had travelled some fourteen miles by canoe and counted eight more live beaver houses, giving Trapper a total now of nineteen live beaver houses on Wakami Lake. He had yet to check the river, but it was getting dark, and the river would have to wait for another day.

Dusk settled down over the lake, darkness closed in, and the wind died down. The lake lay motionless, and the very earth seemed to have stopped breathing. As Trapper paddled, I sat and watched the moon and stars in the water. It was apparent that God had brought darkness to the earth and had lighted the heavens. The waters were likened to a jeweller's case with diamonds resting on a mirror surrounded with deep blue velvet. They glistened and twinkled from far below. I reached to pick a sparkling gem from God's jewellery box, but all shattered in an instant and was gone. There was no hum of the wind in the pines, no lap of the water in the flood wood along the shore, no song of the birds, and no whisper of the breeze. The world had fallen into a soundless sleep. A dewdrop touched my cheek as God kissed the world goodnight.

6

On the Wood Trail

Wood pile at camp.
(Photo by Paton Lodge Lindsay)

I scooped up the crystal-clear, ice-cold water and tossed it onto my as yet half-asleep face. It dripped from my chin and elbows as I crouched at the shoreline and gazed in awe at the magnificent golden sun that warmed the treetops and lit a pathway across the still waters directly to my feet. It was as though I could have just stepped onto that golden ribbon and walked my way to heaven. The magnificent splendour and peace of the river was interrupted by a stentorian roar that came from up at the cabin.

"By all that's holy, I'll bet there is no corner left on that damn blanket of yours!"

Stretching with a great groan I asked what on earth he was talking about.

"Well, sir-ee now, I'll just bet you swallowed that goddamn blanket last night!"

I laughed and blushed, having to admit that when I was really tired I could indeed snore with the best of them.

This was the beginning of yet another day, and once more, if the forecast of our woodland inhabitants was correct, the prospects looked inviting. Trapper would always say, "At this time of the year, when old man winter might just decide to camp on your doorstep any night, you have to be ready ahead of time." Wood was the order of the day.

It didn't take Trapper long to erect a sawhorse, and without even the assistance of a solitary nail. He just threw a log down onto the ground and at each end pounded in a pair of sharpened, crossed poles, and there it stood. He made sure the teeth on the saw were sharp and then stuck the file into a crack on the log. It was an old saw that had served him faithfully for years. He called it "Liza." It seems a peculiar habit of bushmen. All of their equipment is given a name, usually female in gender. The cookstove was "old Bertha," the saw was "Liza," the shotgun was "Bess," the old pickup was "Lizzie," etc. I couldn't decide if this peculiarity was due to the fact that these tools did all the work so they were considered female, or because of a solitary life alone, these men enjoyed the company of anything called female. It was at least encouraging as well as reassuring to note that these were all useful items he couldn't do without.

As we made our way up the hill behind the camp, he pointed out the various types of trees and described their state of being and evaluated each as to its worth for fuel wood. "A dry pine that is dead but is still standing, that's the best for kindling or for a hot fast fire. That's called a 'Chico.' When a tree dies and falls to the ground, it isn't long before it's covered in moss and fungus and then it gets punky. It's no good for burning, then; smokes like a bastard. An old red pine root is the best to start a fire. It's got enough pitch in it to ignite right away. White birch and yellow birch are as close to hardwood as you'll get in these parts. We use green Jack pine most of the time for the body wood. It's not the best but it's often the best you can get."

He and Tracker headed their way on up the hill ahead of me. The way they manoeuvred, it seemed as though they both had the advantage of travelling on four legs. I trod on with camera in one hand, and the .22 magnum in the other. The hill I found to be very steep, and the climb made more difficult by the loose debris of needles and moss and branches, and the slippery wet leaves that had accumulated in years and years of degeneration. Several times, I slipped on moss that hung precariously to a rock or punky log. It was beautiful up there on the hill; a mixed forest of black spruce, yellow tamarack, red pine, and white birch. God had seen fit to place these varied species together on earth and they managed to live in harmony with one another. They all lived beneath one sky, gaining nourishment from one source, living in total independence, and yet meshed as reciprocal partners in Nature's intricately woven chemistry of life. I wondered why man, who has supposedly been gifted with intelligence and humanity, could not attain that same peace in his existence.

"What took you so long? You look like a young calf moose that hasn't found its legs yet."

"It's hard to climb that hill. I'm too short in the legs to get over half of that stuff and too big to get under the rest of it."

"Built like a brick shithouse, we used to say. Well, that has its advantages, too."

"Like what?"

"Oh, like you won't have to fill your pockets with stones to keep from blowing away in a storm!"

"You'll never get that tree down in here. It's too dense."

"You think not, eh? I'll put that Chico down just exactly where I want it. You just watch."

With that, he swung the axe into the air and limbed the surrounding trees of all dry and protruding knots and branches. Wood chips and lichen flew in all directions.

He worked and narrated, "It's not hard to gut yourself on those things, you know. They are so damn hard they are like stone. When you fell a tree, you have to make sure it's clear all around so that your axe won't catch on anything or the tree won't get hung up on its way down. Make sure your axe is sharp, too. There is no more dangerous weapon in the hands of a greenhorn than a dull axe. If your axe should glance off a knot you might just cut yourself and bleed to death back here. You got to *think* when you're in the bush. Be aware of everything around you all the time. You're out here all alone. You can't just call up Daddy any time you need him. It's a lot easier to be careful in the first place than to have to crawl forty miles for help."

He sat down on a log and took off his left boot and sock. "Just look at that. See that scar on my foot, from my big toe right to my instep? I was felling a tree, and the axe slipped on loose, wet bark. The blade of that axe went right through my boot and cut my big toe right in half lengthwise. Look at that! Right down the middle, and cut the cords in my foot. It was in winter, too, and the snow was over two feet deep. I had to walk out twenty-two miles to get help. I couldn't take my boot off or my foot would freeze. Every step I took, the blood would ooze out of my boot and leave a red track in the snow." He put his sock and boot back on, and rolled a cigarette.

Walking around the tree, he eyed it from all directions. He held his axe out at arm's length so that it hung vertically beside the trunk of the tree and he decided the tree should fall to the south. The tree was leaning to the south, but most of the larger limbs were on the east side. He proceeded by laying the blade of the saw to the butt of the tree on the south side and made a horizontal cut to about one-third of its diameter. Then he made a second horizontal cut above that, but on an angle that freed a wedge-shaped piece from the trunk. Stepping to the opposite side of the tree, he swung the blade onto the trunk. The sharp teeth chewed into the wood and a funnel of wood chips falling from the saw created a pyramid as they piled at the foot of the tree. As this final cut moved to the centre of the trunk, I watched the top of the tree as it began to shake and vibrate. The tree began to crack and sway, and slowly, the top of the tree leaned toward the south. With saw in hand, Trapper took a step or two back into the bush. Now, intimidated by this descending monster, I, too, took to the bush and, just as fast as my short, stalky legs would allow, I ran in the opposite direction. There was a great cracking and tearing overhead that culminated in a roaring swoooosh and a mighty thud. The earth virtually jumped with the impact of this fallen monarch.

Branches, needles, leaves, and dagger-like knots all took to the air as flying missiles that all seemed bent on puncturing my hide. I crouched beneath a fallen tree seeking protection from this storm of forest debris. As the air quieted and the forest debris settled, I looked up to see this massive pillar half-buried in the soil. The ground was like black powder. All little things had been uprooted. The earth had truly bounced with the impact of this monarch of bygone days. Awestruck, I stood in silence and took in the devastation and thought: if this is what one tree can do, just think what a bomb could do. I couldn't seem to focus on such a picture. For me, fortunately, I had never had to live through hardship, poverty, or war. These were things that happened in books or movies; at another time; in another place. However, in the peace and solitude of this northern wilderness, the devastation unleashed by a solitary pine certainly brought the thought to mind.

Out of this solitude, Trapper came raging toward me like a mad bull moose. "What in *hell* are you trying to do? Are you trying to get yourself killed or something? You scare me, sometimes. I don't think you'll ever make it outta here alive."

"In self-defence, might I just ask such a stupid question as what the hell are you yelling at me for?"

"You're going to get killed. What did you run over here for?"

"Beats wearing that thing," I said, pointing to the felled monster.

"You are supposed to move at right angles to a falling tree, not run away from it. When that tree crashes into the other tops surrounding it, it bends them right back and when all the energy in that tangle lets loose, a dry knot or limb could gut you. You are always talking about your ancestors who were knights in medieval times. That acts just like a catapult, you know; it can kill you."

"Well, I just didn't think about it."

"If you don't soon start to think, the opportunity to do so might not occur again."

I nodded in the affirmative. He tousled my auburn curls and began to cut the Chico into four-foot chunks to be carried down the hill to the camp. He wheeled that old saw about with great skill, moving on to the next block as each fell free. In mere minutes, he had the Chico piled in a heap.

"There, you old bastard—you'll keep Old Bertha warm tonight." He sat down to light up yet another cigarette.

"Don't you know you shouldn't smoke in the forest?"

With narrowed eyes seemingly held in place by the crow's feet wrapped about the corners, he glared at me and snapped, "I've never yet started a forest fire but I've helped put many a goddamn fire out."

Never changing his glare, he looked directly into my eyes, plucked a leaf from a nearby tree, and spat into it. Rolling the cigarette butt in the saliva, still glaring at me, he crushed the leaf in his bare hand and put it into his shirt pocket. Then he spat on the ground and turned away. "A man who doesn't have brains enough to put a cigarette out oughta not light it up in the first place."

We rose together, and he hoisted a four-foot block of wood to each shoulder and started down what from then on would be known as the "Wood Trail." Seventeen blocks in all were piled up by the sawhorse. Trapper then cut each of these into three blocks and split each of those into eight pieces. As he did that, I piled the split wood in the woodbox and under the washstand. When that was filled, I started to pile wood outside. One by one, I cradled eight pieces each time into my arms, carried them to the cabin, and piled them along the full length of the cabin wall. As the pile reached five feet in height, the forces of gravity took over, and refusing to stand any longer, my nice pile toppled in a heap to the ground.

"Oh, shit."

"What's the matter with you? Can't you curse without swearing?"

"Oh, the hell with it; who cares if the damn wood is piled or not, as long as it's here."

"You will, Miss know-it-all. If you don't pile that wood up, when the snows get deep, you won't be able to find half of it and what you do find will be all wet and the size of a truck tire with snow. Pile it up again."

"Are you kidding?"

"No kidding. If you pile that wood up against the walls that get the brunt of the winter's wind, the camp will be a lot warmer. When it gets to sixty below zero, you'll think there are cracks in the wall of that camp big enough for the dog to run through. Did you ever think about that? No, I'll bet you didn't. I don't know if you city folk think at all. You couldn't last out here one night alone."

"Okay, okay, okay. Will you please stop yelling at me all the time? Every time I try to do something, you make fun of me. I am trying to absorb some of your way of life but if I get hollered at every time I ask a question, I just won't ask. If I get laughed at every time I do something, then I just won't do anything. And if my being here upsets you so much, then I just won't be here."

"Now there is a thought! Oh, just hold on there, now, don't go gettin' all in an uproar. Just don't go gettin' a knot in your shirttail and your English all mixed up! I don't yell at you all the time and I don't laugh at you, either. I never said your being here upset me. I never said any of those things."

"You did too. You said everyone down south is a crazy bastard. You said they don't know how to eat and they don't know how to dress, and they all live in a pile of cement holes like goddamn groundhogs, and they're all crazy. Well, I come from down there and I like it. It's a good place to live."

"You mean it's a good place to come from," he retorted.

"Oh, go to hell. You are the most conceited, egotistical, self-satisfied, hypocritical, pompous goddamn old frog I ever met."

Well, he started to laugh and he laughed until he staggered, and he staggered until he backed onto the scattered firewood and backed over that until he buckled backwards and went ass over teakettle over the sawhorse.

"Come on, kid. We got to pile that wood up today. If it snows tonight, we'll never find half that wood."

He started to pile, showing me how to properly pile the wood, making piers at either end to support the pile. I piled and piled until my back was breaking and my fingers felt raw to the bone.

"Well, now, that's a job well done. Good thing we got that wood done today; those loons'll soon be flying backwards."

I scowled at him, and he grinned back, his sexy, crooked kind of a smile; his dancing eyes held captive in those crow's feet. He was a hard-living man with his hand to gun and knife most of the time. He lived totally independent and unto himself, asking nothing of the world but to be left alone. I once heard him say that if you didn't take chances in life, it was like being born dead and waiting a lifetime to be buried.

He stood some six feet tall; was ruggedly handsome; had a superbly powerful body even yet. His hair was still raven black, just beginning to grey at the temples. His cheeks were hollowed in skin yet unwrinkled but tanned by the weather. Those crooked crow's feet about amber-green eyes flanked a nose as chiselled and straight as any belonging to a Roman centurion. He was clean-shaven but for a trimmed black moustache above pencil-fine lips. As stubborn and dogmatic as he was, it was difficult not to like him. He was idealistic, compassionate, and honourable. He had a very strange sense of honour; he would take the shirt off your back if you weren't wearing it and give it to someone who really needed it. At the same time, he would take the shirt off his back and give it to you if you needed it.

We sat on the woodpile, our backs against the wall of the camp, taking in the warmth of the sunlight.

To the Rescue

Otter climbing onto log.
(Photo by Paton Lodge Lindsay)

My experience with the big Chico and the thoughts of war made me think of Trapper's earlier comments regarding his time spent at the military base at Petawawa.

"Trapper, tell me about your time in the army."

"I wasn't in the army."

"Well, you said you spent time at the military base in Petawawa."

"I did say that but I didn't say I was in the army."

"So what were you doing at the base, then?"

"Put me up a brown sugar sandwich and some tea in my tea pail, will you? Like I told you, that was another story. When the war broke out, they were looking for volunteers to fight the battles. You could have to dodge bullets and fight the enemy but you might have a roof over your head and a crust of bread in your belly and a dollar in your pocket. All the young lads in the settlement and small towns volunteered to serve their country, to fight for freedom. I went down to the recruitment office and volunteered, too. I could write some. I was young and strong and healthy and good in the bush. I could live off the land, was a good shot, and didn't need no damn map or compass to get around the country. I figured I had a pretty good shot at getting in. When all the young men left town to serve I was left alone in town with only those too young or too old to serve and the women. The army said I was too scrawny to carry a pack. They said I had flat feet and wouldn't be able to walk. Well, I decided right then and there that I'd show those pencil-necked bastards who could carry a pack, who could shoot a gun, and who could walk their mile.

"There was a cannon and artillery range at Petawawa where the government trained the troops with live ammunition. You couldn't get ammunition, but we still needed it to hunt and to trap. One day, those crazy bastards had their guns aimed right into the settlement and they put a shell right through the wall of Gramma's house, right into the kitchen. Well, now, I'll just tell you I knew where there was lots of ammunition, and it was free, too. At night, after dark, I'd go with some old trappers and we'd sneak out onto the cannon ranges and collect all the duds—artillery shells that hadn't fired. Then we'd spend all night in the dark sitting around a campfire and with a coal chisel and an axe and we'd pound the plug out of the base of the shells so we could get the powder out. We'd collect the powder in old metal tobacco tins, load up our packsacks with several tins each, and take it home to load our own shells. I don't know how we weren't killed sitting there in the dark, some of us smoking and pounding on loaded shells, with gunpowder and dynamite and a campfire. More than once we got a run outta there, but we got our ammo to hunt and trap.

"It didn't matter if you had any money or not—you just couldn't buy ammunition during the war. We got lead to melt down for bullets; and the copper bands from the shells were worth a dollar, too, but you had to be careful where you sold it. With all the men gone, the women were left home alone with the children to look after. There was no one there to put food on the table but me, so I did it. I shot fifty-four deer one year and lots of those deer came from Algonquin Park to feed the families whose men were gone to war. It wasn't like now, either. Some of those men were away from home for years. Some of those men never came home.

"I poached fur and hunted deer in the park all through the war. I ate well, too. I hunted the odd moose and partridge. Beaver would average twenty-five to thirty dollars a pelt, and I could get several a day. Twelve to fifteen beaver a week would give me $300 a month. At a dollar a day, that was a year's wages in a month.

"The army said I was no good, too scrawny; couldn't carry and couldn't walk. I showed them what I could do. Archie Belaney, better known as Grey Owl, wasn't the only goddamn bastard that could carry a gun across Algonquin Park and go undetected. I crossed their damn park hundreds of times and kept their goddamn park rangers good and busy, too. They hired extra rangers and even had their air patrol. That stopped the small-time poachers that were around but it didn't stop the King of the Long Runners. I knew the secret trails and hideaways and had the skills of the old-time voyageurs. Goddamn young rangers today, they'd get lost in the back of their pickup truck."

I went into the cabin and readied some brown sugar sandwiches for him and packed a lunch in his tea pail as he had asked. "It's all ready for you."

"Did you put in my enamel cup?"

"Oh, no, I forgot it. I forgot a fork, too."

"I don't need any damn little pitchfork to dig out the back of my neck. I eat with my belt knife. Goddamn little pitchfork is about as useful as tits on a bull or ribbons on a piss-pot. Come on, Tracker, let's get outta here." He picked up the pack and rifle and was off again to count beavers.

It got cold in the camp. Being used to the convenience of electric heat at home, I had forgotten to keep the stove fuelled up. The stove was dead out and the camp was perishingly cold. I ripped up some cardboard boxes and stuffed them into the stove along with some pieces of wood. Together they flamed up red and hot. Happy with my one-match fire, I settled down to read. Within minutes, the stove was again out and the camp cold. A cold wind breathed heavily on the camp. Lazily, I crawled in under the arctic sleeping bag to read and get warm.

Sometime later, I awoke and, half-stunned, rolled over, rubbed my eyes, and tried to see through the two red slits swollen from sleeping. A fierce wind lashed out across Wakami Lake. The spruce islands were heavily laden with snow. Streaks of white foam galloped across the lake to the far shore, which was totally invisible from sight. The white foam rose and fell in the expanse of raging black waters that rolled to the other side of the lake. It was four o'clock, nearly dark, and Trapper wasn't back. He'd never make it in that twelve-foot canoe. I decided that I'd best take the boat and go and find him.

Quickly I pulled on my insulated boots and heavy parka. Then, for some reason not known to this day, I changed into rubber boots and nylon ski jacket, neither of which was suitable for the weather. Getting to the boat, I quickly checked it out for life jackets, rope, gas can, and bailing can. It was all there. I untied the boat and shoved it out into the water. Tracker jumped in, and I followed. As we drifted out into the green turmoil, I pumped up the pressure in the gas tank. I had never run a motorboat before but I had watched Trapper several times. All was ready to go. I lowered the motor into the water, squeezed the rubber ball on the gas line, turned the handle to start, and gave the pull cord a good crank. The motor purred into action without hesitation. Happily, I was reassured that there really wasn't much to it at all. I then realized that though the motor was running I didn't seem to be under power. I was just drifting in the rough water. Long tentacles of water seemed to climb the sides of the boat in an effort to get in and would fall away just as they reached the gunwales. I turned the handle back and forth to start, slow, fast; but no change. It finally sputtered and quit. Once more, I set the handle to start, pumped up the gas pressure, pulled on the cord, and away it went. The same thing happened.

Distress overtook me as I realized just how far from shore I had drifted. The waves now battered the boat and crashed over the deck, tumbling inside. Several inches of water had collected in the bottom of the boat. The camp was all but out of sight as I drifted around the point. My breath all but stopped. How did I get myself into these messes? Trapper must have taken both paddles with him. I had to take some definite action quickly, as within minutes I'd be beyond the shelter of the islands and at the mercy of the open waters. I had only one choice. If I stayed with the boat, I'd drift to God knows where, and Trapper wouldn't be able to find me. I was beginning to wonder if he would even bother to try. He might just figure good riddins! The alternative was to jump in and try to swim to shore, a shore that I could no longer see. It was only from the direction of the waves that I could figure out where the shore should be. To jump in was against all my better judgment but I had no choice. I sat drifting in the midst of a raging sea. Snow had closed out all sight of the shore. I cautioned myself against panic and took off my rubber boots. If they filled with water they might pull me under. I picked Tracker up and threw him overboard. Taking hold of the bow rope, I jumped in.

The icy November waters closed in over my head. I really had to fight panic. I pulled on the rope and looked up through the water to see a giant shark-shaped object looming above me. It was the boat. Pulling on the rope, I broke through the surface. Brushing aside the hair that blinded me, I looked about to get my bearings. A huge wave crashed down on me rolling over and over and over, its icy tentacles grabbing at my limbs. Fear choked me as I became intensely aware of the situation I was in. This could be it if I didn't keep my wits about me. Without the boat, I'd never make it. I'd never stay afloat in the icy waters. From behind, another wave crashed down on me, knocking the wind from my lungs. That great black shadow loomed overhead again. It faded, and soon the waters parted to let me through to the air I so desperately needed. I licked my lips. The taste of salt told me I was crying.

Something sharp caught at my leg. What if my pants should get caught on an old log? This was all flooded land. The water had been raised by the building of the Wakami Dam. Hidden forests lay drowned beneath all the waters in the bays. It didn't seem possible to drag the boat back, but without it, there was no hope at all. I was thoroughly exhausted. My limbs were numb and reacted involuntarily. For me it really seemed as if the battle were done. My body stiffened with renewed fear but somewhere I found another burst of energy. In what would be my final struggle for shore and survival, I reached for the water and pulled on the rope. "Reach and pull . . . Reach and pull." In an effort to maintain sanity, I finally coached myself out loud as I had many a young swimmer in previous years. Reach, pull, inhale, and glide; reach, pull, inhale, and glide." This rhythmic motion I repeated time after time. Was the shore really getting any closer, or was it my imagination? Something caught at my pant leg again. It was the sharp knot of a tree. The water was deep yet, far over my head, but I could now see the muddy line where the sandbanks rose. If I could just keep going long enough to reach them, I might be able to stand up. I could hardly see anymore, and my arms just fell at will; but there is no fight as great as the fight for one's life.

Ahead, I could see logs and stumps in the water. My knees finally hit the wall of the drop-off. For a moment, I lay there resting against it, the waves crashing over my head. I staggered to my feet only to be knocked down by a wave and washed into the shallows. Literally I crawled on all fours up onto the snow-covered bank, where I collapsed in total physical exhaustion. After some unknown period of time, I began to regain my senses and pulled the boat up out of the water as far as I could and tied it off to the large clump of alder stumps. Somehow, I made my way to the cabin and for a time just sat on the step and shivered.

"Where was Trapper?" That thought made me come to my senses. I had to get things straightened up before he got back. He must never find out about this. Quickly, I stripped down and dried off and got warm, dry clothes on. I hung all my wet stuff out on the clothesline behind the camp and returned and tried to dry my hair from the heat of burning boxes in the stove. I wiped up the floor, and all looked normal. I turned to look out the cabin window. In the deep blue light of dusk I could just see Trapper standing at the shore looking at the boat.

"What's going on here?" he shouted up to the camp.

I didn't answer. He came directly to the camp and posed the question again. Very directly, he said, "I asked you what's going on here. What happened here?"

"Nothing happened."

"Your hair is all wet!"

"I just washed it."

"You wash the damn dog, too, and the floor?"

In furious strength he grabbed my arm and swung me around to face him.

"Your coat and boots are in the boat. They are all wet. And the dog, did you give him a bath, too? You can't hide anything in the bush from me and I'm telling you right now, don't you ever lie to me." He smashed his fist onto the table. "Don't you *ever* dare lie to me. NOW, I want to know what happened here."

I related the entire story to him as though reliving it all over again. He was enraged, common sense lost in anger.

"What the *Christ* were you doing in the boat?"

"I was coming to get you. I was afraid you couldn't make it in that canoe or you'd get into trouble or get lost in the storm."

"LOST!" he bellowed. "There we go again. LOST? That's a good one. ME, LOST? I've been on my own since I was eleven years old. I've trapped in the bush on foot, and travelled in canoes for months at a time and never seen another human being, and in weather that you wouldn't put that dog out to piss in. I've slept out with no tent and no blanket at forty below zero and lived off the land all my life and now, NOW you think I need some spoiled, wilful greenhorn of a kid, and a female at that, from Toronto to look after me? Well I DON'T. And furthermore, I'm telling you right now you stay outta that boat and you leave my stuff alone. You're goin' to get into some shit around here that you can't get yourself out of. And, I'm tellin' you, if I have to take you in hand, I will—and don't you ever think I can't."

"Yah, you and whose army?"

"Don't you ever dare me!" he yelled as he slammed his fist down on the table again. "Just don't you ever dare me, you orphaned, ill-bred, misbegotten relict of a sea cook."

"I was only trying to help you!" I yelled back in retaliation.

"WELL DON'T!" he roared. "I don't need your help. Now you'll probably end up with the grippe or something, and how can I look after you back here? Get into bed, and I'll get the damn fire stoked up and get some hot tea into you and get you warmed up. Go on. Get into that bed before you get your ass burned and I'm in about the right mood right now."

I crawled into bed with Tracker at my side. We were all safe now, but I shook uncontrollably. Was it the cold or was the real fear of it all just beginning to settle in? I don't know why, but it was then that I really started to cry silently. Trapper brought me a cup of hot, sweet tea, and a bowl of hot soup. He added his blanket and sleeping bag to the top of mine. I remember seeing him sitting at the table in the flickering glow of the oil lamp, marking new beaver houses on the map. Feeling warm and secure in his care, I fell asleep.

8

Midnight Visitor and the Sea Monsters

Charlie, camp pet.
(Photo by Paton Lodge Lindsay)

Sometime in the night, Tracker awoke me with his growling. He was staring at the camp wall, eyes gleaming, front legs stretched straight out in front and rear end stuck up in the air. His eyes moved from side to side as though he were watching something. A low, guttural growl rumbled deep in his chest and kind of gurgled from between clenched teeth. Immediately I held my breath, stopped breathing, and listened. He growled again and jumped back from the wall. There was something outside! Then I heard it. There WAS something out there! I listened very intently. No, there was something INSIDE the cabin! It was an animal. Oh, my God, there was a wild animal in the camp! I pulled the sleeping bag up over my head and slid down to the bottom of it so I could pull it tightly down under my face and arms. There was a veritable marathon going on in the wall. They streaked from one end of the wall to the other and back. I could hear claws scratching on the logs, and squeaks, and screeches, and it would reverse and start over again. I folded back the corner of the sleeping bag to peek out. Tracker's eyes were all afire with excitement. They travelled back and forth along the wall following every lap these mysterious dragsters made. Suddenly they were right at my head. I dove under the sleeping bag again. A terrible shriek emitted from the wall and bones cracked and crunched.

"Oh, God, I'm going to be sick. Trapper, are you awake? TRAP-PER?" There was no response. How could he sleep through that racket? "Are you asleep, Trapper? T-R-A-P-P-E-R, are you asleep?"

"Well, I'm not, now. Jesus, Jesus, Jesus! It's only mice. Go back to sleep."

"MICE? If there are mice that big up here, I'm going home tomorrow!"

"M-m-m," he grinned. "Now, I'm about to tell you there are mice ten times bigger than that up here, so I'll help you pack to-morrow."

"There isn't a mouse in the world could make a racket like that."

Not satisfied with his reply and edgy with the continued rum-pus going on right at my head, I turned the flashlight on and shone it on the wall and followed the sounds in the wall with the beam of the light. Suddenly, the light reflected off two eyes in the wall.

"Trapper!" I yelled, "there is an animal in here."

"Jesus Christ, will you be quiet and go back to sleep? It's only mice."

"It's NOT mice. It's a big animal. There it is. Look. Look at it. It's looking at me through that knothole in the wall. Oh, my God, it's coming into the camp! Look at it."

"Jesus Christ! I can't run around in the bush all day if I can't get any sleep at night. What the hell is the matter with you, any-way?" He rolled over and propped himself up on one elbow. "Well, I'll be a son of a sea cook! Go to it, ole boy. In a day or two, there won't be a mouse in the house. It's a weasel. He'll clean the camp out. Every camp should have a weasel."

That weasel visited the camp periodically and could always

be sure of finding a snack on the top log of the camp. Trapper put a sardine tin up there and every day we'd put some little tidbit of meat in there; every three or four days, we'd find it empty and know that Charlie the weasel had been back. Before the winter was out, he brought a girlfriend. We called her Charlotte. Charlie and Charlotte would run about the camp and wrestle and play and give us endless joy and entertainment. Tracker seemed to know they belonged and never bothered them.

It was early, five in the morning, but now that we were awake, Trapper decided we might as well get up anyway. Today he was going to the head of Wakami Lake and count beaver houses on the river, and then go up to the Janette Lake portage and maybe over to Efby Lake and Efby Creek. After a rather intense altercation, I convinced him to take two canoes. He could go and count beavers on Efby Lake and creek, and I could take Tracker and count beavers at the head of Wakami Lake. We packed our gear and readied everything for the day. Tracker seemed to sense that something special was planned, as he kept pacing from the door of the camp to the shore and back. Every once in a while, he would leap into the air and bark with the anticipation of another day on the trail. Trapper took the green twelve-foot canoe, and I took the grey sixteen-foot Chestnut canoe. I preferred the sixteen-foot canoe to paddle, but, as Trapper said, "When you have to do a lot of portaging, the shorter the canoe the better. Some portages are so thick with brush, and some small creeks so crooked, you'd have to have hinges in the middle of the canoe to get around the bends." He always said no matter what a canoe looked like, or what it was made of, or how small it was, if it would float, he'd go in it.

Once readied, it took us an hour and twenty minutes to paddle up to Roger's Bay. At this point, we parted and went our separate ways. Trapper went into the Efby portage and I paddled on up to the head of Wakami Lake. As I paddled, I made use of the "pitch" stroke that Trapper had taught me. That is a stroke by which the direction of the canoe is governed by the angle or pitch of the paddle blade in the water. You never have to "J"—just keep paddling ahead with a steady forward stroke. You simply adjust the angle of the paddle to compensate for water and wind conditions. Then I tried another stroke that Trapper had shown me, one where you draw the paddle blade through the water in the usual manner but keep the paddle in the water with the knife edge of the blade forward to return the paddle to the forward position. You never remove the paddle from the water, so this is a very quiet stroke when properly executed. I found it a little tricky at first, as the paddle kept trying to twist in my hand and would then reef on the canoe. As Trapper had said, "If you don't watch yourself doing that stroke, you can find yourself drinking standing up." It took me a while to feel comfortable with that stroke but I can honestly say I never got wet.

Trapper had made me a small cedar board on which he had wound some fifty-pound test fishing line, the green line that looked like green butcher's cord. It was well armed with a big number three Muskie Killer, the variety with a copper spinner and a gang hook hidden in a red bucktail. The bay through which we were paddling was mainly flooded land; stumps, deadheads, and roots all came close to the surface and at times even touched the belly of the canoe. This proved to be true as we rounded a point into the river. There was a multitude of black stubs standing upright in the water. I had to manoeuvre the canoe among them to make my way out into the open water. It really bothered me to have unknown objects just beneath the canoe and out of sight in the black water. I just knew there was some creature lurking down there waiting to reach up over the gunwales and yank me from the canoe down into those cold, black tea-coloured waters. I paddled on and on, never seeming to completely get away from the stubs. I stopped paddling and laid the paddle across the gunwales to shift position. Not a ripple disturbed the waters as we proceeded into the narrows.

The hills to the west were reflected in greens and yellows in the water. They were a mural of exquisite skill painted by the greatest artist known to mankind. Tracker, who had been sleeping in the stern of the canoe quickly rose up and extended dilated nostrils to the air. What was it? What did he smell? Just ahead of me, one of those black stubs was bobbing up and down in the water like a floating pop bottle. I stared at it intensely and in disbelief. Then two more stubs bobbed up and down. The largest of the three remained erect in the water and started to cough and spit at me. The two smaller stubs turned and swam away. As I dared to drift closer, I noticed the elongated snake-like neck, the wide, flattened head, grey about the mouth, the long whiskers. It was an otter. As she lay out on top of the water, a long, sleek, fur-covered tail at least half the length of her three-foot body lifted out of the water and swung over her back. She looked like a miniature sea monster. It was a mother and her two little ones. The she-otter escorted her two little ones several yards away and then turned to whistle and cough and spit at me again. She would float about fifty feet away from me and snap and crack her teeth at me, advising me to stay away.

"Go on, on your way, now. Go on. You just leave me alone, and I promise faithfully that I will leave you alone. Go on, now. Please," I quietly begged her. She departed, lifting that snake-like tail out of the water as she went. Thankfully, we had gone our separate ways without incident. As I continued to cruise the west bank of the river, I found bits of green poplar brush and white sticks floating in the water. These were a sure sign that beavers had located somewhere close by. Trapper had said there were seven houses on the river last fall. As I paddled along, I found six beaver houses, but they were all dry. There was no new mud, no new sticks, no fresh feed bed. It presented a dismal outlook. Had Trapper taken all the beavers last year, or had they just moved for some reason?

Farther upriver, I came to the remains of an old log cabin. There were two old remains there, one partially submerged in the river. Trapper later informed me that it was an old Hudson's Bay Company Post. The Wakami River was on the Arctic watershed. Not far past the old post, we finally reached the head of the river and the Janette Lake portage, where Tracker and I got out and stretched our legs. We walked along the riverbank and followed a well-used game trail in the small peninsula that led around to an old log slide. It was a kind of cribbing built over the creek and rapids, going about a half-mile uphill to the next small lake. Loggers used to slide their logs from the above waters down through this huge wooden trough or slide and into the Wakami River, and thence to the mill.

"It's three o'clock, Tracker. You know what the boss told us. We have to be back at the Efby Portage by four-thirty."

Once settled into the canoe again, we headed straight across the river to the far side. Just below the portage was a beaver house all freshly mudded and with the beginnings of a fresh feed bed in front. We paddled our way along, trolling the Muskie Killer all the way. Where the river opened up into a small pond, we found another new beaver house. This house was freshly mudded and a few green poplar and birch branches floated about in the water, but there was no feed bed. Poplar and birch trees were felled along the bank. Beaver runways led into the bush all along the bank, but no feed had been brought to the house. There seemed little doubt that someone would be residing there. I made two complete circuits about the little pond in the hopes of catching a fish, but no such luck.

Proceeding on along the east bank, we came to a huge beaver house hidden behind a point that stretched out into the main body of water. This house was well-mudded and had a feed pile in front of it that must have been eight feet wide, fifteen feet long, and the full depth of the water, which must have been at least ten feet deep. I could see yellow leaves in the water and a huge poplar that had fallen into the bay. We found there a beaver house of massive proportions with a feed bed equally tremendous. There had to be a huge family here. The tracks in the mud were as large as my own hand. There were really big beaver tracks, and medium and smaller tracks as well. There had to be at least three years of beaver kits in this house.

It was now three-thirty, and darkness comes early in autumn. We paddled along the east shore in the light of the setting sun and made our way down to the flood wood bay, where we frightened a school of mergansers. Resting the paddle upon the gunwales, I shifted about, flexing leg muscles that had become stiff from immobility. As I took up a new position, this time with my derriere upon the seat, I heard a considerable amount of splashing in the distance. Looking carefully among the flood wood entanglement, nothing gave away its presence. Again, I heard the splashing. I saw nothing.

Perhaps it was a school of ducks after minnows. I listened keenly to the wind. An unbelievable sound came to my ears. It resembled the sound one would expect to hear from a table full of little boys indulging in a feast of spaghetti and meat sauce. Once

again, that same sound teased my ears. This time it was accompanied by the crushing and crunching of bones. Slowly, I glided forward without moving my paddle from the water. My eyes burned
from their intense, unblinking stare searching the entanglement.
Suddenly my heart jumped, then skipped a beat, then stopped, I'm
sure, momentarily. There it was. There by a huge, octopus-like
stump, was that whistling, coughing, spitting, bobbing pop bottle.
This time there was no going around her. I kept silent and made
Tracker lie down in the bottom of the canoe. The wind was right.
Tracker would never smell her, but it wouldn't be long before she
got a whiff of him again. Was a she-otter with young as unpredictable as a she-bear with cubs? I didn't want to find out.

Quietly, and as motionlessly as possible, I manoeuvred through
the water so as not to disturb her, lest she feel I was too frequently
invading her territory. Keeping a wary eye on those behind me, I felt
like I was being stalked and hunted. Another glance . . . that long,
snake-like neck was stretched high out of the water. It bobbed up
and down a few times and then held steady. Her snorts crossed the
water. She coughed and spit and gnashed her teeth. A high-pitched
whistle came to my ears. She climbed up onto the huge stump and
let a loud whistle out to the wind. Carried on the wind, her whistle
was answered from a flat rock at my back. From the rock, a huge
black animal whistled in response then slid into the water, bobbed,
growled, and gnashed its teeth, and the four were mobile. Daddy
otter was here, too, and I was caught between them.

Now there was a marathon race, and I was out in front—but
not for long. The gap between us was swiftly closing, and the four
coughed and spit as they came. Tracker balanced precariously on
the gunwale and seat and growled and barked, which only encour-
aged them. I paddled as an Olympic athlete striving for the gold,
but the only gold I was looking for was the gold of the poplar at the
Efby portage, which was nowhere in sight ahead of me. The otters
behind me sliced through the water as a team of Olympic scullers.
It definitely seemed as though they were up for gold. If lucky, I
might catch the bronze, if they didn't catch me.

As the canoe touched shore, I got up and ran the length of the
canoe, only to find that it had actually passed backwards beneath
my feet, and there was twelve feet of water between the bow of the

canoe and the shore. I leaped over the end into the water and flogged it to shore. I then legged my way down the trail just as fast as my short, stalky legs would go. In a mental frenzy, I fully expected the otters would cut through the bush and head me off. I was terrified. Many times, I had seen otters cavorting and playing in the movies, but this was different. This wasn't Walt Disney. This was for real.

I ducked under a fallen tree, jumped over a rotten, moss-covered log, tore headlong around a massive stone, and connected with a seemingly immovable object. To my great horror, I lay sprawled out on my back, and Trapper was laid out flat on his back on the trail. In totally stunned disbelief, he got up, brushed needles, bark, and other debris from his clothing, picked his packsack up from beneath a spruce where it had landed, fetched his cap from where it hung precariously on a birch branch, and in total silence turned and stared at me.

He began very quietly, but each word increased in both enunciation and volume. "Might I ask just what the *roarin'* Jesus you are tryin' to *do* to me?" Removing his hat from his head, he threw it to the ground and said, "What are you tryin' to do, outrun the north wind or something?"

"No, Trapper. It's the otters. They are after me, the two big ones and their little ones. They were in the bay when I came across it and now they are after me."

He laughed. "Look at you. You're all wet again, and it's cold. It'll be damn cold as soon as that sun is gone. Let's get back to camp. You think there is a wild animal behind every tree in the bush. If that were true, I'd have been dead long ago or else been a millionaire. I spend all my time looking for them. I wish they'd come lookin' for me instead. It would sure make life a lot easier."

Of course when we got to the shore, the canoe and paddles were floating well out from shore. We looked at one another. In total silence, he just stood there and grinned. That sexy smile, the amber-green eyes framed in the crow's feet; he just stood and looked me right in the eye. Finally, being the gentleman he could be, he took his canoe and went and got my canoe. Seeing as we were both returning to camp, he took a rope and tied his canoe behind mine with a bridle hitch, and we both paddled the canoe together back to camp.

When we got back to camp, Trapper cleaned the partridge. He pulled the feathers and skin off together in big fluffy pieces and tossed them into a burlap sack. The feathers removed, the pink, shiny flesh showed. They looked just like little Cornish hens you'd see in the meat department of the local grocery store.

"Yuk! Are you going to eat them?"

"It may be 'yuk' now, but it's 'm-m-m!' at the table."

A green, pimply sack hung at its neck. It was translucent. You could see through but not into it.

"What's that?" I asked, pointing to it.

"That's the crop. They store the food they've eaten in it. If you were to break it open, you'd know what they'd been eating."

"Really? Let's open it!"

He looked at me as if he truly believed I was totally demented. He took his knife and opened the crop. It was very delicate, tissue-like skin and it hung in a sack separate from the body but attached at the throat. A connecting tube that resembled the hose on a vacuum cleaner joined it. Within the crop were yellow tamarack needles, pieces of green leaves, and bright red berries. I picked through the feed and looked at each kind.

"Now, with this autopsy—or whatever kind of biological research you care to call this—done, do you suppose I could finish cleaning the damn things?"

"Permission granted," I quipped.

He cut off the wings and the legs and the head. Then he split the bird along the rib cage and folded it back on a hinged spine and emptied the innards out. He cut the tail off last, washed the bird, put it in a pot, and said, "There! See what you can do with that. That's more in your line . . . maybe?"

I took special pains to prepare his partridge. As he puttered about outside the camp, I laid three linen tea towels across the table and arranged some sprigs of pine and yellow poplar leaves in a glass for the table centre. I covered a plate with aluminum foil to serve as a silver platter and set the roasted partridge dripping with butter, fried onions, and bacon bits in the centre. Then I surrounded them with pan-browned potatoes and carrots candied with brown sugar and honey. Two candle stubs glowed atop little foil-covered milk cans on either side of the table centre. A small glass of warmed cranberry juice topped off this gourmet trapper's dinner. I stepped to the door of the camp and leaned out with an iron frying pan and a large steel spoon. Banging the pan with the spoon, I rang the dinner bell.

"*Votre diner est prêt, Monsieur.*" My eyes lighted up and the corners of my lips curled to see the delight and surprise in his face.

"Don't know 'bout your French, but you sure are capable in the kitchen!"

He buttered a hot scone, sipped the warmed cranberry juice, and believe it or not, with a fork broke free a piece of partridge breast dripping with butter and hot honey and raised it to his lips. He held it in his mouth savouring the flavour, then chewed on it easily, sat back with eyes shut and let the butter and honey drip from his chin.

"What are you doing for the next twenty years, kid? That is food fit for a king. Fit for a king, and I'm just a trapper." He started to laugh. "You are a real princess, and I am a real pauper. It's true. Here we are, 'way back in the wilderness in this little log cabin, and it is no fantasy, it is reality. We are the Princess and the Pauper."

"And you, Sire, are a real king. You are sovereign of all you survey. Maybe that dinner will help you to forgive me for all the trouble I've been to you."

"Oh, Christ, it's only because you are young and eager and want to learn and want to do a good job. I know all that, but you've got to listen and you've got to do what you're told. You may be a mature adult where you come from, but up here in the bush, you're like a baby away from home. It's different here and this is a goddamn big backyard you're playing in. You know, it's a hundred and fifty miles to the 17 Highway, and a hundred and fifty miles to Highway 11. You are at the end of the road in this part of the country."

The darkness turned to blackness, and the old gas lantern hissed its whistling tune as I did up the dishes. It seemed the gas lantern did nothing but whisper Christmas carols, dozens of them, one after the other. Perhaps I was a little bit homesick and was subconsciously looking forward to the return south for Christmas with my family. As I finished the domestic chores, Trapper oiled the firearms. We completed our chores together and both decided to turn in, as morning came early. Once I was in bed, Trapper turned off the gas lantern. Its hissing slowed to a whisper.

Only the moonlight shone through the window. Three spruce spires were silhouetted in the full, white face of God as He looked down with love on our darkened world. A long, lonesome, "O-O-O-W-W-W" prowled the hilltops to call the night life together. It was the end of the day for one-half of the world, but only the beginning of the day for the other half.

Nature's Meteorologists

Male timber wolf along the trail.
(Photo by Paton Lodge Lindsay)

This is my Father's world;
The birds their carols raise;
The morning light, the lily white,
Declare their Maker's praise.[7]

In the fall of the year, the Canada geese make their annual migration to their wintering grounds far to the south. Other than the loon, there is nothing more a part of the Canadian North than the Canada goose. Trapper's trapline appears to be right on the flyway. Never in my life have I seen so many geese. The days were cold and clear. The bays and ponds were frozen. The geese were on the move. Summoned by the mellow "honk, honk" from the leader of the flying wedge, on came the long-necked wild geese from their northern nesting grounds. They streamed across the sky so far above that their large bodies appeared like two lines of dots in a great "V." In spite of their height, one could distinctly hear the call of the temporary leader, some old veteran, answered in deeper tones by the rear guardsmen as the long array moved in impressive unison across the clouds. The fanning of their wings was distinctly audible, too. Sometimes, the two diverging lines came together into one, and a serpent seemed to crawl with snake-like undulations across the sky. Other flocks would come on in In-dian file and shoot straight as an arrow across the sky. A slow, lazy drift down a slope of a mile or two on almost motionless wings brought them to the surface with majestic grace, and, flying low until the precise spot was reached where they wished to rest, they leaned backwards and settled with a heavy splash onto the water. Their call haunted the lakes and hills for days and nights without cease. On the third day, the snows began. The logs along the shore became gem-clad with white wilderness diamonds and twinkled in the few sunny periods. There wasn't a sign of bird or animal life. At mid-afternoon, the wolves began to howl a ceaseless "O-O-O-W-W-W" that prowled the hilltops and valleys until six o'clock the following morning.

"Just watch out, now," warned Trapper. "When the wolves howl for hours on end like that, there is something on the wind."

"Did the old people tell you that, too?"

"You laugh! Go ahead. You can laugh now, but I'm tellin' you, you won't be laughing tomorrow."

During the night, Mother Nature had truly redecorated. The pine and spruce were all robed in white velvet that kissed the snowy carpets beneath. Long curls of snow swirls entwined among the old logs and resembled great, white, sea waves rolling into the shore. Granite stones that once rimmed the islands took on the softness of giant marshmallows. During the night, twenty-two inches of snow had been laid down to blanket the earth in prepara-tion for the long sleep.

"There, now: What do you think of the wolves now, eh? They

weren't too far from being right, were they?"

It was true, just as he had said. There it was. The weatherman, with all of his advanced equipment and intricate radar and modern meteorological devices, has problems forecasting the weather accurately, but these creatures of the wild seemed uncannily capable of doing so. Was this another of Mother Nature's wonders? Trapper felt strongly that this snow would not stay. Why? Because the animals were not ready for winter. My not-very-well-concealed display of doubt annoyed him.

"They're just not ready yet. They know when winter will come. They know if it will be a long winter or a short winter, open or bad."

"Oh, come off it, Trapper. Man is the most intelligent creature on earth and *we* can't tell that."

"You are wrong. Man is not the most intelligent creature on earth; he only thinks he is."

"Oh, use your head, man. Just look at civilization today. Look at the marvels and wonders of communication and transportation, and medicine, the health and wealth of our country and our standard of living."

"Yah, just look at it! Education is going to be the ruin of this civilization. We know too much for our own good, but we don't know enough to sustain life forever. In the past, people were born and raised the best way people knew how. Everyone was self-sufficient. There was plenty for everyone. People worked together to support their small towns and traded and shared and everyone prospered. Today, with all their 'scientific miracles,' as you call them, people live to miraculous ages and they don't die off. They don't leave the earth offering food and space and shelter and work for the young. Don't you see that if so many didn't live so long, but just passed on when their time came, we wouldn't have a world population problem. We wouldn't have food problems. You said you want to manage the natural resources. Well, those educated people you always talk about say we have to have hunting and trapping seasons to control the animal population so the animals don't become overpopulated and get diseases or eat themselves out of house and home and starve to death. By controlling the numbers of animals, we are being humane. It prevents thousands and millions from starving to death or dying a terrible death with suffering from disease. What of the human population? No! Man is too blind to see that the same end awaits him." He lit a cigarette.

"No, instead, when children are born sick, we spend billions of dollars to keep them vegetating in lives that will not likely amount to anything. When people grow old and diseased, we hook them up to machines and dope them up for years and subject them to long times of agony in the hopes that they will live longer. If your dog were suffering like that, they'd charge you with cruelty to animals and force you to humanely put it out of its misery; but if it's your parent or your kid, they force you to keep them living and suffering. It's against the law to let the animal live and against the law to kill the human. Now I ask you, where is the sense in that?

"In the animal world, when they grow old, they die and make room for others to follow. They give birth to and support their own. There is no welfare in the animal world. No taxes, either, no imposing factors from society. No, Man should look to the animals and he'd learn something. Man can't do anything that animals can't do. Not when you look to the real necessities of actual life. He might do things differently and extravagantly, but he'll pay for it. Man has lost track of what life and living are. Kids today, hell, there is no point in even talking about it. A few generations ago, by the time you were fourteen or fifteen you were a man, out working, had your own home, maybe even a family. There was none of this runnin' home to Mommy and Daddy, 'cause Mommy and Daddy had a half-dozen more kids at home to keep. Today, the kids arrive back home with their spouses and all their kids, too. Mommy and Daddy keep everybody.

"No, damn it, you were a man. When my mother died, I was eight years old. Me and my sister went into Algonquin Park with the old man to live in the logging camps and cut down the big pine. When I was twelve, I was in charge of all the horses in the lumber camp of 200 men. I'd take a team of horses and a wagon or a jumper sleigh and go miles out to the railroad to meet the train. They'd throw off all the supplies along the track and I'd have to find them and load them all onto the wagon alone and tie it all down and get it back to camp. Sometimes I'd be gone overnight.

I knew every trail in the bush for miles. Today, you take a kid of twelve, shit; the only trail he knows is the trail from the idiot box to the refrigerator and the microwave and back to the computer."

"Okay, okay, okay. Trapper, you said the animals can tell when winter is coming and that they weren't ready yet. How can you know . . . how do *they* know?"

"Well, we've been checking beaver houses for a couple of days now. In the small lakes and ponds where the waters have frozen, the houses are all mudded up and their winter's feed is in. Those beaver are ready because where they live, winter comes early. In the big lakes and the river, where we are still paddling, the waters are still open. Big lakes take longer to cool down, and the wind can get at them and keep them from freezing. In the river, the current keeps the water from freezing until it gets really cold. Winter won't set in until much later for those beaver. Those beaver have just started to mud up their houses. They have just started to cut and put in a feed bed. They won't require that food for a while. They know it. They have to know it. Their lives depend on it."

"Mother Nature sure did endow the animals with instinct, didn't she?"

"There you go again," Trapper snapped, "thinking man is smarter. It's a peculiar way of thinking. In the animal world, the ability to get along and survive is considered mere instinct. In man, it is considered a superior thing called 'intelligence.' Who in hell does Man think he is?"

"Trapper, you really astound me. You talk about yourself as if you were one of the animals."

"I AM, no more, no less. 'And they went in two and two into the ark, the male and the female as God commanded. And take thou unto thee all food that is eaten and it shall be for thee and for them' . . . that is what the Lord said . . . 'This is the token of my covenant which I make between me and you and every living creature that is with you for perpetual generations.'"[8]

More than an hour passed, neither of us speaking, just thinking and being with the Maker Himself in our own ark of the wild creatures.

My Own Line

Paton out on the trail.

(Photo: Keith Harlen Hoback)

I sat up in my bed, shedding my sleeping bag as a caterpillar would shed its cocoon; but I was not nearly as graceful as an emerging butterfly. With a loud groan, I stretched my "wings."

"Don't stretch too far," he laughed. "You'll have to walk back."

"What's up? What plans have you got for today, Trapper?"

"Today . . . today we'll sit tight right here in camp. We'll stay close to the ole box stove, eh, Tracker? We'll stay right here in camp and keep ole Bertha hoppin'."

"But Trapper, it's so beautiful out."

"It's goddamn shitty out there, that's what it is. You just touch one Jesus balsam and you'll see just how beautiful it is. The son-of-a-whore'll pour half the snow in the bush down your Christly neck. No, it's not for me. Not today. I'm just going to keep ole Bertha puffin' today."

The remainder of the morning was spent reading. Trapper was thoroughly engrossed in the tales of the Old West. I dwelt on my books of biological content and environmental management. Rachel Carson and Aldo Leopold and I had become conversant acquaintances. This quiet morning when there was nothing else to do, I spent some time thinking. Is that when most of us find time to think—when there is nothing else to do?

"Trapper, do you think that I could have a small line of traps of my own?"

"You, don't be crazy! You, the lover of animals, protector of the wilderness? You want a trapline? Are you serious?"

"I was never more serious about anything in my life. I don't know that I agree with trapping but then I don't really know anything about it first-hand. Everything I hear about it is always one-sided. People are always for it or dead set against it. There is only one way to find out the truth and that is to go with you on the trapline and see for myself and do it for myself. Then, I can speak with first-hand knowledge and experience."

He paced the floor, scratching his chin and stroking his moustache, and then cast a sceptical eye in my direction.

I said, "You are the King. Tell me, show me, and share your life with me. I want to know about your lifestyle. Nine generations ago, your ancestor came here from France to negotiate a trade alliance with the Natives. You say your ancestors were granted the rights to the fur and the rights to hunt and fish whenever necessary. You say they were granted by the king."

"You're goddamn right they were. They are mine by right from the king. My family has trapped these lands for nearly 400 years, and we are still trapping them. When the Lord made this world, He didn't make Algonquin Park first. There were lots of beaver, they were mine by right, and I made goddamn sure I got my share. They can have their goddamn Algonquin Park. I've got my own park now—Wakami Park."

"Tell me your story; share your story and your life with me. When your generation is gone, the first-hand history is all gone and it will forever be gone. Show me your way of life."

"Okay, grab a packsack and let's get at it. You'll need some wire and fencing staples, an axe, some Conibear traps, a belt knife, some leather gloves, and a rifle. Put in your compass, a map, some waterproof matches, and some pepperoni sticks. Throw those fish and partridge guts into a bag. You'll need them for bait."

I rushed about, frantically gathering all the items he said I'd need and trying not to forget anything.

"Get a hitch in your git-a-long. There are lots of things to do, so let's get going."

Quickly I pulled on my jacket, toque, and mitts and, with rifle in hand and pack on my back, we ducked through the door on the way to set out my trapline.

"I sure wouldn't want to be goin' on a long trip with you," said Trapper.

"Why?"

"The plane or boat would be halfway to its destination before you got there to board it."

"Oh, yah? Well, I'll have you know that when I was in school, there wasn't a boy I couldn't outjump, outrun, or outfight. I was a real tomboy."

"Was?"

"I still am, I suppose."

My brother and sister grew up rather normally, I guess. They had the distinct advantage of not being the first, the oldest. I didn't present any real difficulties for my parents, but I certainly wasn't the beautiful, petite model-become-equestrian and artist who was my sister, and I certainly wasn't the trim, handsome, athlete-be-come-professor and world's expert in his field that my brother is. I always jokingly said there were three B's in our family: Brains, Beauty, and Brawn. My sister got the beauty, my brother got the brains, and I got the brawn! My brother would always whimsically retort, "You're the oldest. You were first in line!"

When I was a little girl, I always liked to play cops and robbers or cowboys and Indians with the boys. Then, it was road construction and railways in the sand pile. By the age of nine, I would be nothing other than a female Sergeant Preston of the RCMP in the wilderness of the Arctic patrolling about by dogsled and bringing law and order to the frozen north. By eleven, I was determined to be a test pilot for the new supersonic jets coming into the world. By my teens, I was going to be a conservation officer just like Chief Ranger George Keeley. I patrolled our ravine and Black Creek to ensure that no one disturbed the birds or animals there. I played baseball and basketball and football. I was on track and field teams, swimming teams, and won a local table tennis championship. Of course I also took ballet, acrobatics, highland dancing, music, and equestrian lessons. All of these were of course an attempt to make a lady out of me. Ha! Whatever had gone wrong? What had Mother ever done to deserve me? Now I was going to be a trapper.

Trapper and I trod along an old wagon road used to portage supplies into the old logging camps many decades before. The only telltale signs were the two wagon ruts, hidden beneath inches of accumulated pine needles and leaves, that wound about between the poplars and birches and pine trees, now forty to fifty feet high.

"Look there! See that old blaze on that tree?"

"Where? I can't see it."

"Look! Right there on that old birch. It's an old blaze to mark the road."

"I must be blind. I can't see any blaze."

"You people are something else! Those great white hunters from down south come up here every fall and we're always hauling them around somewhere because they couldn't see a blaze, either. They're always lost. They'd get lost in the back of their four-wheel-drives if they didn't have a keen nose."

"A keen nose?"

"Yes, a keen nose. Most of them never get far enough away from their campsite and fifth wheel to lose the scent of that antifreeze they bring up here in cases of twenty-four." He tramped about, obviously completely disgusted with me and all aspects of civilization.

"There!" He pointed. "Do you see that?" he said as he tapped his finger on the tree trunk. It was a scar long healed over, the lips curled outward and hardened with time. He slashed at it with his axe and bared the white tree flesh once more just as it had been fifty years before.

"Here's a good spot. A fallen log is a natural. Hollow the rot out of the centre a bit more till it's a couple of feet deep. Then cut a long, dry pole and bring it here. I'll show you how to set this." With the end of the log hollowed out, and a six-foot pole at my side, I awaited further instructions.

"Okay, now get a trap out of the pack and about a foot of wire. Then cut a forked stick, just a small one, and shove the partridge legs onto it . . .

"Good. Now, reach as far back into the log as you can and push the forked stick with the bait on it into the log. Make sure it's stuck in good . . . Now, you're ready to set the trap. Get one of those one-twenties out of your pack."

"One of these Chinese jigsaw puzzles?" I asked, holding aloft a small Conibear.

"That's it."

I handed it to him and he narrated as he demonstrated.

"Now, make sure when you are handling this that your fingers are never in a position where they can get caught in the jaws in case the trap snaps. Okay, ready?"

I nodded in the affirmative.

"Position the two springs so they are in a straight line with the jaws of the trap. You can place the trap on top of the log so you have something hard to press down on. You squeeze the spring and flip this little keeper over the spring to hold it. Turn it around. That little bar, called a 'dog,' is part of the trigger set. When you get the second spring depressed like this, then you put the keeper on so the springs stay depressed, like that. Okay? Now, you pull the two square jaws together like this, position the trigger where you want it, and flip that trap 'dog' over and put it into this slot on top. There! That's it. Then you place the trap in the end of the log, secure it with some sticks then flip the keepers off the springs and it's ready. Okay, give it a go."

It had taken him only a few seconds. It looked simple enough; nothing to it. I picked up the trap and unfolded the springs as he had shown me. Geometrically, it looked like a square between two triangles. I placed the trap on top of the log as he had suggested, kind of like a workbench. I gripped one spring with both hands and squeezed it as hard as I could. Much as I tried, I grunted and groaned and coughed and farted, but I couldn't squeeze that spring together. It was really powerful. Finally, after trodding several square metres of forest floor in some earthly two-step, I managed to get the spring together and hold it. How was I going to get the keeper on, though? I sure wasn't about to let go. I tipped the trap to one side, and then toward me and the keeper fell into place. That spring was secure; now for the second one. Not as hard. Success achieved. I centred the wire trigger prongs and flipped the trap up in a circular motion; the trap 'dog' flipped around and into place over the jaws. I held the trap dog down in place as I let go of the second spring.

It was at that moment I realized I had not been breathing. I was so tense setting that trap, I had been holding my breath. As I knelt on my knees, I set the trap into the front of the log with sticks as he had shown me. I covered the trap and the end of the log with conifer greens so the trap wasn't visible to birds; and also, he had said it would prevent snow from accumulating on the trap and freezing it. I wired the chain to the six-foot pole I had placed alongside the log. Carefully I eyed up everything I had done. I even lay out flat on my stomach for a ground-level view into the log and the set. It looked pretty good to me. If I were an animal, I'd go in there for that bait. I stood up.

"It looks good to me."

"You think so. Well, you better look at it again."

Again, I took stock of everything I had done. Bait in place, trap secured upright with sticks, trigger set and centred nicely, greens over top, trap wired to the pole. It looked good to me. I fiddled and moved the greens about a little.

"I don't see anything wrong with it, Trapper."

"You might scare the hell outta something but you'll never catch anything." He looked at me for a long while. Then the crow's feet at his eyes wrinkled and the corners of his mouth twitched.

"What about the keepers on the springs?" he questioned.

"Oh, I forgot them." I bent down on one knee and reached in with both hands to remove the two keepers. Snap!

"Oh, shit!" I think I did. Shit, I mean!

I fell backwards from the log and could feel a warm, wet sensation about my knees.

"Scared the piss out of yourself, eh?" he laughed.

"You just shut up. Just get me out of this damned contraption. Hurry up!"

"No way, you got yourself into it. You get yourself out of it."

"Trapper, this isn't funny. Get it off me NOW."

Once again, the crow's feet about his eyes wrinkled and the corners of his mouth quivered. All at once the silence was broken with a laughter that surely stirred every beast in the bush. He staggered from tree to tree, holding his ribs in agony and laughing and crying at the same time.

"I hope you die of your agony!" I yelled at him. "Get this chunk of scrap metal off me."

"Setting it was your first lesson. The second lesson is getting yourself out of it. What if you were back here all by yourself? There'd be no one to help you. Go for it. Get out. I'll watch."

"You're a warty old frog, you son of a sea cook."

"Oh, oh. Watch your tongue, young lady. Okay, I'll help you get out this time. Here's a rope."

"What am I supposed to do with that?"

"Put the loop over the toe of your boot, then pass the rope twice through the spring and pull on it."

I did as he had instructed, and the spring compressed. I put the safety keeper on. Then I removed the rope and transferred it to the other spring and did the same thing. I was out; but I would have to carry a rope in my pocket for emergencies so I could get out when alone. Once out of the trap, I reset it, and we headed off to do the next one. By the end of the day, I had thirteen traps set along a four-kilometre trail. It was definitely a new experience, a challenge, and I was not sure of the results. Not a word was spoken on the way back to camp.

We approached the little log cabin in the mist of dusk. The aroma of partridge, dark brown gravy simmering with potatoes, onions, parsnips, and carrots wafted through the air, teasing and tantalizing our nostrils. We ate heartily and went directly to bed. Early to bed and early to rise makes a trapper healthy, wealthy, and wise!

Woodland Wigwams

Reddy came to eat every day, too.
(Photo by Paton Lodge Lindsay)

"You better get dressed. You'll catch cold sitting about in your nightshirt like that," he mumbled as he came through the door.

"Oh, Trapper, it is so different out there today. Each day is so splendidly different." I've been looking out the window pensively, remembering a poem I once heard but I don't know who penned it:

> The world was black and white,
> The black of pines, the white of snow
> Until the sun burst into flames and set the sky aglow.
> Compassion burned within my heart for those who do not know,
> Pines etched against a rose red sky above new fallen snow.[9]

The morning ritual done, we packed up our gear, and Tracker and Trapper and I were in the boat and on our way to town. Tracker sat up in the bow, I was seated in the centre, and Trapper was in the stern. He started the motor up, and when he turned the handle, the bow lifted out of the water. We were on our way to the park grounds at Brown's Bay in Wakami Provincial Park, and then via truck to Chapleau.

The wind was fiercely cold and, even though we were bundled in heavy sweaters and hydro parkas, it bit right through to our bones. After some twenty minutes on the water, the red and white rails of the Ministry of Natural Resources dock came into sight. Wakami Park itself is a magnificent wilderness area. Though not overly big, it is surely one of the most beautiful parks in Ontario. Besides its great beauty, it is abundant with wildlife of all types and better-than-average fishing that would include northern pike, pickerel, whitefish, and perch. I believe the campsites are larger than in many parks, and they are separated by clumps of spruce, Jack pine, and birch that are as yet young enough to afford privacy.

Wakami has all the conveniences of most parks and then some. The Pioneer Logging Exhibit in my opinion is as interesting as the one in Algonquin Park. There are trapper's trails and a trapper's cabin, all kinds of nature trails, an amphitheatre, and an old Native burial ground. At the head of the lake is an old Hudson's Bay Post, unfortunately now partially submerged by the raising of the waters in Wakami Lake. The restored trapper's log cabin is on an island near the foot of the lake. A sixteen-foot birchbark canoe is on display for all to see. A good hiking trail surrounds the fifty-four-mile shoreline of the lake. A canoe trip, which takes several days to make the round, is also most enjoyable.

The entire area is dotted with trails and old roads that served trapping and logging camps from bygone days. One has only to walk the creeks and rivers and shoreline, or the old rutted roads, now overgrown, to find them. Rummaging through the long grasses is likely to turn up some interesting artifact such as an old kettle, an axe head, a cant hook, or a shanty dish. I have just such a collection of my own. Here in the park, the pages of history really come to life. As we drove out the park road to the park gates, my imagination turned back the clock to see these old logging times come to life. There were horses and sleighs and men at work in the bush. The teams clomped along in the crunching snow, bells on harness jingling. Logs were piled high, and atop the pile, a teamster sang out,

Come all ye brave shanty boys whereever you may be,
I would have you pay attention and listen to me.
For it concerns a shanty boy so noble, true, and brave
Who broke that jam at Pig Pen Chute and met with watery grave.[10]

I visited the old cookery filled, in my mind's eye, with eighty men all dressed in their checked shirts, woollen pants of Melton cloth or cavalry cord, and high, leather, cork boots. The slab tables were filled with monstrous bowls of salt pork and beans; raisin, apple, and sugar pies; scones and molasses cookies; and great tin pitchers of tea. No one spoke but to request that something be passed. They just ate and got out. In the evening the men sat about the bunkhouse camp playing cards and listening to others playing the mouth organ or the fiddle . . .

Trapper's voice interrupted my visions. "We're goin' to town, Tracker, to see them city dudes. Do you want to see all them city dudes, Tracker? We'll get a bag of chips for Tracker. All those city dudes and civilized boys eat that bagged dog food that looks just like dried-up moose shit, eh, Tracker? That's no damn good. That beaver meat is far better, eh, Tracker?"

We drove out through the winding Wakami Road that was lined with an honour guard of Jack pine and turned left down the old Kebskwasheshi Road. It was just an old forest access road barely wide enough for two vehicles to pass. The Kebskwasheshi Creek followed the road through grassy beaver meadows and marshlands. Where a creek crossed the road, there was a little sign that read "Mink Creek." The forests here seemed so remote to me—yet there were small villages here and there throughout the north woods. As we drove along the old road, I thought back to the times of the voyageurs and the Natives who would have been here.

"Just imagine what it was like here a hundred years ago, Trapper. I'll bet there were Indians living in wigwams and everything back then."

"Back then!" exclaimed Trapper. "Look at that. They're here right now."

There in the Jack pines beside Mink Creek, at a place known locally as The Pole Camp, was a long clothesline sagging with the weight of blankets and sleeping bags. Farther back, close to the river, was a real honest-to-goodness teepee. I presumed they were probably American hunters of the Black Powder clan, but no, they were not hunters of moose at all. They were Natives down from Moosonee and Moose Factory to trap for the winter.

A young Aboriginal woman flagged the truck down. She had a very tiny baby in her arms. She and her husband and another couple and all their children had come down from Moosonee for the winter trapping season. It was the only way they could keep going through the winter months. The mother told us the men were away hunting and the baby hadn't eaten in several days. Could we possibly take her to town to get some food? Of course. Trapper backtracked and took her into Sultan to the little store, where she bought some milk, Pablum, and bread.

The Native trappers had twenty beavers so far, along with some otters. They snared a lot, and their beaver pelts were stretched on round hoops made from bent alders or ash. The hides were then sewn into the centre of the wooden hoop, and the spring of the green boughs would stretch the hide tight. They were then hung out in the trees, and the frost would freeze-dry them.

Once back at the Native encampment, we were offered a cup of tea. We met the older woman and the five children. The children were delightful, as are children anywhere. They were shy but eager to see company; and of course wanting to play. Two walked alongside of Trapper, each with an arm wrapped about one of his legs. Their little bare hands were red and chapped. Winter had already gnawed at their wee noses and split brown lips. Their home consisted of tarpaulins hung over a teepee frame of sapling pine. Green boughs covered the floor to a depth of several inches. A firepit in the centre supplied both heat and cooking facilities. It was very difficult for me to understand why, in Ontario, the wealthiest of all provinces, people had to live in a tent at forty and fifty degrees below zero.

Trapper remembered, "I found a birchbark wigwam, one time. That was the nicest thing I ever seen. That old Indian, boy, I'm tellin' ya, he made a good job of that.

"He went up there in the summer. He had to have gone there in the summer to get that big birch because he had to have got it in peeling time. There were chunks of birchbark there twelve feet long and eight feet wide; great big chunks of bark. He must 'av had a long piece to go, because it's all Jack pine country up there. He had to go up into the hardwoods to get them big birch and take them big chunks of bark. He had big poles, fifteen poles wigwam style, and took them big chunks of bark and had them all put on the poles like shakes. There was a round door in it and a fireplace and everything.

"I found that in the dark comin' on evening. One time, Uncle and I stayed there two nights, 'cause it rained for two days. There was no goddamned beaver in that part of the country at all. The Indians must 'av had a canoe hid up there and cleaned all the beaver out. That was up on the Bonnechere River in Algonquin Park country I found that place."

The forty-mile drive into Chapleau was truly scenic. The area is right on top of the Arctic Watershed and was a great Jack pine flatland that extends for miles. When you leave Chapleau, it is eighty miles to the next gas, so you make sure your tank is filled up. As Trapper would say, "If you don't come well prepared when you come to this country in winter, you best not come at all. I would never think of coming here without a good spare, a jack, four-way wheel wrench, chains, a tow cable, spare tire and pump, an axe, matches, a box with some dry food and tea, and a can of gas in the back. It's a big backyard up here."

You seem to virtually jump out of the bush into Chapleau. It's a small town of about 3,000 people. Most of them work at logging, or in the lumber mills or on the railroad. A glance at the homes will tell you the inhabitants are very involved with tourism. There are boats and canoes about all over. Everywhere, there are signs offering rentals, guide service, and bait for sale. When we emerged from the MNR office, I had my helper's trapping licence in my pocket. As we passed the local hotel, a big, burly Native stepped up to Trapper and asked him for some money.

"What did you say?" Trapper asked him.

"Have you got a dollar to spare?" he repeated in a deep, guttural voice.

"You're damn right I do but I'm not about to give it to you."

"Come on. You're an American, you got lots of money."

"You damn lazy son-of-a-bitch. You're a big, healthy man not even thirty, I'll bet. I'm over sixty. Why don't you sober up and get yourself a job. There's lots of work in the country, 'less you're walking around lookin' for work and prayin' to God you don't find it. If you want a dollar, go and work for it like the rest of us." Trapper pushed him aside and took me by the arm.

"Come on," said Trapper. "Let's get outta here before I crucify one of those bow and arrows on a hydro pole." I laughed. It wasn't what you'd call "politically correct" today, and it wasn't a very pleasant thing to say, but it *was* rather funny.

We hadn't gone much farther down the street when an old fellow who had seen much better days stepped up to Trapper. This fellow was rather unkempt and looked far older than he actually was. You could smell tobacco on his clothes, and the fingers of his right hand were stained dark, yellowed and brown from smoking over the years. The smell of cheap whiskey hung in the air about him when he spoke.

"Hey, there, neighbour, you got a couple a dollars to spare so I could get some lunch?"

Trapper stopped and chatted with him for a few minutes. Before we left, he took out a five dollar bill and gave it to the old man. They chatted a few more minutes, and we turned to leave. We had gotten about ten feet away when the old man called out to Trapper, "You wouldn't have another five, would you, so as I could get a good lunch?"

Trapper stopped dead in his tracks. He turned on the spot and strode back to the man. "If I gave you another five, you'd have just enough to go and buy a bottle. Now we both know that would be the last thing you need." He snatched the five dollar bill back out of the man's hand and shoved it into his coat pocket. "You'll get no money from me," he said. "But I'll take you and buy you lunch." The two of them headed off into the Sportsman's Hotel for lunch.

"Why were you so rude and hard on him, Trapper? Maybe he was hungry. We don't know how some people live. We don't know what hard times are like."

"WE don't know hard times? YOU don't know hard times. I well remember hard times and I never begged anyone for a goddamn cent. I lived in the bush like a damn animal and hid in caves and slept in old log piles and ate anything I could find. I worked or I'd die tryin'. Don't you ever tell me I don't know hard times."

We walked in silence.

Brown Sugar Sandwiches

Red squirrel.
(Photo by Paton Lodge Lindsay)

A silent eternity passed before he began to speak. "It was the spring I was eight years old. Mama was waiting for a new baby to give us a little brother or sister. We waited, hopin' each morning that when we woke up the new baby would be there. Every morning, we would run together to the rocker by the fireplace; but no, there was no new baby yet. We wished it would hurry and come. Mama said she wished it would hurry and come, too. We thought it would never get here. Early one morning when we were still in bed, we heard horses and a wagon coming to the cabin. We were sure it was the new baby coming at last. It was old Captain Young to see my father about business. They talked about the coming river drive and about the Depot in Algonquin Park. Father would go as soon as the baby came. It wouldn't be much longer, he said. It was long overdue now.

"'But Captain Young made it through the mud,' said my little sister, 'so we know for sure that the baby can make it here, too.'

"My father asked Captain Young if he'd take my sister and me to Gramma's in Black Bay for a few days and if he'd send the doctor out for Mama. Gramma, Lizzie Turcotte, was married to Michel Chartrand. He was an old retired voyageur, and they lived in an old log house at Black Bay on the Petawawa River. Papa packed up some clothes for us in a bag. We gave Mama a hug and a kiss and said goodbye. She told us to give Gramma her love. Papa made us promise to be good, and in a few days he and Mama would bring us a surprise. They'd bring the new baby to Gramma's and come and get us. We ran excitedly to the wagon, and Captain Young drove us to Gramma's house at Black Bay.

"We loved to visit with Gramma and Grampa. They were old French, hard workers, lived in the bush, and lived off the land all their lives. Grampa always had such wonderful stories to tell, and we'd sit on his lap and he'd tell us all about the French king, and the old voyageur days, and the logging days in Algonquin Park, and all about the poaching and the trapping they had to do to keep the family going. Gramma was busy sewing a dress for Mama. It was a surprise, and she was busy knitting little clothes for the baby. For two weeks we stayed at Gramma's. Then one evening, in the dark of night, we heard horses and a wagon coming to the house. Grampa took the lantern and went out to see who it was. In a few minutes, he came back to the door and told Gramma it was Papa's wagon. They were here. The baby and Mama and Papa were here at last. Grampa told us to go and wait in the kitchen until they called us and not to peek. We ran gleefully to the kitchen and hid waiting. The wait seemed long. Would they ever come to get us?

"Finally, Grampa came and told us we could come. I took my little sister by the hand and led her into the front room toward Gramma's chair. Gramma sat in the big old wooden rocker with a bundled-up patchwork quilt cradled in her arms. Our eyes glued to the colourful quilt, we tiptoed quietly up to her side and peered at the wee face that peeked from beneath the corner of the quilt. Gramma rocked the bundle back and forth in her arms. My sister reached tiny outstretched fingers to touch the doll-like face. Her gentle touch made the baby squirm and open its blue eyes to look toward my sister, who mutely turned and looked at Gramma. I looked at Gramma, too.

"'This is your new baby brother. He has come to stay with us, and you can help look after him. His name is Joseph. Isn't he just beautiful?'

"My sister, not taking her eyes from the baby, nodded agreeingly. For some reason, I didn't think Joseph was very beautiful at all. He certainly wasn't quite what I was expecting for a brother. In fact, I really felt like I didn't like Joseph very much at all. I looked away from him and about the room.

"'Where's Papa?' I asked my Gramma.

"'He's outside talking with your Grampa.'

"'Where's Mama? Gramma, where is Mama?'

"In the silence, I saw Gramma's eyes well up and overflow. Her pale face wrinkled and contorted with pain. Two big tears fell down her quivering cheeks. She leaned forward and pulled us toward her and said, 'Joseph has come to live with us. Your mama has gone to live with God. Before she went with God she said she loved you both very much and she sent this very special baby for you to love and to remember her always and know that she will always love you. She asked your father to always keep you together forever.'

"My little sister tore her eyes away from baby Joseph to look at Gramma. 'When is Mama coming back?'

"'Your mama is going to live with God forever.'

"'Emma's Mama left her and went to live with another man but she came back. You'll see, Mama will come back to us, too.'

"Gramma picked my sister up and hugged her. 'Your mama will rest in her favourite place down by the river where you would all go for picnics, remember? Your mama will rest there forever and live forever with God.'

"We stayed another couple of days with Gramma. Father was quiet and didn't talk to us much. Mostly he and Grampa talked, and Gramma was busy with the baby. Then the day came when

Papa packed up our stuff in the bag and said we were leaving. Gramma wanted him to leave us with her, but he said no. He would leave the baby with her, but he would take us to the camp in the bush with him. He packed the wagon and told Gramma we'd stop by the river to visit with Mama for a few minutes on the way to camp, and we were gone.

"At the Chutes below Black Bay, Father stopped the wagon, and we walked down the trail to the river's edge where Mama always liked to lunch. My sister was so happy we were going to visit Mama. She skipped along swinging her little arms and singing the hymn she and Mama used to sing whenever we'd come there. Papa knelt on the grave and talked to Mama and told her what he did with the baby and promised her he would keep us together and that he loved her and missed her very much. My little sister brought out a paper sack with brown sugar sandwiches that she had made all by herself for the picnic she thought we'd be having because Papa said we were stopping at the river to visit Mama. We stood quietly by the river looking at the place were Mama was buried.

"In a few minutes, we walked back to the wagon. Papa reached to lift my sister into the wagon. She yelled, 'No!' and ran back down the trail to the river. Papa and I followed after her. She knelt and laid the paper sack of brown sugar sandwiches on Mama's grave and turned to Papa. 'Mama didn't eat for a long time and she will be hungry. She'll find these sandwiches and know we came to visit her. Mama will eat them when she comes back from God's. She won't stay with Him. You'll see, she'll come back to us.'

"Well, of course Mama never did come back, and my little sister didn't understand. Papa took us with him into the old logging camps in Algonquin Park and we lived with the loggers in the camps, and from that day on, I knew what hard times were. I was just eight years old—and boy, did I know what hard times were."

I walked silently by his side as memories clouded his face and the tears dripped from his chin.

Childhood Memories –Gramma and the Orphans

Remembering back.
(Photo by Paton Lodge Lindsay)

"So, my mother died when my brother was born. He was raised by my mother's people. They were Irish and spoke English. My father's people were French and didn't speak much English. My little sister and I went to live with my father at the logging camps and the depots in the park. When we weren't there we were at Gramma and Grampa Chartrand's at Black Bay. We had an awfully hard time of it because we didn't speak any French, and Gramma and

Grampa didn't speak much English. We were so lonesome with our family all gone and no one to talk to but we had each other. My sister was about four and I was eight. We never went to school because it was too far; we grew up in the square timber camps speaking French and Indian. If it wasn't for Gramma, I know we would have died because we would have starved or froze to death.

"I remember back when Gramma wanted a sewing machine so bad. She had a few chickens and a cow and would sell stuff to the loggin' camps and the townspeople to make some money. She sold eggs for ten cents a dozen and hand-churned butter for fifteen cents a pound. She saved all her extra money for a year and a half and at last she bought that new treadle sewing machine.

"Gramma looked after us orphans. We had no clothes. She took old wool pants and cut the backs outta the legs to make pants for me. A workingman never wore out the seat of his pants, so it was good material, and she made me some fine pants. Once she had a woman's coat, kind of white and black checkers, and she made two real nice shirts outta that. Boy, I wore them a long time . . . and they were really warm. She'd made me deerskin mitts and deerskin moccasins, too. Yes, yes, yes . . . when I think back to old times. One time I didn't have any coat to wear, and Gramma gathered up all the heavy material she could find and pieced it all together, so I was fitted out with my own coat of many colours. Another time, I had a coat made from a plaid blanket with the fringes sewed across the front and back like an Indian jacket. I was so proud of my new coat. Jeez, we lived poor.

"When I was ten years old, I remember I wanted a bike so bad. My father said I didn't need one; I was old enough to go to the logging camps and work. My Gramma made him leave me at home that year. Well, sir, I made five cents here and ten cents there, but I was going to have a bicycle. One time, I split a half-cord of firewood, and the lady gave me ten cents. I got ten of those great, big, brown coppers. Boy, did I feel well paid. Another time, I split and piled a cord of wood, and the lady gave me a quarter.

"I'd walk for miles into the bush. Leave at daylight in the morning, and I was just a kid, with a couple of pieces of homemade bread and butter and some brown sugar on it, and that was it. I'd go and stay out alone and fish all night and sell those fish.

Carrying them home was the hardest part, but I got five cents for each big catfish, and bass or pickerel, and ten cents apiece for eels. I worked real hard for the whole summer and managed to save up some money and I paid two dollars for an old bicycle with wooden rims.

"Then, I wanted a gun. The men wouldn't let me have theirs. I said, to hell with them, I'll get my own, and I did. I remember the potato sacks I'd tie on the handlebars and I'd push that bicycle and walk for miles and miles along the gravel road and pick bottles. I picked 150 bottles for 150 cents and I bought an old .22 Stevens rifle. I had to hide it in the bush, because the old folks were going to take it away on me. By ten years of age, I was hunting partridge and I could sell them for a quarter each.

"That fall, my uncle went trapping and I went with him. He used big bear traps to catch the beaver and that way he only caught the big beaver, and they were caught by the head and killed right away. He set a trap on one end of a dam and helped me set my first trap on the other end of the dam. On our return, we each had a big blanket beaver and Uncle had to help me pull mine out of the water. I was determined to be a real trapper, but my father said I was ten years old, and it was time I started working.

"The next fall, I went to the logging camp and took my end of a crosscut saw. My sister worked in the cookery doing dishes and carrying in wood. She was just a tiny wee thing but by the time she was nine years old, my father had her splitting and piling all the wood for the cookery, and there were two hundred men in the camp. No wonder we never grew. We were worked half to death.

"I tried to learn to read by looking at old Western comics the men would buy in town. My father beat me and said, "A working man doesn't need to read; a working man doesn't have time to read." No, back then you didn't sit around watchin' TV or playing games on the idiot box or askin' for a handout. If you wanted money, you earned it. I spent many winter nights in a cold woodshed with no blankets and no dinner. At the age of thirteen, I took my old .22 Stevens rifle and a bear trap and a packsack with a couple of pieces of bread and jumped the train. From that day on, I was my own man. You say we don't know hard times! Well, *I* know hard times. You're goddamn right I know hard times."

Improvising

Old Log Trap Camp
(Painting by Paton Lodge Lindsay)

"When I was a little gaffer back just after my mother died, I always went to the bush with the old men. They were men in those times, born back in the 1850s and '60s and '70s. They always had a way to do everything. They never said, 'No' when they might be stuck. 'Never say whoa in a bad place.' That's what they always said.

"Well, one time we were all back in the bush at breakup, and I didn't have any snowshoes. I couldn't go anywhere. I was only about four feet tall, but there was four feet of powder snow yet. My old Uncle Michel says he's going to get me a pair of snow-shoes. You'd never believe where he got them! He took his axe and walked over to a dead cedar tree about eighteen inches across and he dropped that old cedar into the snow. Then he cut out a block about three feet long and split two cedar boards or shakes out of it. They were about ten inches wide, and maybe an inch thick. All the while, my eyes watched in wonder, and he just kept a-winkin' and a-grinnin'. He sat himself down on that old cedar log and began to whittle away on the cedar shakes with his Henry Boker pocket knife. In an hour, those two cedar wedges took on the exact shape of a pair of beaver-tailed snowshoes. He then cut a "D" shape into each one where my toes would fit. With the point of his knife, he bored a hole on each side and tied on a couple of cords. I'll tell you they worked just fine, and I was one mighty proud kid. I could get about all over, just like the rest of them.

"I'll just tell you, though, when the freezing rains came, and there got to be a crust on the snow, now that was something else. I couldn't even stand up. My butt would kiss Canada pretty quick.

"Those snowshoes were solid. There was no mesh in them. They were just like a pair of skis. Well, sir, now my uncle had an answer for that, too. He took out some old leather packsack straps and tacked them onto the bottom with little shingle nails, and there was no more problem.

"In old times, you had to rely on your own methods to get along for yourself. The Lord put everything on the earth for mankind's needs. If you didn't know how to use it and look after it, you just had to do without. We never did have much money back then. We weren't wealthy, but boy, we sure were rich. Hard times . . . you betcha, I've known hard times."

15

The River Drive

An old logging camp.
(Photo by Paton Lodge Lindsay)

"I was working in a logging camp the winter I was thirteen. They didn't want to give me a job 'cause I was too young and too small. I told him I knew I wasn't a man, but I had to eat, too.

"I cut trails for the log makers and trails to get the teams in to skid the logs out. After a month, I drove a team of big bay broncs from out West. They were a crazy, wrangy pair. They were three years old and had never seen a harness. They'd throw their heads and jump the pole and turn crossways in the harness. We were both young and new at the job, so we learned together. You couldn't fool around with them or pet them or rub their ears, or anything. They'd kick you and bite you anywhere they could get hold of you. You'd have to watch them all the time, 'cause you knew they were watching you. The mare, she had a brand on her hip, a big circle 'O' with a 'B' inside.

"I took my end of a crosscut saw after another month and then I was sure I was a man. I thought so, anyway—I was doing a man's work. Some of them log makers could really cut logs, a hundred or hundred and fifty logs a day, with a crosscut saw. If you got into timber two or three feet on the stump, they'd cut fifty logs a day. You had to have an eight-foot saw, sometimes even longer. There were different kinds of saws, too. There were pulp saws four or five feet long, narrow-backed saws for cutting pulp, and pine saws, and hardwood saws. My mother's grandfather brought one of the very first pine saws into the valley. He walked all the way from Pennsylvania carrying that saw.

"When we got done makin' logs and the camps were all a bustin' up and the drive was settin' out, I went on the drive. Oftentimes I wondered if I'd ever make it. They were a breed of men them times you called *men*. You had to be good or you were good 'n dead. If you wanted a roof over your head and something in your belly, you worked for it, and you didn't say no to work of any kind, no matter how little they paid or how long the days were. You didn't quit, 'cause it was a seventy-mile walk outta the bush. No one would drive you out. Oh, you got a drive out, all right—on the river drive!

"In the winter, you'd cut logs and then skid them with a team of horses down to a big landing called a skidway. You'd pile all the logs along the riverbank or out onto the frozen lake. They'd be piled up there twenty, thirty, forty feet high, thousands and thousands of logs. Each company had its own brand on a stamping hammer—like a huge sledgehammer—and you'd go along and stamp your mark into the bark of every log. That was called a 'bark mark.' It was the same idea as brandin' cattle. Then in the spring, you'd shove all the logs out onto the ice or into the raging, flooded rivers, and the force of the water would take the logs downriver. River driving or log driving was the only way to move the logs from the bush to the sawmill.

"The logs would float downriver to a lake where you might have to gather them all into a ring of logs joined together with chains. There would be thousands of logs collected in these rings, called 'booms.' They'd be floated or towed down to the foot of the lake and then loosed and driven down the next section of river to the next lake, or to the mill. Once at the mill, each company would sort out all their logs according to their bark marks, and the logs would all be delivered to the right mill. You could tell who owned every log by the brand that was stamped into it with the company stampin' hammer.

"On the river drives, you worked long hours for little money, and it was dangerous work. Many a poor bastard got killed on a log drive. Sometimes, in the back bush by a rapids or an old log slide or chute, you can still come across a small clearing with a few derelict old wooden crosses stuck into the ground. You knew some poor bastard had met with a watery grave. I'd always take a moment to pray and think, as Grampa always said, 'There but for the grace of God go I.'

"Sometimes on the drives, the logs would get upended and stuck in the bottom of the river or against a big rock, and a log jam would develop. Then you couldn't move any more logs downriver until the jam was cleared. Breaking a log jam could be deadly. You might have to climb onto that jam out in the raging, icy waters and use your peavy or pike pole to loosen the logs one at a time and roll them out into the river. Sometimes, with a really big jam, you might have to load the jam with dynamite and blow it. You always stayed on the upper side of a jam. You always have to know how you are going to get off that jam and how you are going to stay out of its way when it lets go. You could get yourself killed or someone else killed pretty easy.

"My very first drive, I was only fifteen years old. It was 1930 and we were on the Petawawa River. Back in those days, we were driving the big white pine on the Petawawa and Bonnechere and Ottawa rivers. You'd often ride the logs downriver literally standing on the logs with a pike pole or a peavy in hand for balance and to move and guide the logs. It was kind of like walking a tightrope at the circus. The logs would always want to roll beneath your feet. The trick was not to see how fast you could roll the logs but how to keep the logs from rolling in the first place. Anybody could roll a log—hell, they'd roll themselves. After a drive, you might play at log rolling or log jousting, but you never played about on the drive. The water was too cold and you could get injured or killed all too quick. You just wanted to finish the drive alive and pick up your money.

"There were times you might see a problem developing across the river and you'd have to cross the river on the logs to get to the problem. You'd run across the moving logs as fast as your cork boots would allow. You always looked for the biggest logs, as you knew they would hold you and support your weight. If you couldn't see a really big log, you might lay your pike pole or peavey across several smaller logs and then you could balance and kneel on the pole and rest for a minute before you took off again and ran for that big log.

"One time, I was running across the logs in the river and I headed straight for a huge white pine log. I leaped onto it and be damned if I didn't go down right over my head into the icy waters. The other logs had banged and bumped it so often that the log had slid out of the bark, and there was nothing but the huge hollow tube of bark floating there in the river. It wouldn't support the weight of anything. I was damned lucky to get out of that alive. I could have drowned or been crushed by the other logs or just died from the temperature of the icy waters. Those were very dangerous and hard times. You damn near had to kill yourself just to live.

"I remember a time we were running a pointer boat downriver following the logs and the men decided to run the log slide instead of portaging the boat. That water was just raging and a-roaring through that slide, and the boat started to wobble. I thought it was going to splinter apart, and we'd all be dead. It moved back and forth across the slide, bumping against the timber side walls. It would slide along the one side and then bump over in the current and rub along the other side. That boat was moving so fast that every time the boat rubbed against the wall of the slide, a cloud of smoke would come off the gunwales of the boat. The friction was so great the boat would actually ignite and start to burn when it touched the wall. When we came out of the slide, we rode a huge plume of water the old fellas called a 'rooster tail.' We rode that plume for over a hundred feet through the air before the boat bottomed out on the fast-moving waters below the slide.

"Somehow, weeks later, we got to the end of the drive, and I was still alive. A walking skeleton—I had worked too hard to have any meat on my bones. I'd been gone from Gramma's seven months since I'd left for the logging camp. Time had come for the spring beaver hunt. I'd go and see Gramma and Grampa at Black Bay and then I'd head up to White Partridge Creek in Algonquin

Park to do a little beaver trapping. The beaver were mine by right. Grandfather Michel Chartrand was one of the last living voyageurs. He said his great-grandfather's great-grandfather said his grandfather had told him the king of France gave all the lands and all the fur and the rights to hunt and fish to our family."

"When you start to think back, the things you done and the places you went, how far away from home you were . . . You didn't want to see nobody in there. If you saw somebody, you ran away because you didn't know who they were. So when you left home, they didn't know whether you were drowned or killed or in jail or something until you got back home.

"I'll tell you what, some of my people . . . My dad, boy, he used to give me hell. He said, 'You're goin' te get killed in there. One of these trips, you're not goin' te come out of there, you're goin' te die in there.'

"I told him, 'Oh, I don't know. You used to be a tough man one time. Maybe a little bit of it rubbed off on me.'

"I used to take my young brother with me sometimes. And my dad would give us hell, M-M-M-M. He'd say, 'Where were you? Where'd you young bastards go?'

"'We walked back to Lake Lavieille.'

"'Lake Lavieille? Holy Jesus Christ, it takes four days to walk in there from Traverse Station. It's about thirty miles in there.'

"'That's nothin'—we left Lake Lavieille yesterday and we came across the trail by Lake Traverse and we're here today.'

"Oh, my old man used to give me the height of shit. Well, it's just one of those things. We used to make some nice money. We used to get twenty-five or thirty dollars for a beaver at that time; that was all you got. We'd make a living; them days you got thirty-five dollars a month in the lumber camps. Kill one beaver and you had a month's wages. That's why we went to the bush.

"There was some people worked twenty-five or thirty years in the loggin' camps and lumber mills. They were broken-down men when they were fifty years old. Workin' in the loggin' camps all winter bullin' those big logs and then shovellin' snow and drivin' the horses or old trucks. Up at four in the mornin' and go to bed at ten at night all winter for eight, nine months. Then you'd come out and work ten hours a day in the sawmill in the heat and bullin' that green lumber; work then, by fifty years old you were all crippled up. Some of us fellas who went to the bush are still gettin' around yet. I can't work no more, too old now."

"Oh, you still do pretty well, Trapper. You're seventy-five years old and you still put in all your own firewood every year and you still trap. You do all right yet."

"I made four thousand dollars this year; I don't owe nothin' and still got a hundred dollars left in my pocket. Guess we're doin' okay. As old Grampa used to say, 'It's not a shame to be poor, just goddamned unhandy.'"

16

Ridin' the Rails

Riding the rails in the old locomotive days.
(Photo by Paton Lodge Lindsay)

"You'd never give seven dollars for a railroad ticket to ride a few hundred miles. Seven dollars was a week's wages. I'd worked hard for five months and had a few dollars, maybe a hundred and fifty dollars. I worked for a dollar a day, twelve, fifteen hours a day. It was hard work but it was honest work. I figured that the train had to stop to take on water. I'd go and hide under the trestle bridge. When the train went to pull out, I'd jump the freight. You had to know the ropes when you rode the rails. When pulling out of a station, sometimes the fireman would slow the train again and the railroad police would chase you off. If you weren't fast enough, they'd take you away to jail. I'd always do pretty good, 'cause I'd travel alone. Another fellow might get you caught. You always stayed away from strangers 'cause you never knew who was riding the rails.

"Well, it was black dark and freezing cold when that engine started to puff and pull away from the water tank. I got my pack and moved to the end of the trestle bridge. When the train slowly passed, I climbed a car and got onto the roof of the boxcar so that if they checked the cars they wouldn't find me. When the train got really moving, the wind was so strong it was goin' to blow me off, so I had to tie myself to the walkway on top of the boxcar. I got so cold, I was sure I'd never reach home alive. I'd freeze to death in the night. More than one poor bastard was found frozen on top of or beneath a boxcar.

"When at last the train slowed to go into the station, I could hardly untie myself I was so frozen. Nobody knows what cold is until they ride 119 miles on the top of a freight on a cold night. When the train stopped, a whole bunch of railroad police ran out and jammed all the boxcar doors shut. Then they started checking them all one by one and they'd take the people away. I ran along the top of the cars and threw my packsack to the ground and jumped down after it. They shot at me. Mind you, I wasn't a criminal or a bum—I was a thirteen-year-old kid lookin' for a crust of bread and a bed. Now they were going to kill me.

"You know, a kid isn't much different from a dog. Hit at him and kick at him enough and he'll turn mean. I ran into the dark with them after me. I thought to myself, *If I had my .22 here tonight, you bunch of trigger-happy bastards, those bright brass buttons shining on your chests would make perfect targets. If I ever live to be a man, let them try and kick my butt then.* I tripped and fell in the dark and crouched hidden and quiet. I was so cold and so hungry and so tired. I lay shaking in the bulrushes, hugging my packsack and praying to God they wouldn't find me. Hard times . . . you want to know 'bout hard times?"

The Old General Store

Lizzie "Turco" Turcotte and Michel Chartrand.
(Courtesy of the Chartrand family)
Marriage Registration of Michel Chartrand, voyageur, and Elizabeth Turcotte,
7 July 1879, Pembroke, Renfrew County, Ontario.
*(**search.ancestry.cacgi**-bins/s…&db=OntarioMarr1858-1899…ga&indiv=1)*

"The spring drive over with, and having safely escaped the railroad police, who were doing their best to puncture my hide, I walked with pack on my back the thirty miles home to the depot settlement.

"Now, in the 1930s, times were not easy for anyone. I'd have to find work somewhere because Grampa and Gramma had a house full of their own; they didn't really have the means to feed me. A man had to look after himself. I had worked hard for five months to get the hundred and fifty dollars I had hid in my hatband. I always kept my money hid in my hatband. If someone tried to steal your money, the first thing that fell off was your hat, so the money was away from you and you didn't have any money on you; or, if you fell into the river while drivin', your hat would always float. Mind you, when I was a kid, my hat was always so big it looked like I was about to fall out of it, but at that time, the money folded in the hatband made it fit just right. As I hiked my way to town, I thought I'd stop and get some supplies for Gramma to help them out at home. I would be stayin' there for a while, so I should at least help fill the larder and the pantry.

"General stores back in those times were a special place. They were one-stop shopping centres and community meeting places, and post offices and hardware stores all rolled up in one. You got meat, vegetables, staples, hardware, tools, harness, guns and ammo, building supplies—everything at one general store. One time, a bunch of the ladies were gathered to get their mail and they got talking about their weddings. One of the ladies had actually gone on a honeymoon. Well, her story sounded so wonderful and exciting that her little girl piped up and asked, 'Was I there with you, too, Mommy?' The mother answered, 'You were not with us going, but you were with us coming.'

"Another time, late in the fall, everyone was talking about the cold weather. Old man Towns was in the general store. One of the ladies was a little shy on firewood for the winter. She turned to old Mister Towns and asked him if he could maybe bring her some firewood. Well, the old man just kind o' grinned a little and in his Irish lilt answered, 'Well, if he stiffens up in the night, I'll slip it right into you in the morning.' Everyone had a grand ole laugh at that. General stores were the first mini-marts in the country. Grandfather always said, 'They had everything from a clap of thunder to a bee fart!' I figured that must of covered just about everything.

"I was walking pretty tall when I walked into that old store and kicked the fresh wood shavings that covered the ole plank floor. Old Mic looked at me and asked where I'd been and what trouble I'd got myself into over the winter. I kind of stretched a little taller and proudfully told him I'd been logging all winter and now I wanted to buy some supplies for Gramma if he'd deliver them in the wagon and drive me out to the settlement. After assuring him I had money to pay him and it would be worth his while, he agreed.

"I wanted six bags of flour, ninety-eight pounds at two dollars eighty-five; two bags of brown sugar, ninety-eight pounds at five dollars that was for bakin' and to eat on bread; ten pounds of tea at twenty-five cents a pound; two ten-pound pails of corn syrup at a dollar-fifty; and two ten-pound pails of molasses at a dollar-fifty each. We ate lots of homemade soup and beans back then, so I'd have twenty pounds of macaroni at a dollar-fifteen and twenty-five pounds of rice at two dollars; a seventy-five-pound bag of beans at two dollars, and a seventy-five-pound bag of peas for about the same.

"Old Mic tallied up and I still had money left over. I told him I wanted the heavy Mackinaw shirt with the double back, and a pair of leather gauntlet gloves for Grampa. There was a bolt of real pretty blue and white material. I'd been eyeing that for a while. I'd have that whole bolt for Gramma. She could make aprons, and dresses, and even nice little curtains out of that. I needed the thread for it, too. Mic got my stuff all packed into the wagon and I sat up right on top of the load. As he climbed up and took hold of the lines, he tossed me a pack of cigarettes. I lit up my first cigarette and smoked it as we travelled through town on the way out to the depot.

"Gramma was out front at the old log house at Black Bay. She was busy working the soil in the garden when we arrived. She was so happy to see me and know that I was all right. When she saw all the supplies we had, she broke down and cried. She thought they were for a jobber and that Mic just gave me a ride home. When we got everything all stashed away, Gramma made the finest dinner any man ever sat down to, and while we ate, I told them all about my winter experiences. It was so good to be home again.

"Not long after dinner, the dog started barking out in the yard. Someone was arriving in the dark of evening. My father came through the door. He walked over to me and knocked me off the chair. 'What the hell are you doing here? If you can't stick around and work and earn your keep in the winter, you don't need to think you're goin' to sit around here and eat all summer. Go on, you get outta here. We don't want to see you hanging around here. You're nothing but a bum.'

"He kept hittin' at me until Grampa yelled at him if he hit me one more time, Grampa would put the police onto him himself.

"I swung my pack onto my back, took my hat off the nail, and put it on my head, pushing the peak well back so I could see out under it, as it was now much too big again. I left with no food, no money, and no place to stay. I would head for the old root house on White Partridge Creek up in Algonquin Park and live there until I found a job. A workingman can always find a job."

Springtime, Syrup Time

Emmett in centre with father to left and brothers and sister.
(Photo from Emmett Chartrand)

"I had spent the last six months waist-deep in the snows cutting down the big pine and making logs. One morning, the heat of the sun would put a warm glow on your face, and the boughs of the pine seemed to have a new green in them and the chickadee sat perched overhead singing, 'spring time, spring time,' and you knew spring was here. Streaks of black threads stretched like giant spiders across frozen rivers. Gurgling waters burped at the open air holes, and you knew it was breakup time. It was maple syrup time.

"In the spring of the year, you'd round up all of the old men and two or three teams of horses and you'd head thirty or forty miles into the hardwood bush. We all used to look forward to the syrup-making time. The camps were there and they were all built of white pine logs and had a scoop roof. The scoop roof was made with hollowed logs split in half with the two halves placed hollow up, and then a third scoop placed with the hollow down was laid over these to cover the joint. They didn't leak a drop.

"There were two camps, one a stable for the horses, and the other camp for the people. Each camp was about twenty by thirty feet. The camp for the men had a cookery at one end, and a sleep camp at the other end with all pole bunks. There were no spring beds in them times.

"There were three great iron cookers or cast-iron pots that each held about fifty gallons of sap. Once you got to camp, the first thing you did was to start cutting wood. You'd be about three weeks making syrup, and there were the syrup fires, which never went out for three weeks, and then there were the cookery and sleep camp fires. You cut about fifty double cord of green wood, all with crosscut saws, and piled it ready for the next year. Then you'd start to tap the trees. Back then, we didn't use metal spiles or plastic pipes. We used cedar wedges about eight or ten inches long and hollowed basswood troughs to collect the sap. You made one crack upside-down on the tree with your axe and hammered in the cedar wedge and then set the basswood trough underneath. When the tree would start to bleed, the sap would run down the wedge and drop into the trough. It would take three or four days to tap about two hundred and fifty trees. Then we had big wooden barrels on stone boats about ten feet long and five feet wide and we would travel around with the horses and collect the sap from the troughs and dump it into the barrels.

"When you'd start to boil, that would go night and day. The fires never went out. We built a long fire and hung the iron cookers over the fire. One cooker had cold sap in it, one would be half-boiled, and the third was ready. You never added cold sap to boiling sap. You'd keep canting the sap on into the next cooker to keep boiling. We'd wire a piece of salt pork to the handle of each pot so the sap wouldn't boil over. Each time the sap would boil up and touch the salt pork the sap would settle back down into the cooker. When the syrup in the last cooker was ready, we'd dip it out and fill up the eight-gallon cream cans with the thick, golden syrup. We didn't get one gallon of syrup from forty gallons of sap like today—we made it thick, almost like corn syrup. When you got to the end of the syrup, it was always thicker and cloudy in the bottom, and we'd really love to scoop out about a gallon of that and spread it over the snow and make snow taffy. You could eat taffy until you were stuffed. We ate it until we were sick. A dill pickle would settle your stomach then.

"When you were done with the boil, and the syrup was all into the cream cans, you took out all the cedar wedges and stacked them along with the three bush cords of basswood troughs and the green wood piled for the run the next year. With the syrup all done, we'd all head into the big moose yards—that's where the moose congregate in winter when the snows get deep. They choose a place where they have shelter from the weather and a good food supply and they'll gather there together for the winter. They have protection in numbers, too, from wolves. We'd shoot ten or twelve moose with those old black powder guns, gut and skin them, and throw all the moose quarters in the snow until we were ready to leave for home. One team of horses took all the cream cans that were filled with syrup; another team took all the moose meat packed in the barrels and all the moose hides, and the third team took out all the men. Once home, we'd take all the moose meat and cut it into strips and salt it or smoke it and store it in barrels. Then we'd have meat for the summer. The hides were made into moccasins, cuffs for gauntlet mitts, head straps for tumplines, and lines for the horses. They call them 'reins' today, but we always called them lines. They were eighteen feet long by about two inches wide. A set of lines cost twenty-two dollars in those times. That was a month's wages, so you'd make them yourself.

"Once the syrup and the meat were in, you were ready for the river drive. From September to March, you made logs. In April, you made maple syrup, and from the end of April to August you drove the river. It was always the same. Six months of logging, one month putting in meat and syrup, and five months with 150 men and 300,000 to 400,000 logs comin' down the river.

"That's how we got along in old times. You always went to the bush with nothin' and came home with plenty. Springtime was a special time. The Lord gave new life to everything, to everyone."

19

Spring Beaver Run; the Orphaned Cubs

Toughy

(Photo by Paton Lodge Lindsay)

Tiffany

(Photo by Keith Harlen Hoback)

"Late spring was always the time for the last beaver hunt. I'd go in to Algonquin Park for three or four runs every spring. I had no camp; no tent. You'd just take a single blanket to roll up in wherever darkness took you. It was like that all winter. Sometimes it would be forty below zero, and you'd just roll up in that little threadbare blanket close to a small fire with only the stars for a roof over your head. You'd wake up in the night with one side of you burnt and the other side of you frozen. All you could do was put another piece of wood on the fire and roll over to thaw one side and cook the other side. Many is the night I near froze to death from sleeping so close to the fire and trying to keep warm that my blanket caught on fire. Then I'd have to spend the rest of that trip with nothing but the shelter of some blowdown or a cave and a small fire built against the rocks to keep me warm. Later, when it would start freezing rains, if you still had that blanket, you'd stretch it fiddle-string tight over a pole, and once it got wet, it would shed the rains and then you'd just sit up around the fire all night and try to keep warm.

"I'd carry tea, scones, and brown sugar. That was it. On a long run, I'd bring a poke of flour. That was the leg cut off an old pair of pants. I'd sew the bottom and put a drawstring in the top and put in the flour, salt, and baking powder. When it got wet, it would get hard like a cast on the outside and preserve what was inside. When I wanted scones, I just opened the bag, made a well in the flour, and poured water right into the bag. I'd stir it with a stick and all the wet flour would form into a ball you'd lift out to use. The rest stayed dry for the next time. Tea, scones, and brown sugar—that was it! You ate meat you caught if you had time to cook it and if the park rangers gave you time to eat it. You did your hunting by day and you travelled by night or skinned by the firelight at night. You could never stay long in one place; never more than one night. You had to keep moving.

"In fifteen to twenty days on snowshoe and on foot, you'd travel three hundred miles or more. You lived like a dog and worked like a dog, living on bread and water with no heat, no bed, and no roof over your head, and always on the move. You never slept much at night 'cause you always knew someone was tracking you down like a criminal. Sometimes you'd think jail would be better. You'd at least have shelter, be warm, and have something in your belly; but who'd feed the old folks at home? In those times, you worked until the day you died. There were no old-age pensions, no unemployment insurance, and no welfare.

"People in town would kick your butt. They didn't have nothing to feed you—they could hardly feed their own. There wasn't much work. A logging company wasn't going to hire a scrawny kid of thirteen or fourteen. The only place you could make money and survive was to go to the bush. You could pick cones and princess pine and guide fishermen in the summer and log and trap in the winter. Either way, it took me into the park. I lived in the park.

"I'd get a stake of cash and buy flour, sugar, tea, and a box of shells for my rifle and I'd be away again. It got so as I'd keep a beaver tail in each hip pocket and when I'd stopped for the night, I'd skin the beaver, shove a gad[11] into the beaver tails and cook them over the fire. The scales would all blister up and you'd pull them off and put it back into the fire to cook the meat. They'd get all golden and crispy just like pork crackle and that would be my dinner.

"I remember one time I had shot and skinned somewhere around fifteen beaver. My pack weighed almost eighty pounds, and I was heading home. Home then, was the root house. It was an old, fallen-in, abandoned root cellar from the Depot Farm on White Partridge Creek. I'd fixed it up a bit and had a firepit in it and a pole bunk with spruce boughs to sleep on.

"I was in about fifty or sixty miles and figured it would take me a few days to get home. There was no snow, now. The snow had gone, and I stashed my snowshoes. The ground had got bare and I headed for the root house. When I got around thirty miles from home, I ran into an old she-bear with cubs. She was determined to have the beaver skins she could smell in my pack. A bear can hear and smell good, but they can't see very well. You can't outrun a bear and they can climb fast and well. I was willing to leave her alone but when she got a whiff of those fresh beaver skins I was packing, she got up on her hind legs and started cracking her teeth at me. Then I had no choice. I had to shoot her. Well now, those cubs were there and they were scared and alone and so small. I knew what that was all about after your mother was dead. I didn't need no extra load, but I tore my blanket in two and I tied each cub up with only its head sticking out and put them in the top of my pack. They weighed about six or seven pounds apiece. They'd whine and scrap on my back, but we got along okay.

"That night when I made camp and we settled down beside the fire, we seemed so much alike. We were all so young, and left all alone with no mother, all alone in the wild to look after ourselves. We were all cold and hungry. I had nothing to feed them. That night, I had nothing to feed myself. They curled up beside me to get warm. It felt good to cuddle in beside something alive. I remembered how Mother had felt when she was here. My tired eyes looked up through the big pine boughs to the full moon. Mama had told me that the Man in the Moon was God. He was always there. He was there again now, His full, white face watching over us. I thanked God for being there. I knew someone had to watch over us orphans.

"I named those two little bears Toughy and Tiffany. They hung about for a couple of years, and I'd see them sometimes when I was around the root house. Toughy left first, and later Tiffany. They each found a mate, I guess, and then had their own families. Of course, over the years there were lots of little four-footed orphans who shared my life."

Chitter and Chatter

Chitter and Chatter.
(Photo by Paton Lodge Lindsay)

Living in the bush, you have so many opportunities to see wildlife. If you keep your eyes open and your mouth shut, you can often sit quietly and watch them for a long time. The nicest part about living far in the bush in remote areas is that most animals have never seen humans so they will stay and watch you. When you know the habits of the animals, you really learn to understand them and know how they will act. When you learn to respect them, then you can love them. You can't truly love anything without having respect for it first.

When wildlife is part of your world and always about you, it becomes part of your everyday life. The animals become personalities and friends that truly gain your respect and your heart. Those feelings are even stronger when some of those animals give up their lives to save yours. Animals have kept me clothed and eating all of my life. Whenever I can, I do my best to help animals in distress.

We humans seem to find it easy to criticize. We find fault with someone because he is rich or because he is poor; because he is educated or because he is not; because his religion or his colour is different than our own; because he wears a turban or a kippah, or she wears a burka; because they wear furs for warmth or because they wear a mere loincloth to keep cool.

In nature, we are blinded by fairy-tale stories of beauty. Old Mother Nature is not always kind. Nature is the true story of "Beauty and the Beast." Birds and animals eat meat. Some animals kill others and steal the babies of others for food. Big birds rob the nests of little birds. Owls capture and eat little animals alive. Trapper was always involved with nature and animals. He had come to respect it all and he loved it all. I really loved it every night after dinner when we sat in the flickering light of the lamp and listened to the wood crackling in the wood stove, and he would always have a story to tell.

"Now, I'll just tell yuh one time I was about eighty miles back in the bush, sitting by a creek. I had just drunk some ice-cold water that I had scooped up with the peak of my cap. I heard a moaning in the bush. There was muskrat sign, and beaver had been feeding along the creek. I heard the moan again, and there was a funny little chatter. As I walked carefully along, I came to a beaver trail going up into the bush. The moaning came again. It was coming from toward the creek. Slowly, I made my way along through the alders and willow and there on the trail lay a big 'coon, its insides trailing along behind it. It had been feeding along the creek, and by the looks of the tracks, it seemed as though a bear had got hold of it before it reached the safety of a tree. That racoon lay there looking up at me. Its belly was torn open but it was still alive. I made things right for the raccoon.

"Unfortunately, it was a she-'coon. Her breasts were long and full of milk yet. From the flood wood I heard chattering again. Searching the flood wood logs, my eyes met two wee black eyes that looked up to mine. At first I thought it was a muskrat or a baby beaver, but there were two baby 'coons. I took them by the back of the neck and worked them free. They didn't seem to be hurt any, just scared and lonely. They snuggled against my chest and whined just like little puppies.

"I put them inside my shirt where they'd be warm and carried them for several days till I got back to the root house. Once there, I poured some canned milk into the thumb of a leather mitt that I had punctured. It wasn't Mama, but by now they were just eager to eat. When I put them down, they just lay in the grass. They didn't try to run away or anything. Once, a while later, I pulled them back to my side. I'd made some partridge soup that night. When I was done, I put my shanty dish on the dirt floor, and they ate up the rice from the bottom of the dish. That week, I found they liked grass, rice, turnip, and carrot. A dried-up wrinkled apple was a real treat to them. I cut some tiny poplar and alder shoots, and they'd chew away on them as they lay at my feet.

"I'd have to watch them all the time for fear of stepping on them. I called them Chitter and Chatter because of the incessant 'chitter-chatter' everywhere we went. They'd follow me everywhere in the bush. When I'd stop for the night and stretch out by the fire, they'd come and curl in beside me. I'd listen to their contented snoring and stroke their downy beige-brown fur. Little masked bandits! They felt warm curled up inside my shirt. Together, we spent the night watching, listening in the flickering firelight, waiting for the ever-present crack of a twig that would announce the arrival of the ever-hunting enemy, the 'snap' telling us it was time to get up, time to run again. The setting sun had gone to bed. Night was coming and day was done. As the face of God rose behind silhouetted spruce spires the whippoorwills chanted their vespers."

21

Making Snowshoes

Paton made her own mukluks from beaver and moosehide trimmed with marten.

(Photo by Keith Harlen Hoback)

"Grandfather always said, 'It's not a shame to be poor; it's just damn unhandy.' Someone else said, 'Money is the root of all evil.' We never had any money, so I don't know about that.

"Gramps taught us to be handy, because to be handy was to have money. To be handy meant you could make everything you needed for yourself and sometimes you could sell your wares to others. Fact is, when you lived back in the bush, you didn't need much money. Where would you spend it? It was too far to travel to buy things. We didn't run to town every day like today. You had to be able to look after yourself and make do for yourself. We always made our own canoes and snowshoes. Grandfather always said to make your canoe in the winter and your snowshoes in the summer. Then you were always prepared. As this is summer, it is snowshoe time.

"Snowshoe frames have to be made from very select, straight-grained, clear, knot-free hardwood. Rock ash is the very best.

Grampa and I would tramp through the bush, axe in hand, until we found suitable timber. Then we'd fell the trees, cut them into eleven-foot logs, and portage them home. Then each board was hand-split with the grain. If you made pointed Iroquois snowshoes, you'd cut each strip of wood in two, as they are made from a two-piece frame. We usually made the beaver-tail-shaped Algonquin snowshoes, which have a one-piece bent wood frame, so you needed the full eleven feet for the frame.

"With the beaver tail snowshoe you had to be very careful to whittle the frame at the very centre front, making sure to stay with the grain until it was a very thin, round shape. Then you steamed the wood and bent it to the oval beaver tail shape and bound the two ends together. You then whittled the toe and heel crossers and mortised them into the frame. You had to drill the frame for the stringers and steam the toe so it had a slight lift to it. There was several days' work just to prepare the frame for lacing.

"The next job was to prepare the *babiche* or rawhide thong to lace the frame. This was a great deal of work. Most often, we used moosehide, but cowhide or horsehide works well when you have it. We'd take the hide and with a very sharp knife shave off as much of the hair as we could. The hide was then placed in a barrel of water and lime to soak for several days until the hair would pull out of the hide. At that time, you would remove the hide from the lime solution and soak it in clear water. We would then stretch the hide out on boards and with a graining knife remove all hair and stubble until the skin was clean. Then we'd turn the skin over and grain the inside of the hide so there was no trace of fat or meat on it that would rot the hide.

"With that done, the hide was placed into a mixture of water and lactic acid to soak for a day. Back in the bush, you could get lactic acid from fermenting potato water or soaking hemlock bark until it fermented. Then the hide was rinsed again in clear water. Then you took the wet rawhide and with the sharpest knife around, you cut by hand the rawhide thong from the full hide. By cutting around and around and around in a circle, you'd cut one long thong that in the end might be a hundred feet long and about one-quarter of an inch wide. The *babiche* was kept wet to work with or it was dried and rolled into balls and stored for use later.

When stored, it would dry out and become hard and stiff. To use it later, you would have to soak it until it became soft again.

"The triangular weaving pattern in the lacing of a snow-shoe is another feat. The pattern has to be followed exactly. The *babiche* is strung wet, and the stretch has to be pulled out of it as you work. Rawhide shrinks as it dries, so as the snowshoes are hung to dry, the *babiche* lacing dries tighter and tighter. Once the *babiche* is totally dry, five coats of the best waterproof marine varnish are applied to protect the frame and *babiche* from moisture.

"Snowshoes and canoes were the main method of travel in this country in years back. The Indians followed deer and moose runways. The earliest settlers followed a trail of hoofprints. These were the 'blazed' trails to the interior of yesteryear. These were the trails to the Promised Land. Hoofprints were the Highway to Heaven."

Pickin' Cones
and Gettin' By

Trapper at age seventy-four, high atop a Jack pine picking cones to sell.

(Photo by Paton Lodge Lindsay; used courtesy of North Shore Sentinel)

"The first year I picked cones for the Ontario Forestry Branch, I was fourteen years old. The Ontario Forestry Branch was before the Ontario Department of Lands and Forests, which was before the Ontario Ministry of Natural Resources.

"With a pack on your back, you'd head off into the bush with a small axe and a couple of sandbags or small canvas sacks. You had your paper sack with your brown sugar sandwiches and a bottle of water for lunch. You didn't use no tree spurs for climbing, or no safety belts or safety lines in those times. Nobody gave you anything. You went to the bush to make money so you didn't sit around daydreaming or you didn't make anything. You just got yourself in gear and shinnied your butt up that tree trunk. Climbing a red pine with no branches for the first forty feet wasn't an easy job. Your shins were all skinned raw on the inside from climbing and hanging on and sliding and trying not to fall. You'd put a couple of small sacks into your hip pockets or a small sack over your shoulders and cut a long pole with a forked hook on the end, and up that tree you went.

"Once you got to the branches, you could walk up them like a ladder but you still had to be real careful. You'd get yourself all settled and placed on a branch and then with your hook you'd reach out and hook the end of a pine bough and pull it toward you until you could grab hold of it. All the cones grow on the ends of the boughs. You'd hang tightly onto the bough with one hand so it wouldn't pull away from you and you'd pick all the pine cones off the end of the bough with your other hand and put them into your sack. You used your legs to wrap around the trunk or other branches and hoped you didn't fall. When your first sack was full, you'd tie it off with the rope and lower it to the ground and then fill the second one. Once you had dropped both sacks, you'd have to climb down and empty them into a burlap bag and start climbing up that tree trunk again to start over. The kind of cones you picked changed from one year to the next, depending on what kind the Forestry Branch wanted. Sometimes they wanted red pine, another time white pine, or white spruce, or Jack pine cones.

"It's hard work picking cones. You have to climb all through the brush and slash and fight flies; and a bag of cones must weigh seventy-five to eighty-five pounds to carry out of the bush. It is good exercise, fresh air, and a good dollar. Even at fourteen, I could pick a bag a day. That was two-and-a-half bushels a day at ninety cents a bushel. I was making two dollars and twenty-five cents a day.[12] Kids today are just too darn lazy. They don't want to work for ten dollars an hour, and some parents are out there working for less just to keep them. Today too many kids are content to just hang out with their thumb in their bum and their mind in neutral. Somehow seems the whole world is dumbing down. The Bible says, 'The meek shall inherit the earth.' Seems to me the whole world belongs to them today."

The Little
Wood Splitter

Young enough to be holding a teddy bear but instead has an axe in hand.
(Photo by Keith Harlen Hoback)

"I had been living off the land in the bush for many months. I didn't have any friends and I hadn't seen any family. My heart ached for my little sister that I hadn't seen in months. We only had each other, and I needed her now. I jumped a freight car and headed for the settlement and Gramma's. My sister would be in school by now. She'd be livin' with Gramma.

"At Gramma's, I got all cleaned up. I got my hair trimmed up, shaved the two whiskers off my chin, got my clothes all washed. I was scared for my sister. She wasn't at Gramma's. The Old Man had taken her to the camp with him, said she didn't need no schoolin', she was old enough to be useful and he could use her. With pack on my back, I headed out the door and put one foot in front of the other and headed down the old Cadge Road toward the camps.

"There were lots of men from eighteen to eighty headin' out for the bush and the winter's work. You weren't fussy them times. Just to get hired on meant you had a roof over your head and a bed to sleep in, even if you shared it with a million lice, and you had to cut the mould off the bread, and pick the mouse shit out of the oats, and scrape the maggots off the meat before you ate it. That was life for those who were well off. At least they had a job. Beggars couldn't be choosers. You took any job you could get and were glad to get it. My father hired hundreds of log makers and teamsters and drivers each year. I wouldn't work for him 'cause he figured I owed it to him to work for nothing all winter and then at the end of the drive, he'd kick me out for the summer.

"As I got nearer the camp, I could smell the pungent wood smoke and hear the men hollering and the horses coming in for the night. The Old Man was hollering at some poor 'son of a bitch' to get the water barrels in the sleep camp filled. He bellowed at another poor bastard to finish getting the wood split and the wood racks in the cookery filled if they wanted any dinner.

"The kid at the chopping block was a tiny, scrawny, little kid in filthy, oversized clothes and with long, dirty, greasy, unkempt hair. Another poor orphaned kid to work to death. The kid staggered under the weight of the splitting axe. After he made several attempts to split a block that wouldn't let go, my father knocked the kid outta the way in a long line of curses. The little guy curled up in a heap, crying. The Old Man kicked at him and the kid got up to run. My father grabbed the kid and, hitting at him, dragged him back to the splitting block. When the kid turned around, it was then I realized this filthy, scrawny little guy was my kid sister. It was her job to keep the cook camp wood racks full. She was nine years old.

"Hate burned in my eyes as the fiery tears rolled down my cheeks and I streaked to the log pile and grabbed a cant hook. I charged at the Old Man and lay that cant hook right across the centre of his back. I had laid him out flat on the ground. In a ferocious rage, I bounced the cant hook off his cheek and told him if he even dared to try to get up, I'd take his goddamn windpipe out with the hook. I looked at the poor little heap that was my sister. In explosive rage, I threw the cant hook at my father, picked up my little sister, put her piggyback-style on top of my packsack, and headed out the road. We were birds of a feather, her and I; we'd have to flock together if we were ever going to survive. Many is the time I wondered, would we ever survive?

"Her dirty wee hands were wrapped about my forehead and her tiny legs tightened over my shoulders. As her warm tears trickled down the side of my face she leaned over and with her trembling, wee voice, she whispered in my ear, 'Did Mama come back yet?' I'm just tellin' you . . . you want to know about hard times? I do know all about hard times."

The Little Town

The little town of Sultan.
(Photo Courtesy of GNU Free Documentation Licence version 1.2)

I did understand his point. No one could have worked harder for less than Trapper had. He had been on his own in the bush living off the land since he was eleven years old. At that time, his father had remarried—a girl only a few years older than Trapper. With a stepmother only a few years older than he was, the home front was anything but peaceful. Hardship as well as experience had moulded him. He was an extremely exceptional man. There was neither man nor woman nor beast that would tame this being. He was powerful in body and determined in mind. If you failed to agree with his thoughts or his deeds, that was your right. However, he was not to be outdone by the proverbial bulldog. His theory of "What we have, we hold" couldn't be toppled. What he had, he had worked for. What he had worked for, he had earned. No one would take it away. He'd fight at the drop of a hat for his rights and he'd expect you to do the same. If you didn't, "well, there wasn't much bottom in you anyway." Everyone in this world had rights, but those rights came with responsibilities. He believed they were a "packaged deal"—one did not come without the other.

It seemed to have been a very long day in town. We had encountered the two strangers who wanted money. Trapper said the old fella wasn't such a bad fella. He had just run into some hard times. We had done a little shopping, and I had done some sightseeing on my own. I met Trapper back at the truck. He and Tracker were sharing a bag of chips.

"We have to get going, got to be back to camp before dark. We can't risk the cold in the boat trip after dark," said Trapper.

"Trapper, I have to make one more stop before we leave town. Could you lend me forty dollars?"

"What do you want it for?"

"Never mind, just lend it to me or don't. I'll give it back to you later. Please? Please lend it to me. It is really important."

"You're something else. I know what you want that money for. You're going to buy that wool and knit stuff for those Indian kids. I can see right through you. You are a diamond in the rough. Actually, you are a polished diamond."

"Well, are you going to lend it to me or not?"

"I can't. We have to survive on what I've got until after the trapping cheque comes in, and that could be another month. Get in. We have to go NOW."

He started up the truck, and we were on our way out of town, over the bridge and down to the CPR station. Right before my eyes there was a grand old steam locomotive, the king of the rails, enthroned for everyone to see. I had never seen a big locomotive before. This massive king boasted a power that can't be felt even in the new diesels. Old 5433 rests firmly in Chapleau at the CPR station and, with defiant arrogance, eyes the new diesels as they pass by in the yard behind. This old Lord Chamberlain of the Rails carried the King and Queen across Canada in 1939.

Adjacent to this grand old "Iron Horse" is a monument to those pioneers and lumbermen in the area. The Chapleau Centennial Centre is a beautiful log building built with the co-operation of the local community. It houses the tourist information centre and is full of wildlife specimens and mineral samples from the local area. It is a virtual heritage museum for the town. We stopped for a few minutes to take in the locomotive.

"Wow, that was a real step back in time. I could have spent

hours there, Trapper. We'll have to come back again sometime when it is open. There is so much to do up here and you can do it all for free. It's so peaceful and quiet, too."

"Now you've said something. You're damn right. Up here, you can do what you want and do it when you want and go where you want. There's nobody to bother you. It's not like down south in those cities, where every time you have a barbecue, your neighbours know what you're eating. And they're always bitching about something . . . 'Johnny walked on the grass,' or 'Your dog was into my garbage,' or 'Your cat shit in my window box.' A poor kid has nothing to do down there and nowhere to do it.

"You've got to have a long pocket and plenty of money in it to live in the city. You can't go for a walk anywhere because of private property and 'no trespassing' signs and 'don't walk on the grass' signs. It costs ten bucks to go bowling, two bucks to go skating, five bucks to see a movie . . . by jeez, you can't even have a shit if you don't have a quarter."

I had to laugh at his impression of the city because it was actually true. I had lived in the city all my life and never thought of those things. I was blind to my own surroundings.

"Nope," he continued, "this is the country for me. There isn't a dope addict holding up every hydro pole, nor a cottage on every square inch of waterfront. It's green, here, and it's clean, here. It's alive and you're free. This is my kind of Canada, and it suits me just fine."

We arrived back at the little town of Sultan. Sultan was indeed a little town. The houses were small and constructed of rough lumber and various types of insulating material. Every little house seemed to have a little picket fence that seemed to balance precariously about a little yard wherein one would find multitudes of little children and the ever-present little dog. Yes, Sultan was indeed a little town.

In this town of apparent poverty and bleakness, barren of trees, there stood one glowing ray of sunshine. It was a little white frame church with a white spire reaching to the golden heavens above and drawing warmth from the evening sunshine. It was as a beacon in the night, as a light in the dark, it shone so brightly in the evening sky. Much to my surprise, this Roman Catholic church was the only church in town; but as Trapper said, with a population of Tremblays, Fortins, Longpres, Desbiens, Berthelots, Turcottes, and Chartrands, what did you expect?

Every time we took a trip to town, Trapper had to stop and talk with Joe, Tim, Paul, Ron, Ross, and Philippe. The talk of the town, so to speak, was always hunting, fishing, or trapping. Lorraine, Jenny, Rose, Elsie, and Ida became my best friends, as they could speak English, and my *parlez-vous* left a great deal to be desired. At the little general store, Trapper got into a grand chinwag *en français*. It was an arm-waving conversation with the owner of the store. They both ended in peals of laughter.

"What was that all about?" I asked. "Gee, if someone was to tie your hands behind your backs, you guys wouldn't be able to talk at all."

"Oh, that crazy ole coot, he's been around here all his life, knows everybody and knows everything and can tell you the dandiest stories. You can have a good laugh with him. You want to go to a potlatch tonight?"

"A potlatch? What's that?"

"It's a kind of party, I guess. There's a bunch of trappers and guys getting together to bend their elbows and have a bit o' fun. I want to go, so I guess you'll have to go, too. It'll be fun, anyhow, and you can get to meet some of the guys."

25

The Potlatch

Emmett always carved little souvenir paddles as gifts.

(Photo by Paton Lodge Lindsay)

Later that night, we went down to an old house on the river. On arriving, we were met by half a dozen trappers, all old, all dressed in bush attire, and with varying degrees of unshaven faces. The young conservation officer was there, too. Everybody liked him. Trapper introduced me to some of the men, but I must say I felt somewhat like a little girl at a stag party. The "vittles" consisted of a huge roll of bologna, which they called "Chicago chicken"; bush scones, a whole grindstone wheel of extra, *extra*, EXTRA old cheese that I swear slowly made its way across the table. There were cranberries, cold sliced moose meat, a beaver stuffed like turkey, a pot of partridge, and some loaves of hard black bread. The liquid refreshment consisted of anything and everything you could possibly imagine, including the homemade varieties.

Everyone was busy socializing and imbibing, when one old fella pulled out an enormous shotgun. Clad in woollen cavalry cloth pants that would surely have stood at ease even when he stood at attention, the old man staggered to the middle of the floor.

"Say there, fellas, did I ever show ya my ole shotgun? By God, we've seen a lot o' country together over the years. Ya know I mind them times back a bit; them were hard times back then in the late thirties, but good times. Lotsa people was starvin' te death, but we had lotsa venison and moose and partridge and rabbits here in the bush. I had an ole .44 them times, but no damn money to buy shells. The wife says to me, 'Paul, I think I seen some bullets in the top bureau drawer,' and she ups the stairs to take a look and brung down one cartridge. I had but one bullet to get me some food for my woman and the young 'uns. Now I'm tellin ya, I had a lot o' thinkin' to do. 'By God, Flossie,' I says, 'It's gonna be tough, but those young 'uns ain't ate for a couple o' days now, and I cain't disappoint 'em today.'

"Well, I got my boots on and cap and loaded up ole Bess with that one cartridge and away I went. 'Twas jest that time o' year when the ducks an' geese were all comin' down, and by jeez, now, this ain't no lie. I walked and walked and ne'r saw a thing. I decided to walk along the shore o' the lake, and there right before my eyes was seven partridge, all sittin' on a branch. *By God*, I thought, *if I kin just line up them seven partridge with this ole gun, I could get 'em all.* Well, now, I was jest eyein' up them seven partridge and I seen the suckers[13] comin' up to the shore so thick you'd think you could walk on their backs and not get your feet wet. No lyin'. Well, now, I looked at them partridge, and I eyed up them suckers, and I didn't know what te do. I made up my mind to try them partridge and I raised the gun and was jest getting ready to pull the trigger when a flock o' five geese come in and landed fair behind them partridge.

Now, I'm tellin ya, every word of this story is the gospel. I didn't know just what to do with only one shell. I walked up on the hill and set there an' had a cigarette and did some tall thinkin'. I went back down te the shore and I lined up them seven partridge with the five geese and jest as I was 'bout to fire, two ducks come flyin' into view. Well, sir, I lined up them seven partridge with the five geese and I waited for the two ducks to fly into line and I fired. Well, sir, be damned if I didn't split that tree branch right in two and get all seven partridge, and I got the five geese and I got the two ducks all with one shot. And by jeez, by the time I waded outta the water with the geese and the ducks, my boots was full to the top with suckers."

"You're a lyin' ole horse trader, Paul. You could always lay on a good one. Here, you better turn up the bottom of this bottle or tomorrow you may be dying of thirst for a drink."

"Well, now, I'll tell you a funny thing that happened to me," Phillip started. "I was hunting in those hills back around camp 508 one time and I had an ole .45–70. By jeez, I seen a moose on the side of the hill. By God, I jus' threw the barrel o' that rifle across an ole pine stump and I lined up the sights on that moose real careful and I fired seven shots, and you know what, that damn moose never did fall down. Comes to find out it weren't no moose at all. Turned out it was a damn louse crawlin' on my eyebrow."

"Ah ha-ha-ha! You're worse than ole Alex ever was."

Another pretzel-shaped ole gent jumped to the centre of the floor. "Looky here. Now there's the best dam gun was ever made."

"Where'd ya dig that up, Alphonse?" shouted one old codger.

"Oh, Alphonse," shouted another, "you never shot anything with that in your life!"

"Well, now," says Alphonse, "you don't know the half of it. I was huntin' back of Pot Lake one day and I was walkin' along the creek by where it comes out to that little trout pond. Well siree, you wouldn't believe it. You jus' shoulda heard the racket of them ducks in there. I jest loaded up the ole girl kinda heavy like and put two caps on the nipples and let her roar. Would you believe it, them ducks was froze into the ice and they flew away with the top of the pond!"

"Now just wait a minute—old Ross is goin' to fiddle us a tune." Ross stood and defied gravity in a position somewhat resembling an old bent wood rocker and played several rip-roaring good tunes like "Rubber Dolly," "Smash the Widow," and "Rippling Water Jig." At the same time, old Amos with patched knees and pointed boot toes—turned up just perfect for kickin' the eyes outta bullfrogs, he said—stepped off to the music, and another round of fluids was passed about.

"Wait a minute, now!" someone shouted. "Did I ever tell you 'bout that old pig I had? Smartest pig I ever did see. I wanted to get her bred so as we'd have meat for the winter. So, I put her in the wheelbarrow and run her down the way to Simon's place to get her looked after. Well, sir, a couple of weeks later, I look at my pig an' she looks jest the same to me. So, I put her back in the wheelbarrow and I run her up to Simon's again. Simon says, well this time we'll get her bored twice while she's here and then we'll be sure. Well, ole Delilah, she's a smart pig, like I tell you, and she must-a liked that you-know, 'cause a few days later, I look out my winda and there she is, ole Delilah, she's got in the wheelbarrow all by herself an she's sittin' there waitin' to go back to Simon's again."

Someone held a bottle out to Trapper. "Hey, Trapper, give this a try."

"No, by jeez, try nothing. Good, clean water from the creek will do me."

"Oh, come on. This is the best-tasting water you'll ever try." Trapper leaned forward and took a whiff from the bottle. "Firewater, that's what that is. If I was to take a gurgle o' that, my boots would get so hot I'd melt clean through the ice tomorrow. You crazy ole coots, someday you'll take a drink of that weird stuff and just straighten out right there on the ground. Then they just roll you out back and lay you alongside the shanty for the ravens to clean up."

"Ah-ha-ha-ha, then the ravens'll all be dead drunk, too."

"Well, now," says Trapper, "I'll just tell you a good ole tale about drink, and it's gospel true.

"Old times, they say, were hard times. I guess maybe they were, but they were simple times and they were fun times, sometimes. When I think back, so many things come to mind. I remember back one May and old Great-uncle was leaving the settlement to go to town and spend a day with the boys. Well, now, old Uncle was known to take a sip of the good stuff once in a while. We always said Auntie didn't need ever worry he would freeze to death, as he was always full of anti-freeze. Well, this one day, old Uncle was all dressed up and a-heading out the door, and Auntie calls to him, "Now don't you bother goin' an' getting yourself drunk again. I've been married to you for seventy-three years and I won't take one more day of that!"

Uncle gave her a great big smile and a hug and he was away. Now, wouldn't you just know that Uncle didn't come home that night. Well, Auntie just packed up all her things and us kids and drove in her wagon to a friend's place in town. I'll tell you she was so mad she was just saying that whole Rosary backwards. When we got to town, the folks told Auntie that Uncle was holed up in the Crowbar Hotel. The police had stopped him and took a bottle from him and locked him up for the night. He was charged and had to go to court.

"Well sir now, Uncle was a mighty fine lookin' man, 'bout 240 pounds and six and a half feet long. He stood in front of the judge in a blue suit all wrinkled from sleeping, his fiery red hair all standing on end.

"'How do you plead, sir? Guilty or not guilty?' asked the judge.

"'To what?' asked old Uncle.

"The judge held up an old Jim Bean bottle. 'Is this yours, sir?' the judge asked.

"'It is,' replied Uncle, 'and it's mighty fine stuff, too.'

"'I am sure,' responded the judge. 'It certainly seemed to have lifted your spirits last evening! So, you admit that this is yours and that you were dipping into it last night?'

"'It is, sir, and I was, Your Honour. Perhaps Your Honour would like to try a drop?'

"'Certainly not,' says the judge.

"'I assure you it is of the finest quality, Your Honour. I make it myself,' says Uncle.

"'R-e-a-l-l-y?" says the judge. 'And do you make very much of this, sir?'

"'Every year—I make hundreds of bottles every year,' says Uncle. 'Good dollar to be made in it.'

"'I don't suppose you'd care to tell the court just where you make this, sir?' inquired the judge.

"'Why, right back at Sec Lake. Maybe sometime you'd like to come and see my set-up,' suggests Uncle.

"'I'm certain we can arrange that. There seems to be little doubt that you are guilty of the charges, sir.'

"'I can't argue that, sir. Wouldn't Your Honour like to try a sip? It's the best I've ever bottled!'

"His Honour took the bottle in hand and, watching old Uncle, he removed the cap and passed the opened bottle back and forth beneath flaring nostrils and inhaled the aroma that wafted from the bottle. Tipping the bottle to his mouth, he just wet his lips to savour the flavour. Once more, he took a little sip. The corners of his mouth curled upwards and a twinkle came to his eyes.

"His Honour raised the bottle for yet a third sip. Holding the bottle high, he motioned to the two young policemen to approach the bench and said, 'Gentlemen, I would really suggest you try this. It is without question the finest maple syrup I have ever tasted. Case dismissed!'"

It was getting rather early in the morning, time to break up the festivities. A couple of the guys didn't drink, but most of them did, and most of those had had more than sufficient. One old trapper, drink in hand, kinda shuffled his way over to the young C.O. Leaning forward till he was but inches away, he seemed to study the young lad's face.

"You're the new conservation officer, aren't you? A fella's gotta be a R-E-A-L prick te do your job. But I heard you're a pretty nice one." Everyone broke out in peals of laughter.

We'd had a wonderful time with the folks of bygone days. Stories of old times, music from the long-gone logging camps made us remember the past and our ancestors. We grabbed our boots, parkas, and fur mitts and thanked everyone for the fun, food, frolics, and friendship and hoped we could all get together and do it all again in the future; and we bid everyone a very, very good night.

"Boy, Trapper, they are some wild bunch, aren't they?"

"There are some wild old codgers there, but they are a good bunch. Not one of them would ever harm you. If you ever get into trouble or need anything you can go to any one of them and they'll be there."

"That young Native guy, he's good-looking. Kind of looks like what you'd expect Geronimo to look like. That gets to me."

"He might get to you, all right."

"When I was in my teens, I fell madly in love with a Native. He was handsome and tall and sinewy. Jake was a wonderful dancer. I was truly infatuated with Jacob. I always thought if you married a Native, you'd get a real man."

"Marry one? You marry one o' them and you might find your wig hanging on the bedpost in the morning."

"Oh, Trapper, you are crazy but you're fun to be with!"

It was now well after dark, and we would have to travel by moonlight to get back to the camp. We spent the night with some friends in town. The next morning, on our way out of town, the young conservation officer flagged us down. He was mighty handsome . . . tall, lean, blond hair, blue eyes, a gleaming smile . . .

"Mm-m-m, I really like THAT," said I. "I could marry THAT."

"THAT is something you might do well to marry—but THAT is already taken," responded Trapper.

"Well, what kind of husband do you think I should marry?"

"I think you should leave the husbands alone and find a man of your own!"

Trapper stopped and rolled down the window, and the two quipped back and forth for five minutes saying nothing, just that weird, different kind of country or backwoods talk. You know, on a hot summer day they'd say, "Boy, it sure is dry—we're desperate for rain," and the other'd say, "Yah, it's so dry the damn bullfrogs are six months old and don't know how to swim yet" . . . and they'd go on like that.

Well, the young C.O. said he was going flying tomorrow. They had some beaver counts to do, among other things, and had to get some stuff out of the old Squaw Lake ranger cabin. If the pilot dropped him off at the Brown's Bay dock on Wakami Lake, would Trapper pick him up there and bring him out to town? There was no problem. Trapper would be there. Meet him about three p.m.

The following day, we visited with the old trapper who lived in town and had lunch with him and his wife. The guys talked about trapping and fishing and hunting and fishing and trapping and hunting, the Ministry of Natural Resources, and hunting and trapping and fishing. The old trapper's wife leaned over to me and with a twinkle in her eye said quietly, "We women know why the men like fishing so much. It's the only time someone might say to them, 'Wow, you got a big one!'" I blushed but had to laugh.

The next afternoon, we headed out to Wakami Park to pick up the young C.O. We stopped at the dump to drop off some garbage. Then we stopped at Spring Creek and watched a couple of otters playing on the ice and then we heard the Otter aircraft land at Wakami Lake. We then moved on to head into Brown's Bay. When we got to the entrance to the park, Trapper stopped the truck up short.

"Well, now, what dumb horny-ologist did that? Some damned 'Citiot' up here playing God. How the hell am I supposed to pick him up when there's a gate on the park? They must have put that damn gate up this afternoon. Damned cement heads! They know we go in and out of here all the time."

"What are you going to do?"

"We are going to pick him up at the dock just like we said we would." And with that, Trapper kicked the door of the truck open and jumped out, muttering something about 'bone-headed bastards' and went around the back of the truck. He stomped along the side of the truck and with the chainsaw just growling he approached the brand-new pine pole gate and lifted the saw to bite into the top rung.

"You can't do that!" I yelled.

"Watch me."

"You can't do that!" I screamed.

"I just did it," he retorted. Before my disbelieving eyes he had cut that brand-new gate right in half.

We drag-raced our way through the park as if on a NASCAR speedway and screeched to a halt at the Brown's Bay dock. There stood that handsome young conservation officer, hand raised and waving to us.

"What pencil-necked bastard put that gate up on the road?" yelled Trapper.

"Oh, they were talking about erecting a gate but I didn't know they were doing it now. Good thing it wasn't locked," responded the C.O.

"It was," Trapper curtly snapped.

"Where'd you get the key?" the young C.O. asked.

Trapper grabbed one of the packsacks and growled, "Homelite makes lots of 'em!"

26

Knit One, Purl One

Knitting sweaters from odds and ends for the Native children.
(Photo by Keith Harlen Hoback)

Once back at the camp, I busied myself all night knitting. Trapper was stretched out in his red long-johns, snoring away in his bunk. He only awoke once, at about three o'clock, to tell me to go to bed. I couldn't have slept anyway for thinking about the Native children at Mink Creek. I had four heavy sweaters with me. One sweater would do me for the next few months. I spent the night ripping up the rest of my sweaters and winding the wool into large balls. By early morning, I had finished a pair of mittens and was knitting a toque for one of the little boys.

"Where'd you get the yarn?" Trapper asked.

"I ripped up some of my sweaters. I don't need so many. Each one is big enough I can get enough wool to make a sweater, toque, and mitts for each of the kids."

For several days, I stopped knitting barely long enough to get Trapper's meals. In two weeks, I had four outfits finished. They were in plain, solid colours, patterns, stripes, anything that would stretch out the yarn to make it go further. I was out of yarn and had only four sets done. What now? I couldn't leave one child out.

There, hanging on a nail over the head of Trapper's bunk was a bright red cable-knit sweater. I'd never seen him wear it. He always wore the grey and black sweater. Done! All kids love red. I ripped it and balled it and started knitting. I had the four completed sets all laid out on my bunk when he came in that night. He picked them up one at a time and rubbed them against his cheek and squeezed them in his hands.

"Pretty damn nice bunch of work," he said. "That should keep them warm for sure." He turned and looked at the work in my hands. "Where'd you get that red yarn?" The instant he asked the question, he turned to the wall where his red sweater had been hanging and, turning back to me, quipped, "Guess I'd better sleep with my long johns on or I'll be running about here bare-ass!"

A week later, Trapper took a box with the five knitted sets of sweater, toque, and mitts up to the MNR and asked the young conservation officer if he could get them to the Native children. Tim assured Trapper that they would get the box in to them the next day for sure. The road in was now impassable, but Tim would run it in by snowmobile.

It wasn't much, but we had done all we could with what we had. Trapper had certainly been busy working, too, while I was knitting. In the back camp there were twenty-one beaver, four otters, two foxes, three minks, a dozen martens, and thirteen muskrats. Now the real work and skill would begin: to skin and stretch and dry all the hides and prepare them for market. Tomorrow was another day.

Pure Essence
of Beaver Balls

Heading back to the camp after a day on the water.

(Photo by Paton Lodge Lindsay)

After breakfast, we started in to skin. The beavers were to be done first. Trapper said there wasn't anything I could do to help him, so I just sat and watched him. Much to my surprise, there was no gory mess. I had expected blood and guts, but there was none. He split the hide from mouth to tail along the belly and proceeded to remove the hide from the beaver with a skinning knife, almost as one would remove the skin from an orange. He skinned from the centre line of the belly around to the backbone and then turned the beaver around and skinned the other side from the belly to the backbone. When he was done, there was one full oval hide and one complete carcass. After that, he removed the castors or scent glands from the rear of the beaver and then cut off two large hams to be cooked for dinner; then he hung the rest of the carcass up in a tree for the birds and squirrels and any other small animals to eat.

Trapper held the castors[14] up on his index finger. They looked like two wrinkled pears hanging on a short cord. He twisted the cord between them and hung them up over a wire.

"What do you want to keep them for?" I asked. "Are you a pervert or something?"

"They can be worth a lot of money, those castors, over a hundred dollars an ounce, sometimes."

"Over a hundred dollars an ounce?" I questioned. "You'd better not sleep too soundly—I could use some money about now. What on earth are they used for?"

"From these one acquires the purest essence of beaver balls! Those fine, rich ladies dabble the pure essence of beaver balls behind their ears and on their wrists when they dress up to go out to dinner or a dance; and high-up businessmen rub it on their faces after shaving. It's used to scent perfume and other cosmetics and has some medicinal purposes, too. A lot of old-timers would take a set of beaver castors and chop them up really fine and then place the chopped castors into a twenty-six-ounce bottle of gin and set it aside for a couple of weeks until the castor was totally dissolved. Then they would take a tablespoon of this gin every day to help with their arthritis. I have quite a few people who come to me to get beaver castors every fall. They say nothing they can buy helps their arthritis as much as the castor and gin. Some of the old Indian women would use the dried, cut-up castors to make castor tea; said it was good to keep from gettin' in a family way. Yup! Little did you know that when you pay big bucks for those little wee fancy bottles of elegant perfume, you were buying the pure essence of beaver balls, did you?

"Can't you just picture some pompous, self-righteous old battle-axe attending to her ablutions in readiness for a chapter or institute or society meeting or other ass-ociation gathering to make her sincere plea to stop the barbaric practices of fishing and hunting and trapping? Prior to leaving, she just slips into the powder room to dab a few drops of her exotic new perfume behind her ears and departs, assured that when she enters the room, all of 'the girls' will notice her.

"Naturally, she'd dine at some palatial hotel or restaurant on caviar hors d'oeuvres, shrimp cocktail, a sumptuous lobster hand-picked from a tank and humanely dropped alive into a pot of boiling water. And who's to know what sumptuous meat such a lady would choose, perhaps breaded veal cutlet; or baby beef liver but a few weeks old and having been raised in a dark barn, never allowed to see the light of day, and imprisoned in a tiny pen so it can't move and develop any tough muscles."

I do distinctly remember taking Trapper to one of Toronto's conservation areas. We were enjoying the winter scenery and munching on pepperoni sticks as we walked and talked to one another about future plans on the trapline. Some character who had overheard us as he passed by turned and stopped and asked us if we were trappers. Trapper answered yes, he was. The stranger then accosted him and asked if he wasn't ashamed of being a trapper? Well, Trapper stopped eating and slowly put down his food. He turned and, with legs rather bowed and stiffened like a little bulldog, he walked up to the man. I thought for sure Trapper was about to deliver five knuckles right up the guy's nostrils. Instead, Trapper quietly looked him up and down, then down and up, then very slowly and deliberately circled about the dumfounded fellow, who by now I was sure had a wet warm sensation flowing about his knees.

"And who the hell might I ask are you? Where'd you get that leather coat you're wearing, and that leather cap, your leather gloves, and boots, and even that belt that's holding up your pants? I suppose you think the leather for those things came out of a box of Cracker Jacks. You people are all stunned down here. A bunch of stunned, ignorant-looking excuses for humanity. Guys like me try to make an honest living in the bush taking a few hides every year and ignor-anus-es like you campaign to have it stopped. You say I'm inhumane and I'm destroying the wilderness. You only go to the bush for a couple of weeks every summer. I live there. Do you think I'm stupid enough to destroy my home, the place where I live? All year round, you people come to these conservation areas, and by the Jesus, I don't think you could raise grasshoppers here. Down south, here, there's no fishing. The water is so damn dirty that a fish would need eyeglasses to see the bait.

"You 'Citiots,' you're the ones who are destroying the wilderness. Your rivers and lakes are polluted, not mine. Your air stinks and is rotten with industrial pollution, not mine. Your soil is full of chemicals and waste and garbage that you can't get rid of. You want me to give up my livelihood to preserve a recreational playground for you for a few weeks of the year. Well, it won't work. You have to change your lifestyle, your livelihood. You have to make the changes to save the world. It's just about time you stopped flinging all that crap around and calling names and started to take a good look in the mirror and at your own backyard. You've really created a Garden of Eden for yourselves, haven't you? You've created a hell for yourselves and you know it. That's why you can't wait every weekend to get away from it. You want the poor man like me to give up his livelihood so you can go on your holiday and enjoy nature in its wilderness state. Then you risk your lives to drive like maniacs up the asphalt trail to the wilderness to some campsite with running water and toilets and showers, a fuel supply, and a little store; and you run about the lake in your tin boat and motor or your water jet and you destroy the fish habitat and terrorize the wild animals with your dirt bikes and ATVs; and then you go home and you bitch and bellyache about all the garbage you found. How in the hell do you suppose that garbage got there? Not by the likes of me—it got there by the likes of you and your friends. Now, NOW, you want to ship trainloads of your garbage up to bury it in my backyard. You can't even drink the goddamn water down here, it's so full of shit. Why, you need to put a sign up on the highway, 'Welcome to Ontario, the province where you can't give a dying man a drink of water until it's tested.'

"I might take a few hides out of the bush every year to make a dollar but I eat a lot of that meat and what I don't eat, I put out to feed the birds and the animals. I can live and work in the bush for a lifetime, and you'd never know I had ever been there. You, you go to the bush for a week, and I find cigarette boxes, pop cans and beer bottles, plastic bait containers and monofilament fishing line, piles of shit and toilet paper, sanitary napkins and disposable diapers lying all over my backyard. And when you leave, well, I'm just goddamn lucky if you haven't burned the whole country behind you.

"You don't want me to hunt bear at a time of the year when they are the most dangerous because you think it's inhumane. You get ONE rabid raccoon and you think it is humane to kill every living raccoon, skunk, and fox for five kilometres. I guess it just depends on whose backyard the danger is in . . . It's okay for you to protect your family, but I can't protect mine?

"You don't want me to keep a firearm to protect my family or to put food on the table. No, now I have to keep my gun locked up in a steel box that's bolted to the wall. And I have to keep the ammunition locked up in another steel box. When I see a bear at the barbecue at my back door, I have to run and get the keys to unlock the gun case and then unlock the ammunition box and then run out to the backyard and hope the bear hasn't killed my children. Where is the common sense? Where is the safety for my family?

"I don't live in a cement world like you do. I don't have a telephone. Where I live, there isn't any cell phone service, not even satellite phones, a lot of places. My next-door neighbour may be fifty kilometres away. I have to go 100 kilometres to get any groceries. It is 150 kilometres to the doctor, if one is available. I don't have emergency measures services, or a fire department. The police could easily take hours before they could respond in an emergency. We don't all live on a piece of ground the size of a postage stamp. We don't live in a bunch of little holes all piled on top of one another. It's like a goddamn gopher colony down here. You need to have a goddamn head on you that can turn full circle like an owl's just so you can cross the road. We don't all live like you. Some of us live like people."

I never forgot Trapper's words. I was born and raised in Toronto and, having experienced his ways of living, I certainly took what he had to say to heart.

They say the beauty of the sunset is created by the reflection of the sun's rays on particles in the air. I, too, like to breathe clean air, but not at the expense of never ever seeing a red sunset reflected in the calm, black waters of a northern lake; surely none of us would deny future generations the beauty of such magnificent wonders.

I implore you to allow me to soliloquize but once. If we seriously intend to bring about great changes in the environment, then we'd better start looking in the mirror for the cause. You and I are the greatest cause of all the pollution on earth. Everything we do, from breathing and eating to dying, leaves residue on earth. Can we dispose of mankind? Oh? Perhaps I misunderstood you. You intend to eliminate all forms of pollution but yourself! That is much the attitude that has been shown the peoples of the north. You think their way of living is unnecessary, distasteful, cruel, so you'll just eliminate it, not difficult for you to do. Simply pass legislation and eliminate them from your world. Similar to a type of ethnic cleansing, isn't it?

You seem to feel that you are civilized, educated, intelligent, superior beings in this world. You have congregated in massive, megalopolis communities and gained the power of the vote and then through a supposedly democratic system of government, you—though many in number but who actually occupy perhaps one-tenth of the province—have the power to make the rules that run the entire province. You seem to feel you are entitled to decide who will live where, what type of edifice he can build and live in, what type of livelihood he can derive his income from, how many dogs he can own, even what breed of dog he can own. If you don't like what he is, then you eliminate him by legislation.

We have suffered great wars over just such policy making. Great battles have been fought over the balance of power. Is it right that because the balance of power in the south decided not to have studded tires that those living in the north should do without them? Is it right that because the balance of power in the south suffered so many accidents playing on snowmobiles and ATVs that they inflicted limitations on those in the north who need to work with them? Is it right that because the balance of power in the south wanted to protect Winnie the Pooh and Gentle Ben, people in the north, who are threatened with the reality of what bears are and what bears can do, should be prevented from defending themselves and managing and wisely using the bear population? Is it right that because the balance of power in the south who probably only see firearms when used in criminal acts should prevent people in the north from using them as survival tools? Will it take a civil war to bring some sense to all of this? A war between the north and the south? We saw just such a war on this continent but a couple of centuries ago.

"If a man does not keep pace with his companions, perhaps it is because he hears a different drummer. Let him step to the music which he hears, however measured, however far away." These are the words of Henry David Thoreau, who in the 1840s also penned, "What everybody else echoes, or in silence passes by as true today, may turn out to be a falsehood tomorrow, a mere smoke of opinion which some had trusted for a cloud that would sprinkle fertilizing rain on their fields."

To again quote Henry David Thoreau in an excerpt from *Walden*, "None can be an impartial or wise observer of human life but from the vantage point of what we might call voluntary poverty." So I have gone to the trapline that I may become an impartial observer. Said Thoreau: "To be a philosopher is not merely to have subtle thoughts, nor even to found a school of thought, but so to love wisdom as to live according to its dictates a life of simplicity, independence, magnanimity, and trust. It is to solve some of the problems of life not only theoretically but practically."

It appears to me that the mighty megalopolis of Southern Ontario is the conductor of an orchestra with various instruments spread across a vast stage. Once in a while, the odd beat of the drum is heard in the northern forest, or the crash of the cymbals reverberates from the posterior regions, but the strings and the wind instruments of the south carry the tune to all great northern areas. All people must keep in step, as there is only one tune to dance to, and that tune pours forth from the great bandshell situated south of the natural rock amphitheatre that serves to divide this province in two. Trapper's words were right, and I never would forget them.

Stretching Hides

Preparing pelts at camp.
(Photo by Paton Lodge Lindsay)

"Hey there, daydreamer," Trapper called.

I jumped to with a start. "No, I wasn't daydreaming—I was thinking about us and the two different worlds we live in."

"Here. Stretch this beaver hide for me."

"Trapper, I've never stretched a hide in my life."

"You can do it. You learn fast. Just nail it onto that board in an egg shape. Oval, I think you call it."

As he showed me how to do it, he explained that he didn't hoop-stretch beaver like the Natives did, because hoop-stretched beaver pelts were always round, whereas the animal's hide is actually egg-shaped. It is longer than it is wide and narrower at the head than at the tail. Of course, if you were a remote trapper, you would hoop-stretch. You could hardly portage lumber or four-by-eight-foot sheets of plywood through the bush to make stretchers; you'd use what was at hand. Trapper doesn't scrape a beaver hide,

144

either. It might take him thirty to forty minutes to clean-skin a beaver, but when the hide comes off the carcass, it is ready to be stretched; no scraping or graining of the beaver hide to remove fat or meat as so many people need to do. It takes very considerable expertise to clean-skin a beaver. If any fat, meat or grease is left on a pelt, it can burn or rot the leather. Some animals, such as mink and otter, have to be rough-skinned and grained or scraped afterwards.

He stood what he called a "beaver board" up and leaned it against the log wall. It was made from lumber he had cut from logs with the saw. It was about one inch thick by forty inches wide by four feet high. I questioned why he used such big boards, as they were very heavy to move about. He explained that he got lots of eighty-inch beaver and once he even caught a beaver that stretched to 105 inches. You needed a big board to stretch a big beaver.

"The trick," he said, "is to catch the two big beaver from a house and leave the small and medium beaver. You wait until the house is all mudded and the winter feed is all in and then take the large beaver. You want to get them the first time. Beaver aren't stupid. They'll figure out the problem if you miss them. If you got hit on the head every time you went to go through a door, you'd soon find a new door to go through. They will, too.

"The younger ones are safe from predators once the ice is in and they have lots of feed. They'll make it through the winter just fine. We call them 'seed beaver.' Their hides are too small to be of much value, and by selectively removing the older beaver each year, you keep a young, healthy population. This way, you guarantee a supply of beaver of reproductive age and little disease as in old beaver."

As he spoke, he gathered together a box of two-inch common nails and a hammer. He held the raw pelt up by the nose and tacked three nails in across the nose. The pelt hung like a long, cylindrical tube of dark brown, shiny fur. It hung the full length of the beaver board. He then rolled the hide out to the left and placed a nail by the front leg and another by the hind leg. He repeated the process, rolling the hide out to the right. Then he rolled the belly of the beaver out to the left and secured it with a nail; then to the right and secured that with a nail. Finally he pulled the tail area down and placed several nails across the bottom. He had roughly tacked the hide to the board in an oval shape with scalloped edges.

"There you go. Now you finish it," he said as he handed me the hammer. "You just flatten the hide as you go and put a nail in about every half inch so that it's uniform all the way around."

I did as Trapper instructed and when I was done, there were 186 nails in the beaver pelt. Then I trimmed off the excess skin and fur about the leg area and tacked the four leg holes closed; then I trimmed the loose part of the upper lips. The final act was to take a saw file and pry the hide up off the board and bring it up to touch the heads of the nails. This allowed air to pass between the beaver board and the pelt, which would then dry from both sides. As well, the fur didn't get flattened and hardened as it dried, which it would if left pressed against the board. This method produced a much lovelier pelt.

"Trapper, why do you call it stretching a pelt? Because you don't really stretch it, you just roll it out flat."

"Some people stretch the hell out of a hide. Figure the bigger the hide, the more money they'll get for it; but they're only foolin' themselves. I just lay the hide out on the board and tack it down. Then as the hide dries, it shrinks and the hairs get closer, giving you a thicker pelt. When people buy fur they want lots of fur, not just leather."

"You said yourself, Trapper, that the bigger pelts were worth more."

"Yup, I did—but the pelt is graded for the thickness, length, and colour of fur and not so much for the leather. Animal hair is like people hair, in that some have silky hair and some coarse hair; some have light-coloured hair and some dark hair; some have thick hair and others have thin hair. If you cure the hide by letting it shrink rather than by stretching it, you'll make the fur thicker on every pelt, so it will be of greater value to you. You just have to be sure you have enough tension on the hide while it dries so that it won't rot. The fur slips then, and the pelt will be worthless."

"How long does the pelt have to stay on the stretcher to dry?"

"Oh, they'll take maybe two or three days to dry, sometimes longer. It depends on the heaviness of the leather, the thickness of the fur, and how wet the pelt was when you stretched it."

"Boy, you sure have to know what you are doing to be a good trapper. If you had to do all of that with people, you'd be a bit surgeon, hairdresser, dermatologist, and all. How big is that beaver, Trapper?"

He got out his rule and measured the beaver from the eyes to the tail. It measured forty-four inches. Then he measured it across its width and it was thirty-two inches. The size of the beaver is determined for marketing by measuring its length and width and adding them together. This was a seventy-six-inch beaver. This beaver, caught in November, would bring thirty-five to forty-five dollars at the December auction. On average, the early caught beaver would average twenty-five dollars on the first sale.

We took a break and had a cup of tea and chewed on some pepperoni sticks we had bought while in town. They were always great to have in your pocket while on the trail. He sipped on his tea from the blue enamel mug,

"A friend of mine who traps said last year the fur wasn't any good. No money in trapping anymore. He only averaged eight dollars for his mink. I got twenty-seven for mine. If you were to look at our mink side by side, you would see why. He leaves some grease on his hides and the stretch isn't the best. That cost him an average of thirteen dollars per pelt. Do that with 100 pelts and it is costing you $1,300. He averaged twelve dollars for beaver. I got forty. He handled his beaver well, but they were nearly all kits. You have to know what you're doing to just catch big beaver. You have to handle your pelts properly. You have to watch where you sell, too. I've sold my pelts at the North Bay Auction for over thirty years and I'll never sell them anywhere else.

"When you go to a small-time buyer, he offers you one price and you can take it or leave it. But at the trappers' fur auction, your furs go to the highest bidder, and then you know you got well paid because there are buyers from all over the world at the auction. If you need money right away for your family, they'll advance it to you. If you need to order trapping supplies, they'll send them to you and deduct the order from your fur cheque. You get your money pretty quick after the sale, too. I had a friend who always sold to the local small-town buyer. After showing him my cheques for a couple of years, I finally talked him into trying the trappers' auction at North Bay. When he got his cheque back, he said, "Boys, oh, boys, look at that, the fur, she's gone way up in the air!"

Trapper skinned and grained, and then I stretched a couple of otters after lunch. The otters were skinned in the round, not flat like the beaver. These skins were stretched tight on a three-piece stretcher. The otter resembled a freshwater seal, something like an aquatic dachshund with flippers for feet, if you ask me. Trapper skinned and stretched for the rest of the day until everything was cleaned up. The best of the beaver meat was put into cloth bags and hung outside in the cold. That we would eat ourselves. The liver, which is delicious, we fed to the dog because it had been sitting for a few days. The remainder of the carcasses were put out into the bush; some hung in trees for the birds to eat, some left on the ground for the other animals to eat.

"We'll all eat hearty tonight, eh, boy?" Trapper said as he turned and threw a piece to Tracker. "There's lots of meat on the river for everyone."

29

Checking My Line

Paton at the camp in winter; the snow is up to the eaves.
(Photo by Keith Harlen Hoback)

A couple of days had passed since I set my trapline out behind the camp. It was time for me to make the first rounds. Once more, I collected some beaver meat and partridge guts for bait, a few extra traps, some wire, fence staples, my axe, and my rifle. We stepped out of the camp into heavy new-fallen snow. The trees were all heavily laden with snow, the branches sagging beneath the weight. I began the trek down the trail with Tracker in the lead and Trapper at my heels. We rounded the moose runway quietly alert for any fresh sign of moose activity. I checked specific landmarks as well as watching the blazes along the trail. When we reached the otter trail, Trapper told me to go ahead and he'd go over to the creek and check the 330 Conibear trap. I went on ahead, keeping an observant eye for new tracks in the fresh snow. Once I knew where the animals were running, I could set out more traps. The first trap I approached carefully, as I didn't really know what to expect. My nerves were tense and my muscles tight. If a twig had so much as touched my back I'd have become airborne. There was no sign of anything, no sound. I tossed a small stick up to where the trap was set. Nothing responded. I then walked slowly to the trap and looked in beneath the snow-covered green boughs covering the entrance. The trap had not been disturbed at all.

Trapper caught up with me and we moved on to the second trap. Again I followed the same procedure and again there was no sign of disturbance and no sound. I closed in carefully and stooped to look beneath the green boughs at the trap. There, caught by the neck and chest was a large male marten. It was dead and there was no sign that it had even moved after being caught in the trap. It had died humanely, rendered instantly unconscious. I removed the marten from the trap and reset the trap. Taking a moment to get my breath, I picked up the marten to take a closer look at it. On close observation, it rather resembled a small, thin cat. The dark brown fur was long and fluffy and very shiny. It had a tawny under-coat and canary orange patch of fur at its throat. I put the marten into my packsack and was on my way down the trail once more.

The third and fourth traps had marten, too. I was enthused about the success and thankful that none had been alive. We rounded the swamp, crossed through the alder thicket, and forded the creek to the trap beneath the birch roots. Now that I was aware of what to expect, I approached the trap with a certain eagerness and confidence. Trapper grabbed my coat collar and hauled me back against him.

"There wasn't any stone there when you set that trap."

"If it's there now, it was there then," and I pulled away from him and walked up toward the roots of the birch tree stopping only to drop the pack from my shoulders.

"HEY! Don't speak, don't ask any questions, and don't move quickly. Just move slowly backwards out of there NOW."

As I stood erect with pack in my hand and turned to step back the most unearthly "yyeeooowwwl!" I could ever imagine shrieked out behind me. It reminded me of the wail of a banshee in the old horror movies. I don't recall moving from that spot of ground to which my feet were frozen but I must have literally levitated and in a flash I was standing behind Trapper and peeking out at that now animate stone.

"You want to approach a trap carefully. I told you that. That is no ordinary housecat, you know."

"I can see that. Some stone!"

"Do you know what it is?"

"Yes, it's a lynx."

It lay there just curled up as cats do and glared at us through huge yellow eyes. The ears stood erect with long white and black tufts that curled inward. It was all of five feet long, with huge paws the size of my leather mitts. The body was very long and slim, and the legs extremely long, the rear legs a little longer than the front ones. In colour it was a tawny beige, silver, and black, with a spotted stomach and a black knob of a tail. The cat rose up and took a step toward us. I jumped when the crack! of the .22 Magnum echoed through the wilderness silence.

"What did you do that for?" I yelled.

"You're not in a zoo, here, kid. When it lays those ears back flat against its head and takes that first step, it's ready to make a move."

I walked up to the cat and took its massive front paw in my hand. It hadn't even been caught by a toe. Only the thick matt of fur on the ball of the foot was caught in the trap. If it had made just one jump it would have gone free. It hadn't even tried; it had just lain down and waited.

Trapper cleared his throat. "He's an animal just like me, you know. We are all part of nature's plan, even you and I. All animals eat others for food. Insects eat other insects. Fish and birds eat insects. Animals eat insects and birds. Birds eat other birds and fish. Some animals even lure and trick and bait each other. In some parts of the world, there are cannibals, people who eat people. If we don't control the lynx population, they'll multiply and clean out the rabbit population and the partridge and lemming population that other animals rely on to survive. The law of the wilderness says it's the survival of the fittest. The fittest will survive. This time I survive. It's the way I live. I don't know any other way."

This had been a productive day. I hoped other trips would be as full of adventure and learning. On the way back to camp, Trapper shot several ruffed grouse and a spruce grouse. As we passed by the edge of the swamp, he picked a hatful of low bush cranberries. They were in dark red bunches and were dimpled from the frost. Trapper said that would make them all the sweeter. He pulled up some bulrushes from the edge of the marsh and cut the tuberous roots off the bottom. When we reached the camp, he hung the marten and lynx from the eaves. He then took the rush roots and peeled them.

"Here," he said, "you take the berries in and put some sugar on them and a little water and stew them up. We'll boil up the rush roots tonight and have them with the partridge and cranberries. I'll clean the grouse."

"I'm not eating them."

"Then you can do without; suit yourself. This is what you call living off the land."

This had been an educational morning. I learned to observe my surroundings more. I learned about various animal tracks and the habits and habitats of various animals. I had seen animals I had never seen before and I had learned my place in the laws of nature.

After lunch, the sun came out. The sky was clear as far as the eye could see. Trapper went out to skin the catch. I went out armed with my camera. The lynx had cooled sufficiently that it was stiffening up, yet was supple enough that the legs would stay in whatever position I placed them. I set it up for a posed shot arranging the legs as if it was ready to pounce and wedged the feet into the snow.

Well, sir, when Tracker came out of the camp and got a whiff of that cat, the four brakes went on and he skidded to a full stop with nostrils flared, nose extended to the air, and hair all bristled along the length of his back. He stood there as if suffering from rigor mortis. Finally, he took one step forward and, defying gravity, he stood with one front and one hind foot on the ground. On two feet, he swayed forward, stretched neck and nose to smell the air and then swayed back, uttering a deep, guttural growl. After an inanimate moment, he would literally float another step forward and again hang suspended in time and motion. He took fully five minutes to move five feet.

"Who is that, Tracker? Sssssssssssssssssss, get him, Tracker. Who is that, Tracker? Nail him, Tracker."

Tracker grew tense, did his sway forward, dipped his spine and swayed back, standing on tiptoes with muscles rippled and fully sprung ready for a lunge. At that moment, for no apparent reason the lynx fell forward. Tracker levitated to the air, let out a half-dozen ki-yi-yi's, rotated a hundred and eighty degrees, landed back on the ground at a full run, and virtually ran on the spot, making no escape. His claws finally made contact with the ground and he sprinted back to the camp, hind legs passing his front legs. Trapper and I collapsed in peals of laughter.

It had been a great couple of months. I had learned more about the bush and the wilderness, the weather, hunting, trapping, life, and living in these past weeks than I had ever learned in all the previous years of my life. I had learned to gain shelter, warmth, light, and food of infinite variety; I had learned how to make clothing and snowshoes; I had virtually learned how to survive in the wilderness, and nothing had cost a cent. I had seen life and I had seen death but I had not seen anything that was cruel or inhumane. Trapper said the Lord had put everything on the earth that mankind needed. Indeed, it seemed He had.

The Flat-Tailed Pulp Cutter

The flat-tailed pulp cutter.
(Photo by Paton Lodge Lindsay)

During a hearty breakfast of baked beans, scones, and tea, we hashed over all of Trapper's various types of traps. He had 120 Conibears, about four-inch-by-four-inch double springs, that he used for muskrats and marten. He had 160 and 220 Conibears that he used for otter, fox, and lynx. There were 330 Conibears that he used mostly for beaver sets under water and on beaver dams. To him, a working trap is a trap that catches and kills quickly, because then the animal doesn't suffer, nor is the pelt damaged. Seems with regard to traps, the trapper and those concerned with the treatment of animals seek similar requirements: efficiency in catching, swiftness and humaneness in killing.

Trapper explained that you can be rather selective in what you catch by setting certain traps in certain places. He says young beaver are like young children. They are curious and nosy, always poking about looking at new things. By setting the traps well away from the house, you tend to catch the larger beaver rather than the younger beaver. He always waits until the beaver house is all mudded up and the feed bed in and ready for the winter before he sets any traps. That way, he knows that if he catches the two adult beaver, the kits are protected and prepared for a long, safe winter.

I heard some commotion outside, so knew that Trapper and Tracker had returned from their trip up the lake.

"By the roaring Sam Hill did I have a son of a sea cook of a time this morning!"

"What happened?"

"What happened? By God, I nearly got one-half of me eaten and the other half drowned."

"Really, a little bit of excitement this morning?"

"It's not at all funny. It was close. I showed that damn flat-tailed pulp cutter. He dumped his last wad right there in the bottom of the canoe and that dog, that damn dog."

"You sound like you really had a hard time, Trapper."

"You remember that huge beaver house up by the Portage Lakes? Well, sir, I set a trap up there the other day. I went back up there this morning with the twelve-foot canoe. The trap was gone off the house, so I knew I had something. I'm just tellin' you I looked and looked all over the Jesus bottom for that wire and trap. I pulled a quarter of the damn feed bed out. No, sir, I couldn't find it. I figured the damn beaver got into the trap and broke the wire and got away with it. And then that frigging dog, that damn useless son of a bitch, just kept trying to climb outta the canoe and damn near wet me a couple of times. I didn't feel like drinking water standing up so I grabbed the paddle and swung it to trim him up and make him listen. He ducked and I hit the gunwale and broke the blade on the paddle. Now, I'll just tell ya, THAT really impressed me and improved my humour. It scared him enough, though, he lay down in the bottom of the canoe and he stayed there. I'd just have to shake my head at him and he wouldn't move. I didn't know what the hell was wrong with Tracker. He's usually awfully good to listen to me. Then I saw what the dog was after. I should have listened to him in the first place. The beaver had got the stone off the wire and somehow he'd worked the sliding lock up the wire, and the flat-tailed bastard was sitting on top of the house in a bunch of sticks. Goddamn big beaver, too.

"Well, sir, I had no gun with me, and there we sat, looking at each other. I looked at Tracker and I wondered. 'Catch him!' I yelled. Tracker just flew out of the canoe and the top of that beaver house just exploded. The beaver with the trap and the pole and the wire was into it with the dog. The beaver lunged into the water, and Tracker with it, hanging on to the side of its head. Beaver and dog went to the bottom. I couldn't see nothing, for the bottom was all stirred up and the water all a muddy swirl. They came up under the canoe and were banging about beneath me and damn near turned me over. Then everything went quiet. There was nothing. I couldn't see or hear a thing. I thought the dog was a goner. Then I saw Tracker's ass coming up outta the water. He still had the beaver by the side of the head and he tugged and jerked and pulled the whole thing up onto the house. Finally the beaver rolled over with his four moccasins up in the air and Tracker let go and shook himself off. He did a really good job. Well, I gave that beaver a crack on the head with the axe to be sure it was not in any misery and threw it into the canoe. I'll bet that beaver weighed sixty pounds. I was so Jesus mad, I flung that trap into the lake and got the dog into the canoe, and we headed back."

"Wow, what an experience!"

"Oh, that is just the half of it. When we got out into the middle of the lake to cross to this side, that flat-tailed pulp cutter decided to come around. I'd only knocked him out. He might have had a headache, but once he got his second wind, I'm tellin' yuh, there was nothing wrong with him. That damn beaver and the dog went at it again right there in the canoe. I was trying to keep the canoe from upsetting, and keep myself from getting bit, and I'd have to keep grabbing that buck-toothed bastard by the tail and haul him back to keep him from going overboard. I was scared to hit him over the head with the axe for fear of cutting myself, or cutting the dog or putting the axe through the bottom of the canoe. There's forty-five feet of water out there, you know. Now I'm just telling you that it wasn't a damn bit funny. No more farting around on the river like that, eh, Tracker?"

Several weeks had passed by, and the daily routine became pretty standard. Get up in the wee hours and eat breakfast, then go out onto the trails to check traps. Sometimes we'd return to camp for lunch, sometimes we'd eat on the trail, other times not eat until well after dark at night. The evenings were spent skinning and stretching pelts. Most times, we put in a sixteen-hour day at least. By the time we'd bed down, the moon was always high in the sky.

The snows had deepened to a couple of feet. We had banked the walls of the log camp with snow to help keep the floor and the camp warmer. The ponds and smaller lakes had frozen over. The trapping of aquatic animals was at a standstill until the ice was thick enough to support man or machine. The old trappers would say, anywhere a fox could walk, man could walk. The old trappers were nearly always men. I think some of them thought they could walk on water. I always liked to tease them and ask if they'd "heard about the miracle baby born in town." Then they'd always answer, "No, I ain't heard nothin'." I'd advise them it was on the news: the baby was born half male and half female. In total disbelief, they'd of course want to know all the details. I'd answer, "Yah, it was born with a penis and a brain!"

Over the next ten days, we restricted our travels to Wakami Lake or the land trails, and every day, we would check the line. Travel in the bush was getting difficult. The snows were deep, and we had to snowshoe everywhere we went. As the temperatures had not yet been very low, the snow was heavy and wet, and as we walked, it would stick to the snowshoes and pack on them, making them several inches thick and very heavy. We would frequently have to remove them and bang them together to knock the snow off. Several times, I had tripped on debris under the snow when I had stepped onto the end of a buried alder branch and with the next step my second snowshoe had become caught in the loop of the branch. Down I'd go. There were times when it proved most difficult to get my feet untangled and the pack off my back, get upright again, brush off, and carry on. Travel was often so strenuous that even in the cold, we'd become very warm and we'd shed hat, mitts, sweater, etc., as we travelled and hang them on trees along the trail. On the return trip, we would of course pick them up, and as nightfall approached and the temperatures dropped, we were happy to once again add these layers to our clothing. Each night, we would return to camp fully exhausted. Trapper would look after the fur and equipment, and I would look after the fire and dinner. After dinner, there were always several hours of skinning and stretching hides before we'd sit down to a hot cup of tea or hot chocolate and go over the day's activities and plan the next day.

In the dark, I sat quietly on the snow-covered log at the shore and listened to the water lapping against the flood wood. The moonlight sparkled on the crystal prisms hanging from everything. This was truly a magnificent land, my land, my Canada. I felt so privileged to live here in beauty, in freedom, and peace. It was at the end of a very tiring day. Trapper had joined me and we sat together on the log, sipping tea and making plans for the next few days.

War Games—Parting Is a Bit Like Dying

Trapper portaging a big "blanket" beaver.

(Photo by Paton Lodge Lindsay)

I never went to war," said Trapper. "They said I had flat feet and was too scrawny, said I wouldn't be able to walk or carry anything. I showed them who could walk and who could carry. I'll just tell you I spent the whole war time in the park. I'd make a trip across the park every few weeks and hunt all the way. I'll tell you, the park rangers who wanted to run me never got a chance to freeze their goddamn feet. I hated those bastards; but at the same time, you had to respect them. Most of them were pretty good men.

They could keep up with you; you just had to keep ahead of them or outsmart them. They'd damn near run you to death, but you'd have to laugh after about the things you did to them and the things that happened.

"There were lots of ways to stay ahead of them. They'd never run you at night. They'd always stay in their little ranger patrol cabins or maybe settle down, make camp, light a fire, and stay put for the night. Some nights, we'd sneak up in the dark once you could see the glow of the coal oil lamp in the window. They were usually alone. Sometimes they'd travel with a dog team, but then we'd stay clear of them because the dogs would sense you were around and let them know.

"The rangers would think themselves pretty smart and get up really early and figure on jumping you before you woke up. I fixed them more than once. I'd get up really early and build the fire up. I'd stack up a bunch of green boughs like a statue by the fire and I then I'd take off in the snowstorm. When they found the fire burning in the dark and saw the silhouette, they'd figure they had you. But I would be long gone. They'd never run in a heavy snowstorm, either, but that was exactly the time for me to travel, because the snow would cover the tracks in no time.

"I'd always use the deer runways as much as I could. There was lots of deer in the park back then. If you travelled the deer runways, you could be sure that within an hour, the deer would pass by and cover your tracks. In the winter, I tricked them for a few years by strapping my snowshoes on backward and then I could take my time poaching and packing out the catch. The rangers were following my tracks, but they were going the wrong way. They figured that out after a year or two.

"They used to really watch me. It would be a real feather in the cap of whoever caught the 'king of the long runners.' One time, I dressed up in my Sunday-go-to-meeting suit and packed my suitcase and went down to the train station. They watched me get on the train and I waved to them as they scornfully watched the train pull out of the station. A few miles out of town, I jumped off the train, got my packsack out of the suitcase, changed my clothes, put the two parts of my take-down .22 together, and headed out across Algonquin Park. My pack was empty, so I shoved the suitcase with my suit into it and took it with me. You couldn't leave it where you'd jumped off the train, because if they found it, they'd know where to start tracking you.

"The first night, it was snowing pretty hard by dark. I carefully made my way over to the ranger cabin. If no one was there, then I'd stay in it for the night. It was late, so I didn't have to worry anyone would show up that night, and I'd be long gone in the morning. As I approached the cabin in the dark, I could smell pine smoke. I knew someone was there, so I was very careful. I was sure there were no dogs, because there was no yellow snow. The old fellers always said, 'You never want to eat yellow snow.' As I got closer, I saw a warm, golden glow from the little four-pane window, and white smoke rising from the stovepipe. I peeked through the window. In the faint light, I could see a rope clothesline with their shirts and jackets, wool pants, leather and wool mitts, and wool knee socks hanging to dry over the old wood stove. They were both lying out on top of their bunks with only their red long johns on. I almost laughed right out loud as I picked up a piece of charred wood from where they had dumped the ashes from the stove. They had a small pile of firewood stacked by the door. I peeled a piece of birch bark from a block of firewood and scratched out a little note for them. I silently read the note, 'See you at church on Sunday,' and I tucked the note into the handle of the suitcase. I sneaked back to the cabin really quietly and set the suitcase against the door. Then I quietly backed away from the cabin for a few hundred feet before I jacked a shell up, took careful aim on the stovepipe and pulled the trigger. The commotion that went on in that camp sounded just like a recycling station hit by a tornado. By the time they'd be dressed, I was long gone in the heavy snows.

"There was another time in the fall my cousin and I got a real run. We were both loaded with a heavy pack full of green beaver pelts and a fisher or two. We were poaching close to the boundary of the park. The rangers got on our heels and gave us a good run. There was a bunch of them and they had a couple of trucks, too. I figured this might be it for the king. We played hide-and-seek for quite a while, and then finally they had us trapped. They were all over us. We crawled on hands and knees through an old wooden culvert and snuck up the other side. Up on top of the hill, I saw one of their trucks parked. We made our way through the bush up to the truck. There was no one in it. They were all running us. I opened the door, and would you believe—there, hanging on a hook, was a ranger jacket and cap. Well, now, I just put on that ranger jacket and cap, turned the keys that were in the ignition, and drove that truck right down the hill and passed right by a couple of them. We waved courteously to them, and they waved right back to us, and we were on our way."

"What marvellous stories to share with your grandkids, Trapper!"

"You know we will we have to get the pelts all ready for market and down to North Bay by the end of November. That gives us about a week to get everything done and head down. I thought as we were going that far south perhaps you'd like to go on down, see your family and maybe stay for Christmas."

"I have really missed my family . . . and can you just imagine being able to get water out of a tap, turn a button on the wall for heat, flip a switch for light, pick up a telephone and be able to talk to anyone, have a glass of fresh milk, sit on something other than a pine stump, have a hot bath, put on a dress, go out for dinner, and have someone else do the cooking and the dishes? What luxury!"

"I didn't notice you were getting any flatter on the butt on my pine stools! It's not my fault every time your elbow bends your mouth opens. What do you mean sit on a chair?" We both laughed.

"We could both use some hot water and soap and a haircut. My damn pants are patched with pieces of tarp and blankets and sewn up with string and snare wire. I bet they'd stand up in the corner all by themselves. You'd need a stick, I think, to knock them down. I'll soon look like those long-haired fifties hippies that tramp around down south. Or, worse yet, like those young dudes of today that strut about in baggy pants like a baby with a load in the crotch and their arse hanging out for all the world to see!"

It was decided. The next day, Trapper would go and check and snap all traps. It would be three weeks to a month before his return and he didn't want any animals left in traps. I would remove all of the pelts from the stretchers and brush them up to be nice and clean and fluffy. Then I would catalogue them all as to species, size, and gender and pack all the pelts and label them ready for the auction house. It was a tremendous amount of work, but a trapper was involved in wildlife management and had to keep accurate records, too. It was important to keep track of what you were catching. With marten, for instance, as long as you were catching equal numbers of males and females, or more males, you were safe to keep setting. As soon as you started to catch more females, then it was time to pick up your traps. A few males could breed several females, but if you didn't have the female then you couldn't regenerate the numbers and protect the population.

I tended to each pelt carefully and sorted them into piles on the cabin floor. There were beaver, otter, mink, muskrat, ermine, marten, fisher, fox, wolf, and lynx pelts, and one black bear pelt. There was hardly room in the camp to move about. The beaver were piled skin-to-skin and fur-to-fur so as not to get any oils onto the fur. They were then packed flat into a large shipping bag. The beaver castor was put into a paper bag and added. The castor would be used in perfume, aftershave, and various medicinal products.

All pelts that were stretched with fur out were packed into another bag. Pelts stretched with hide out were packed into a third bag. Great care was exercised in the taking of animals and in the preparation and shipping of hides. Trapper said this was a resource to be respected and managed for the welfare of both wildlife and human populations, and was a legacy entrusted to us for the future.

The following morning was spent closing down the camp. After breakfast, we let the fire go out and then cleaned the ashes out of the stove. Wood had to be split and brought in so the wood rack would be full for our return in the winter. Water containers were filled so there would be some water in camp, but only three-quarters full, to allow for expansion as it froze. The sleeping bags were rolled and hung on wires from the ceiling, to prevent mice from damaging them. All dried, non-perishable foods were packed into metal lard tins to keep animals from getting at it. All pots and pans were turned upside down on the shelves and covered with clean cloths. The shutters were placed over the windows. As I set a new fire in the stove to be left in readiness for our return, Trapper hung the rest of the beaver carcasses in trees for the birds and animals to feed on in the winter.

We gathered up our clothes and what gear we would take for the trip. As I packed up our packsacks, Trapper took them, the bags of pelts, and the guns, and packed the boat. It was a quiet time for me . . . a very, very quiet time. At the shore, I stood and looked across the lake to the far shore, now void of all colour but for conifer greens. I then looked up across the ice-covered bay to the portage, then around to the entrance of the trail, and finally my eyes settled on the camp. I wanted to go home but I didn't want to leave. Quietly I sang out across the waters,

> Land of the silver birch, home of the beaver,
> Where still the mighty moose wanders at will,
> Boom de dee ah da, Boom de dee ah da,
> Bo-o-o-o-ooom.

> My heart grows sick for thee here in the lowlands,
> I will return to thee, hills of the north,
> Boom de dee ah da, Boom de dee ah da,
> Bo-o-o-o-ooom.[15]

As the outboard motor hummed its monotone solo down the lake, the little log camp backed into the Jack pine hills, and the entire picture blurred before my eyes. I didn't want to go back south. I wanted to stay here in the northern wilderness. Sure, I missed my family; but the loneliness, the lack of luxuries and conveniences, the hardships, the independence, the quiet, the peace, and the freedom had become part of my life. Trapper had become part of my life. I wanted it all—ALL of it—to BE my life.

When we reached the dock at Brown's Bay, Trapper tied up the boat and backed the truck down to the dock. In choked silence, I helped to load the gear into the truck and then to drag the boat up onto the shore. Together, we turned it upside down to be left until spring. Trapper stood silently, hands in his pockets, looking out across the lake and bidding farewell to his vast kingdom. I couldn't help but see the magnificent landscape before me through flooded eyes. He wrapped an arm about my shoulders and drew me to his side. With saddened eyes he looked right into mine that were overflowing and softly placed a kiss on my forehead.

"*Partir c'est mourir un peu.*"

"What does that mean?" I sobbed.

"Parting is a little like dying."

I nodded in the affirmative. My throat was so tightly knotted I could not speak.

"You're not very happy about leaving the little ole shack on the lake, are you. Come on, we best get a move on."

After a final last look at the magnificent shores of Wakami Lake, we silently climbed into the truck and settled with Tracker between us. I watched the blurred Jack pines pass alongside the truck. Streaks of pale green poplar and white birch trunks interrupted the conifer green. The sway of the truck on curves, into ruts, and over stones seemed far distant. We drove out of the park, turned left along the Sultan Road, and travelled the twenty-two miles out to Highway 129, where we turned south to follow this winding ribbon of a road almost 150 miles through the absolutely magnificent wilderness of the Mississaugi River Valley.

Seven hours later, we arrived at the fur auction house in North Bay. As Trapper had been a patron of the auction house for over thirty years, everyone greeted him with a smile and a ready handshake.

The pelts were unpacked and each identified with a tag for the auction. The pelts would then be distributed to various rooms about the building for sorting as to species, size, grading, and drumming, which is rather like being tumbled in a clothes dryer. Any dirt or debris in the long-furred pelts falls out and the fur is fluffed up. It is then bundled into lots for the auction to be held in two weeks. I enjoyed a tour of the entire facility, including the auction room. Trapper was given a receipt for his pelts and offered an advance. He took an advance of $400 to look after gas, new clothes, and "Christmas boxes"—his name for "gifts." I wanted to go home, but my heart was indeed torn in two.

Home for
the Holidays

Regular dinner table setting at my parents' home.

(Photo by Paton Lodge Lindsay)

Many hours and several stops later, we arrived in the dark of night and without warning at my parents' home. Trapper, thinking ahead, turned out the headlights and shut off the ignition, and we quietly coasted into the driveway at around three-thirty a.m. Despite our consideration, as we came to a halt, all eight dogs in the kennel sang out in a mighty canine chorus of yips, yodels, and howls that reminded me of the wolf packs howling at the full moon on Wakami Lake. We sat quietly in the truck and began to laugh as we heard my mother calling from a back window: "Kiley and Lady, you be quiet. Shane, Sean, Tyke, be quiet. Duchess, Kerry, Teddy, all of you, be quiet!"

The lights along the path to the kennel and the soffit lights flashed on and off.

"You be quiet!"

All was silent. The kennel and pathway lights went out. The bedroom lights went out. Mother went back to bed, and all had returned to normal. Trapper stepped out of the truck and moved to the corner of the house. He turned and, taking in a huge breath, he raised cupped hands to his mouth. Exhaling slowly through his mouth a long, mellow, melodious wolf howl sang out through the maple and hemlock bush and echoed from the far hills.

"You couldn't leave sleeping dogs lie, could you?" I shouted to him.

Eight dogs again came crashing out of their kennel doors, and a choir of canine choristers once again filled the night air with yips, yipes, yowls, and howls. From the rear window, Mother was heard: "Kiley, Kerry, Duchess, Sean, be quiet. Ted, Tyke, Shaney—be quiet!"

The lights all flashed once more, and Mother called to everyone. The dogs were really upset this time. They had not just heard a vehicle in the driveway. They had heard the call of the wild.

Then there was a basso profundo "QUIET!" Ooops! I knew that deep, stentorian voice. I seemed to recall that it always worked. Father was now awake and up, too. Indeed, it had worked. All was indeed silent. The outside lights dimmed. The bedroom lights went out. Again, everyone was back in bed.

Now was the time to ring the doorbell. It was a wonderful ringer that toned out the Westminster Chimes. We could follow the progress of someone—probably Mother—coming to answer the door by the sequence of lights as she moved through the house. First the bedroom, then the hall lights shone through the guest room, the den, the library, followed by the crystal chandelier in the dining room, the foyer lights, and finally the front entrance lights. It was Mother. She didn't open the door but peered out through the leaded glass windows of the living room. No one was visible as Trapper and I hung close to the wall.

"Bill, there is someone here. You'd better come to the door."

Dad, who doesn't like being roused from his sleep, mumbled all the way to the door about cats and dogs and horses and inconsiderate people who call at all hours of the morning. He opened the door and looked to the right and then to the left.

"Oh, my God, Kathleen, it's the trappers returned from the north!"

My sister came running; the cats brushed against our legs. The chihuahuas, Cha-Cha Linga and Louis Lingo Lopez, danced at our feet. Everyone tried to talk at once. Mom tried to tell us about the new Irish setter puppies and about Kiley's winning Best in Specialty at the dog show. Dad was telling us all about the new STOL aircraft and how it had to be certified by the end of the year. Sue brought us up to date on the new foals and the fall trail ride and all the trophies the horses had won at the equestrian club banquet. We never did get to bed that night but sat about the huge stone fireplace until daybreak talking and laughing and catching up on the past few months. It really was great to be home!

This was home . . . the thick, woollen, military red carpets that spread to black walnut walls; the antique Victorian furniture that came from England and Wales seven generations ago; the huge family portraits in gold-leaf frames that reached from chesterfields to ceilings; the soft, golden light of the fireplace that flickered on the silver epergne filled with red and white poinsettias; the huge, silver pots with massive poinsettias in the four corners of the room. A four-foot holly wreath with swaged garlands hung on the massive stone fireplace.

This was not just a house but a real country home. It was tucked away in the privacy of a hardwood bush thirty miles north of Toronto. Several acres of rolling lawns and wide perennial flower beds were hidden behind cedar rail fences and hemlock hedges. The road and paths that led to the kennels and stables boasted a carpet of purple violets, white and cranberry trilliums, bloodroot, May apple blossom, and a host of other wildflowers in the spring. The canopy in autumn glowed amber-yellow with beech; orange and red with maple; green with hemlock, pine, and spruce. Here and there a pillar of white birch stood out against the colour. In the white of winter spruce spires rose to a cathedral ceiling etched in an iron grey grillwork of sleeping hardwoods. On the south side, the rolling pastures dropped away to a mural landscape some twenty miles to the horizon.

The fully carpeted and heated kennel held some of the most magnificent Irish setters to enter the canine world. The stables, with spotless floors and glistening, varnished walls, were filled with palomino quarter horses, sleek thoroughbreds, spotted appaloosas, and the aroma of hot mash and molasses.

Mom was a master chef and homemaker. A real gourmet chef, she delighted in doing everything herself. Though she had been raised in a home with servants, she always said there wasn't room in any kitchen for two women. At special times like Easter, Thanksgiving, and particularly Christmas, she always went all-out. Christmas at our house was definitely a celebration of the birth of Christ. It was a family time. No neighbours, no visitors. We did always seem to have a couple of special guests who were very senior in years, lived alone, and were in need. Their company added so greatly to our Christmas. We'd always attend the midnight carol service and communion on Christmas Eve.

Christmas Day always started with a fight to get Dad out of bed. Then it was a real effort to convince him to do the tree ritual before his daily shower and breakfast. As we grew older, we were more patient about waiting. Breakfast was always served in the dining room and consisted of fresh grapefruit with a maraschino cherry top and centre, back bacon and eggs, and English muffins with marmalade made from an old Scottish recipe of my second great-grandmother's, and freshly brewed coffee, the beans having been ground only moments before. It always seemed so special just because everyone was back together. After breakfast, Mom would take up her queenly position in the large, white damask wing chair next to the fireplace. Dad would light the tree, put on the Christmas music, and then seat himself on his throne on the matching white damask wing chair on the other side of the fireplace. Sister Sue always acted as Santa Claus and distributed the gifts.

Around November of every year, Dad would always announce that this was going to be a lean Christmas, so everyone please be sensible. It never seemed to fail that he would, each year, have managed to hide about the tree such sensible little gifts as a new stereo or a fur coat, a beautiful show saddle with sterling conches, or a magnificent, hand-carved chess set. There were always the practical gifts such as the clothing, the doggy and catty stuff, the research and reference books for my brother Roderick, who was at university and would within a matter of years become the world's expert in his field. There were always the funny little toys for everyone, once the baby of the family had reached adulthood. Christmas was still children and toys . . . toys and laughter, friends and family.

Christmas dinner was a Louis XIV deluxe. The old English William-and-Mary walnut gate-legged table was of such dimensions that it sat twelve people. There was never anything but a pure white linen damask tablecloth and napkins. The centrepiece was a handcrafted silver epergne. The central vase had bracket supports that held three removable silver basket vases, all with beautiful, silver-pierced cutwork lace about the rims. It was always filled with freshly cut flowers of the season. Two massive silver cornucopias filled with exotic fresh fruits of every imaginable kind reclined to either side. Two tall, five-candle sterling candelabra glowed at the ends. The table glistened with sterling silver; cut crystal stemware; Minton china; Edwardian gadrooned and Victorian bead-cast bordered silver entree dishes and platters; and colourful Christmas crackers. Always, the very special antique dinner plates with a decorated Christmas tree sat upon silver chargers set between the engraved sterling cutlery, which consisted of at least three forks, two knives, and three or four spoons, and an engraved sterling napkin ring with linen napkin at each place setting.

The first course was always moulded tomato aspic jellies that Mother had made. Lovingly, she had spent many hours carefully placing pasta alphabet letters backward in reverse into the base of each mould so that when they were turned out onto a bed of crisp lettuce leaves, each said, "Merry Christmas." There were green jellied salads; crunchy, crisp-leafed salads; a gigantic golden roasted turkey of no less than thirty pounds; the chestnut and cranberry dressing; mashed potatoes and gravy; candied sweet potatoes; turnips; broccoli; homemade hot buttered rolls; nuts; fruits; mincemeat pies; pumpkin pie topped with real whipped cream, drizzled with liquid honey and sprinkled with shaved almonds; and flaming plum pudding. The closeness of family, quiet carols, a crackling fire, and love. This was home . . . this was Christmas.

Red Sky at Night

Trapper ready to "hit the road."

(Photo by Paton Lodge Lindsay)

Four weeks passed. It didn't seem that long, since the outside trees were all aglow with silver tinsel and blue floodlights. Seemed like yesterday that we arrived, but New Year's has come and gone. It was time for Trapper to return north. After many pleading discussions and outright begging and even tears, I finally got permission to return to Wakami Lake. There was a lot of hustle and bustle to get ready for the return trip. Mom and I had busily knit sweaters, hats, mitts and scarves for the children at Mink Creek. I visited all my friends and begged and almost stole snowmobile suits and boots for all the children. They had not been out of our minds over Christmas, and there was no returning without these necessities, as temperatures now would be minus forty degrees. We hadn't been able to round up a baby snowsuit, so we all chipped in and bought a fluffy, white, furry one for the baby.

Five o'clock in the morning arrived early after a sleepless night of anticipation. We were up and at it early, had our breakfast, said our farewells, and the three of us were away. The actual drive took nearly thirteen hours. During that time, we passed through the rich agricultural belt of Southern Ontario and into the scenic tourism area of the Parry Sound District. We continued to drive north on Highway 69 and were seemingly in the middle of nowhere when out of the blue Trapper asked me, "Did you remember to pick up a case of toilet paper?"

"Nope, I completely forgot it."

"Burdock is kinda hard to come by this time o' year, ya know." He pulled off onto the shoulder of the road and got out.

"Where are you going? Oh, well, there's toilet paper under the seat."

"Never mind, I'll get some. Lock the doors. I'll be back in a short while."

He took off through the bush and I sat and waited, and waited, and waited. I looked about the bush and up along the highway. Then I noticed a blue highway sign that said, "Do not pick up pedestrians." How foolish! I'd never ever seen that sign on the highways before. I read my book and I waited, and waited, and waited. Finally he arrived back, threw something in the back of the truck, and we headed north again.

"What'd you throw in the back of the truck?"

"We needed a case of toilet paper; you forgot to get it, so I went and got it."

"Well, where the heck did you get it? There are no stores around here; there's nothing around here. It is desolate and remote around here . . . there is NOTHING around here."

He drove on for a few minutes and we came out into a large clearing, a farm on both sides of the highway.

"What's this place?" I asked.

"Burwash—Burwash Prison. They've got lots of toilet paper in there!"

I was totally stunned. My mind seemed to hang in suspension. My BRAIN went into "lock-down."

"You walked into a prison and stole a case of toilet paper and just walked out?"

"Just gotta know what you're doing; nothin' to it. Pretty cheap place to do your shopping."

"J-E-E-E-S-U-S! You left ME sittin' out in the truck to get caught? You do THAT very often?"

"I kinda consider it a rebate on my taxes!"

"WHEEEW! Let us just get out of here."

We continued to drive north through the desolate mining area of the Canadian Shield. From Sudbury, we turned west and drove through a multitude of those little northern towns that were obviously involved with logging, fishing, and trapping. At Thessalon, we turned north on Highway 129, which Trapper affectionately called the "Mississaugi Special." During the four hours of travel along this route, we met two other vehicles. The "Mississaugi Special" took us through gigantic rock cuts laden with huge curtains of turquoise and opal frozen waterfalls hanging with outstretched fingers reaching into every crevice in the rocks. The Mississaugi River, which in some places dropped a hundred feet below, raged through rapids and massive ice jams.

A few miles farther north, and we travelled through the boreal pine flats of the arctic watershed, turned east onto the forest access road, and made our way toward Wakami Lake. We parked at the park gates and transferred everything onto the snowmobile and sled. Travel from there would be by snowmobile and snowshoe for the next four months. As we rode the trail of the white roller coaster through the park, we dropped down over the hill that declines to the shore, and there she was: the Snow Queen of the north attended by all her ladies in waiting. Majestically they lined the shore in their green velvet gowns now appliqued in white. Tall, lean escorts in black and white accompanied them. The conifer and birch lined this crystal ballroom and swayed to and fro as snowflakes waltzed along the wind-polished dance floor in tune to Nature's symphony. W-A-K-A-M-I, you just need to sound her name and you can hear the music.

We unloaded the Snowbug and hitched it to the sleigh then loaded our gear and grub onto the sleigh and made our way north to the camp. Once there, Trapper took one of his snowshoes and shovelled out the doorway. He checked the roof to make sure the top of the stovepipe was clear and then put a match to the fire we had left in readiness for our return. As the camp warmed, we wrestled our gear and supplies through the more-than-waist-deep snow to the camp. There is no cold like the penetrating, still, cold of a camp that has been closed up in winter. It took several hours for the room to warm up. Once our gear was stashed, we ate and then curled up into the arctic sleeping bags for the night.

The next morning, we awoke to a camp with frost-covered interior walls. That day was spent putting the wood to the stove, as it would take twenty-four hours to heat the logs through and bring the actual camp temperature up to be suitable for habitation. We kept warm and busy unpacking, settling in, and just resting up. It had been a long journey. Trapper was stiff and sore and very glad to be home. The old stove snapped and crackled, the kettle was starting to sing its merry music, and we were beginning to feel the warmth through our parkas. I was HOME.

"My heart is here, you know. This is where I want my bones to rest. Someday I'll just take a long walk back into the bush and not come back," commented Trapper.

"I once sat thinking about that. What would I do if you didn't come back? What items would I need to pack for you for the long trip to the other side?"

"Oh, I won't need much," said he; "and where I'm going, there'll be a fire blazing, to be sure, and I'll keep it going for you when you get there," he laughed.

Through the little window, we took in a flaming red sunset. It was so cold in this natural deep freeze, and yet the entire world seemed to be afire.

"It's unbelievably magnificent. Even the snow is red. Trapper, did you ever in your life see such a red sky at night?"

"Well, now," he began as he warmed his hands over the stove, "when you mention a red sky at night, I just happen to think back to something that happed when I was a mere boy. I heard the old people talking with my grandfather. There was a big fire burning down there in the Ottawa Valley. My father was just a young man

"Red Sky at Night"
(Painting by Paton Lodge Lindsay)

and he went with his father. When they got in there where the fire was burning, there were hundreds of men. Of course, back in those days there weren't bulldozers or hardly any machinery of any kind. There were dirt or gravel wagon roads. It was mostly horses and wagons back then; people had wagons and buggies or double rigs. They called them double rigs 'democrats.' The buggies were a small affair with small wheels on them, and you'd put a single base on them with a board seat and lots of blankets, and they were usually pulled by a single horse. The rich people in town might have a democrat with two or three seats that could sit six or eight people, and they were pulled by a team of light horses that you called drivers. We just had a wagon.

"However, there had been a big company logging up in that part of the country, and how the fire got started, no one knew for sure. Maybe bushmen or fishermen . . . or lightning . . . or someone threw a cigarette on the ground; anyhow, the fire got goin'.

"There were a lot of tops on the ground. It was spruce and pine country. They cut a lot of spruce for pulp and they cut it log length. They'd cut the big swamps in the wintertime and then those swamps would all dry out, and all the dry tops would be left there. That made a real fire hazard.

"There was a big set of ole logging camps where they took all the men and it was called a 'keep-over,' where they used to keep all the supplies like flour, sugar, tea, salt, beans, and so on—all the dry staples. They'd portage all that in when the men would go in to log. The loggers would start from there at the keep-over in the fall. They'd engage a foreman and give him a hundred men and he'd take his men and go into the bush and build new camps where they were going to cut that winter. They'd take all the food they needed from the keep-over and portage it in on the wagons that followed the men as they cut the road in to the new site. There were no roads. You carried everything in with you and cut the road from the forest as you went. Usually you walked in; only the lucky few ever got a ride on the wagons. Old-timers figured the horses had enough to haul the loaded wagons and sleighs. If they could walk and work all day, so could you. They kept maybe a half-dozen men at the keep-over all summer to look after the cattle and pigs and horses and everything. They had no refrigerators those days so they kept live animals at the keep-over and when you needed meat you'd slaughter and butcher it right there. There was no meat inspectors, no packaged meat like today. You walked your meat into the camp on the hoof and you killed it in there.

"However, when my grandfather, and father, and uncles, and the other men were in there on that fire, my grandfather and father and some uncles got cornered by the fire and they couldn't get back to the base camp. The sky lit up bright red like a sunset. They were surrounded by forest fire and were backed up to a big lake about fifteen miles long and three miles wide. They had nowhere to get away.

"Most of the timber in those days was still square timber. They were just starting to cut round logs. Most people don't know the difference between square timber and logs. In square timber days, there were no saws in the country, no cross-cut saws. My great-grandfather paid $1.90 for an eight-foot crescent saw, a pine saw, and he carried it back on foot or by wagon all the way from Pennsylvania. It was one of the first saws in the country. They used to chop the trees down with axes. Then they'd score them with a scoring axe and then took a slab off the side with a broad axe. Both of my grandfathers were good broadaxe men. They got $1.10 a day. A fellow that could handle an ordinary axe got $13.50

a month and his keep.

"Well, back at the old abandoned keep-over there was an old cage crib or a square-timber raft left at the shore of the lake. My grandfather said, 'We are all going to burn to death in here if we don't do something.' Heavy smoke had settled down over the entire area. They got a team of horses and all the food and supplies they could get into an old portage wagon box and they drew it onto the old square-timber raft. They tied the horses there on the raft 'cause they were terrified of the fire and smoke and wanted to bolt. All the men lined up along the back of the raft and shoved it out into the water. Once it floated, they all jumped on. They had two big sweeps or oars, and they rowed out and made their way to the middle of the lake. The sweeps were each about twenty feet long, and four men handled each one to put them out into the lake, and there they dropped the big, eight-foot oak anchor covered with steel sleigh shoeing. They stayed on that crib out in the lake for thirteen days. They had an awful time out there and pretty near died from the smoke. They kept their shirts wetted down and hung over their heads and had to do the same for the horses. Hot coals and hot ash and branches that were on fire blew in the air with the winds created by the fire. One time, the wagon and the raft actually caught on fire and they had to put that fire out. A few days after the fire passed and the smoke cleared a bit, they rowed the crib back to shore.

"They hitched the horses back onto the wagon and drove it up onto the land. All the men who were injured or sick got into the wagon, and the others walked behind. The trees were all burned and ash was all over. They walked in ashes halfway up their boots and tried to find their way out. There was no road left and burned trees had fallen everywhere. They had a dreadful time to make their way out. When they got back to the keep-over, it was burned, as were all the men and animals that had stayed there. Everything was gone. The only way my grandfather and father and uncles had saved themselves was by getting onto the raft and staying out in the lake.

"It was nearly a month from the time they left for the fire until they made their way home. When they got out to the settlement, the people nearly all fainted. They had been presumed dead, burned in the fires, no remains to ever be found. Mass had even been said. The families were in deep sorrow, as all the men had been wiped out, burned in the fire. Now, a month later, at the setting of the sun, a rickety, charred old wagon full of blackened, weakened, hungry men slowly moved down the road of the settlement. As they passed each house, the people standing on the porches looked in total disbelief and made the sign of the cross upon their chests. Many of the women fainted. It was as though the men had risen from the dead and they had come home.

"Gramma made the sign of the cross on her chest and shouted for all the settlement to hear, 'He who dost still the roaring of the seas and quell the raging of the fires dost make the sunset shout for joy!'"[16]

God Reveals His Presence

Rusty waiting for us at camp.
(Photo by Paton Lodge Lindsay)

"Let's take a trip into Mink Creek and see how the families are doing."

"Great! I'll get our parcels ready and you pack them into the sleigh."

Trapper hitched the sleigh onto the Snowbug and loaded the two pairs of snowshoes, axe, rifles, and the boxes for the children. I jumped on, and we were away, with Tracker in hot pursuit. He was used to running with the snowmobile. He had learned that the best place to run was beside it. When running in front, one could be overtaken, with disastrous results. Running behind, he constantly ate the snow flung out from the twenty-six-inch track of the Snowbug.

Out on the lake, a harsh wind lashed at our faces. The cold blast made my eyes water, and it was hard to see. I snuggled my face into the back of Trapper's parka. In a short while, we were within the park proper and the shelter of the Jack pines, which bore the brunt of the biting winds. They served to deflect the winds and in doing so sang their own song of the wilderness.

Even in the cold of January, there was still music in the air; the crunch of snow beneath rabbit feet; the drip of sun-warmed boughs; the chatter of red squirrels; the peet, peet, peet of the whisky jacks as they flitted about overhead and followed us along the trail. It was about twelve miles from the bay to Mink Creek. We arrived to the smell of burning pine, the sound of wood giving way to an axe, and were greeted with wagging tails, warm smiles, hearty handshakes, and some translated welcomes. We hadn't seen the family for nearly two months.

They had moved across the creek from their fall encampment. A new teepee constructed of Jack pine poles erected in a conical shape and covered with tarps formed the roof over their heads. A lazy trail of smoke swirled up and out through the hole in the top. Dozens of hoop stretchers were hung from pine knots on the trees about their campsite. Beaver skeletons were scattered about the camp, with dogs, ravens, and whisky jacks all picking away at any meat that remained on the bones. The head of a moose and a hide lay by a graining pole. Various handmade wooden utensils and tools such as a large spoon, ladles, paddles, clubs, and scrapers were strewn about in disarray.

The kids were hanging onto Trapper, the two smallest ones one on each side with an arm wrapped about his leg just above the knee and they walked along beside him. They would shyly peek out from his side then turn and smile back at me. Trapper took the first box from the sleigh and called all the kids to come over. Black almond-shaped eyes danced in the sunlight as one wee girl untied her box and gleamed over a bright-green snowsuit and boots and a navy hat, mitts, and sweater set. A bright-red snowsuit, hat, mitts, and boots brought a grin to the face of an expectant little boy. Two others stood back, shy but expectant. Trapper handed them each a rolled skidoo suit and boots. Within minutes, they stumbled about with an arm in a leg and desperately trying to effect entry of the other side.

"You're goin' to meet a bear in the bush. You got your boots on the wrong feet," said Trapper.

The young lad just grinned and shrugged his shoulders. We all laughed and I reached and fetched the white box from the sleigh. In that box there was the little layette set we had so tenderly knit and the fluffy white snowsuit for the baby. Trapper handed the box to the young Indian mother. A wonderful grin stretched the width of her weathered but beautiful young face and she sat down on the snow bank and opened it. A cloud passed over her face; the sunlight dimmed from her eyes; rain trickled down her bronzed cheeks. She knelt in the snow and carefully unfolded each piece, held it up and looked at it, clutched it to her chest and then carefully folded each back into the box. Her long slender arm rose and pointed back across the creek to a mound of white snow beneath a white spruce. The cold winds had blown and the snows had come, bringing with them the time for the long sleep for a little seven-month-old child. Winter had taken its toll. God had summoned the baby home.

All became quiet in the bush. Mink Creek had now become a rather sacred place. There seemed to be a holy feeling here among the spruce and pine. The grey jays and the chickadees and the squirrels all went about their daily business, but they, too, were quiet. None made a sound in the hush of this silent nursery. The Indian mother and I walked in silence across the creek to the fluffy white mound. I stood in total disbelief and looked at the little mound of white snow in the wilderness. A gust of wind brushed my cheek and Mother Nature quietly sang with the wind in the pines and seemed to hum a lullaby. On bended knees I knelt and reached out and touched that white blanket of snow that covered the sleeping child. God spoke to us in the silence. A whispered breeze sang its lullaby, rustling the dried grasses along the creek. Through tears and quivering lips I quietly sang,

> This is my Father's world;
> He shines in all that's fair;
> In the rustling grass I hear Him pass,
> He speaks to me everywhere.[17]

Trapper placed a hand to my shoulder. Our eyes met in sorrow and understanding. Our hearts met in sadness and a singular closeness that we each knew would be binding for life. At that very moment we both knew what the future held for us.

35

The Lost King

The Snowbug snowmobile.
(Photo by Robert Foster)

Christmas was a couple of months behind us. We were well settled into the little camp, and it was nice and warm now that the snow was level with the eaves. We literally had a tunnel dug into the wee door and the window that looked out across Wakami Lake. There were several feet of clear, black ice on Wakami now. In areas along the shore, it was covered with hard-packed, windblown snow. In the open, the snows had been completely blown away by the fierce winds of winter, and the ice surface was as polished as a ballroom floor. In the shelter of the heavy bush, the snows were yet free and loose as white granular sugar.

We had been trapping beaver under the ice for about ten weeks. Travel since our return had all been by snowshoe and snowmobile. The Snowbug snowmobile was a wilderness wonder: single ski in front, engine in the rear, a transmission for reverse, chain drive, gas and brake on the floor, and a twenty-six-inch, single track with cleats. It was built in Sudbury and was the best bush machine ever built. Everyone waited for the trappers with a Snowbug to go to the bush and break the trails, and then the fishermen would follow.

The mink season had closed the end of December. Marten, fisher, and lynx close the end of February. Beaver and otter close the end of March, and muskrat would close the end of May. The season for each species closed prior to breeding time. This would guarantee a protected breeding season and the birth of new young each spring so as not to deplete the populations.

Trapper was packed up before daylight. He packed a lunch and his gear, took his rifle and snowshoes, and loaded the sleigh on the back of the Snowbug and headed off to the most distant, remote corner of the trapline to pick up the last of the otter and beaver traps. As he rounded Otter Point, just a hint of morning light glazed the treetops. He stood and waved back to us and was on his way.

He would travel to the head of Wakami Lake and then across to Kebskwasheshi Lake. On the way back, he would check the two small ponds and then head over to Squaw Lake and Nineay Lake, and then along the creek to the farthest lake. It would be about a forty-four-mile trip that day. Very long, very difficult, and lots of hard work. He would not be back before dark.

The weather had been very cold, with temperatures of minus fifty and colder. There was no bottom to the snow. It was just like granular white sugar, and yet somehow, even at those severe temperatures, the snows had provided sufficient insulation so that there was still some slush in the swamps and creeks.

Most trips into the bush, you carried traps in and fur out. This was the last trip of the season, so there would be a heavy load. Holes would have to be chopped through the ice at every set. Even though when trapping under the ice we would cover the holes with green boughs and then with snow to try and prevent freezing, there was still a lot of work to free a set from the ice.

There was as yet a great deal of preparation to be ready for the trip out. All pelts had to be dried and sealed by April 10. There were beaver pelts drying on boards hanging from the ridge and otter pelts on stretchers drying in the corners. Trapper was adamant—there was no option. I had to stay at camp and keep the fires going and look after the pelts, and he would go and look after the final pick-up. He had loaded his gear on the sleigh, jumped into the "cockpit," and was on his way. As I watched him fade into the horizon, the final putt, putt, putt of the Snowbug faded into silence. The pines only seconds before silhouetted against a faded dark blue were now black against a golden hue. Tracker and I watched the hoarfrost twinkle in the first sunlight to hit the alder branches, and we returned to camp.

The first job was to get the fires stoked, and some beaver hams and chopped onions into a pot to simmer. I made up some bannock dough to bake later and then did up the dishes. Beaver, fish, partridge, beans, bannock, and tea had been the mainstay of our diet for months. Fresh vegetables would have been a complete luxury, and fruit only to dream of.

I removed two dry beaver pelts from the hanging boards. Later, Tracker and I took the two buckets, an axe, and a fishing line and headed out to the water hole. I pushed aside the snow and green boughs that covered the hole and then chopped out the ice. I dropped the white and black braided line and hook baited with beaver fat down the hole. I only had to jig it a couple of times before a pike hit it. Great, there was fresh fish for another meal!

Tracker and I took in the warmth from the risen sun. It was now an absolutely brilliantly blinding, warm, sunny day. With the fish and two buckets of water in hand, we returned to the camp. I cleaned the fish and put it out into the meat box on the outside wall of the camp. I poured the two buckets of water into the reservoir on the wood stove and returned for two more. It felt hot out. I stood in the afternoon March sun in just my shirt. It must have been fifty degrees. Tracker kept me company as I split up some firewood and filled the wood rack for the night. The camp chores were all done, and the sun was beginning to get low in the sky. The first evening chill began to settle in. Trapper would be back soon and he would be cold, tired, and hungry.

The camp was toasty warm and all aglow in the light of the coal oil lamp. The aroma of simmering beaver and onions, baking bannock, and perking coffee wafted about the camp. The pine snapped in the wood stove; the beaver pot bubbled and burped on top of the stove and the coffee pot chug-a-lugged like a bittern in the swamp in the spring. We were all ready for Trapper. The hours had passed, the sun had set, and the black of night had enveloped the world. All was dark. All was quiet. I knew all was not well.

Trapper was not back.

"Where are you, Trapper? Where are you?"

Trapper had spent many a night alone in the bush in summer and winter. It was second nature to him. Maybe he just had too much to do. Perhaps the creeks had opened in the heat of the afternoon and he would have to wait until morning and come out on the frost. Perhaps he had decided to skin some beaver in there rather than carry the entire animal out. He had often done that, spent the night in the bush and skinned beaver by firelight. Maybe . . . ?

There was absolutely nothing I could do until daylight. I certainly didn't sleep, just worried. At break of day, I lit a fire in the stove, took my pack and rifle, and on snowshoes headed out the trail to Brown's Bay and Wakami Lake. I snowshoed out to the Old Sultan Road and headed for town. As the temperatures warmed up, the snow started to pack on my snowshoes and I had to keep taking them off and banging them together to remove the heavy, wet snow. Tracker, too, was limping, with the snow packed between his toes, and I would have to kneel and pick the snow from his paws each time we stopped. It was heavy, tough going.

Upon nearing Sultan, I came upon a couple of fishermen on their Skidoos and asked them if they would run me into the MNR office in town. When we got there, I grabbed my snowshoes, pack, and rifle and ran up the steps to the door. I nearly fell through the door yelling for anyone. There was no answer. The two conservation officers were out for the day, gone to the Native encampment. I ran across the yard to Joe's home and told his wife Ida what had happened and asked if she knew when Joe would be back.

As we spoke, Joe arrived. In desperate excitement, I told him how Trapper had left the day before and never come back. Joe was always cool and calm; he reassured me that Trapper would have no trouble spending the night in the bush, said he was one of the most capable wilderness men ever known to the Department of Lands and Forests. Matter of fact, he said, hours had passed since I had left the camp, and Trapper was probably at camp right now and wondering where I was. Joe asked his wife to get him a thermos of tea and said he would run me back to camp. I jumped onto the Skidoo behind him. With little haste, and with Tracker in pursuit, we flew out of town and down the Old Sultan Road past the dump, past Six Mile Dam Road, across Spring Creek, and down the trail to Wakami Lake. Once out on the lake, I buried my face in Joe's parka, and we travelled wide-open to the camp. When we arrived there, Tracker was only minutes behind us.

Upon our arrival, Joe told me to stay with the machine and he would check the camp.

"He's not here!" I yelled. "There's no Snowbug and there are no tracks and no smoke. He isn't here. Something is really wrong."

Joe came out from the camp.

"No, he isn't here and he hasn't been here." Joe lit a fire, put Tracker into the camp, and shut the door.

"We'll go and look for him. We'll find him. You come, too. We'll have some tracks to follow but you know where he was going, you know what he was doing and you'll know what to look for; you always went with him."

We travelled full-speed to the head of Wakami Lake and over to the trail entrance to Kebskwasheshi Lake.

"He's been in and outta here. He must have gone on to Squaw Lake."

We proceeded on. At the trail to Squaw Lake, Joe turned in to Squaw and then on to Nineay Lake and started up along the creek. He stopped the machine.

"Something is not right, here. He seems to be having trouble steering the machine. He's gone off the trail and cut through the bush. All we can do is follow in his tracks."

We followed Trapper's tracks through the bush, through swamps, up and downhill, over creeks, and finally back out to the head of Wakami Lake. We followed Trapper's tracks when we could see them all the way back down Wakami Lake and past where the camp was on the other side. Finally, down by the narrows above Six Mile Dam, about a half-mile ahead of us, we spotted a bright orange spot at the edge of the lake. It was the orange cowling of the Snowbug. Trapper was nowhere to be seen. Joe stopped the Skidoo and we got off. Joe yelled to the bush calling Trapper. There was no answer.

"If he's not dead now, he will be when I get my hands on him," I wailed. "I told him he should never go anywhere in the bush without telling someone where he was going."

We both ran to the Snowbug and found Trapper sprawled out on the ice against the back side of the machine. Joe lifted Trapper's head up onto his knee and checked the pulse in his neck and for breathing at his nose. Trapper didn't move or speak.

"Is he dead?" I screamed. "Oh my God, Trapper, are you dead?"

"No," said Joe, "he's not dead yet. This ole bastard will never ever get to heaven and he's too damned stubborn to shovel coal so I guess he'll just have to stay here on earth. You know, when he came up to this part of the county, the MNR didn't want him here. Trapper had quite the reputation; he was well known to be the best. Nobody could catch him. The guys here said we couldn't afford to have him here."

Joe grabbed the thermos and took a quick drink and told me to do the same. Then he started to throw everything off the sleigh of the Snowbug and hid it in the bush and hooked the sleigh onto his Skidoo. "One time we were at a trappers' workshop the MNR was giving, and an old retired conservation officer, Ernie Young, from Algonquin Park, was there. Ernie figured Trapper owed him about forty pairs of boots that he'd worn out chasing Trapper across Algonquin Park over the decades. Well, Ernie just couldn't believe his eyeballs when he looked across the yard and saw this old bastard standing there.

"The MNR was talking about an upcoming wilderness survival course they were going to give. Ernie and Trapper were silently discharging shots at one another. Finally, Trapper shouted across the yard and said, 'Hey, Ernie, maybe you should take that wilderness course, you might learn how to light a fire.' Ernie hollered back, 'Yup, you old bastard, I never had to light a fire, they were always lit when I got there, and you were long gone.' Ernie wore out many a pair of boots chasing Trapper through Algonquin Park in the old days, and Trapper never ever got caught by anyone.

"Old Oscar Parks, an Algonquin Park ranger, told me one time he grabbed Trapper by the back of his coat and said, 'You're under arrest in the name of the Crown.' Oscar said he got left with a chunk of Mackinaw in his hand and never saw Trapper again. Trapper 'just ran like a deer,' according to old Oscar. Trapper is notorious, you know. He was known as 'The King of the Long Runners'; one of the best wilderness bushmen ever known anywhere."

I helped him lift Trapper onto the sleigh. He said we had to hurry but we needed a hot drink now. I took another sip and handed the thermos back to him. He took a swig and started to put the cap back on.

"Goddamn it, you bastards goin' to drink all of that yourselves, or could you spare a drop?"

"Well, how the hell are you doing, Old Trout?" Joe always called Trapper "Old Trout."

"Don't know what happened. I was way back at the north creek and I got a helluva pain in my arm and then my back, so I headed for home. I didn't have the strength to steer the machine but I just kept plugging on and I made it out to the lake and then headed for the camp. My eyes were all blurred and my vision went and I thought I was goin' the wrong way and then I got an awful pain in my chest and that was it."

Joe told me to get on the sleigh and snuggle close to Trapper to help warm him. Joe flew as fast as the Skidoo would go back to town. As we pulled into the MNR yard, Joe hollered to his wife to call the OPP and an ambulance. "And tell them we'll meet them on the way."

We got into the MNR truck and were off toward Chapleau to meet the ambulance.

At the hospital, the doctors checked Trapper out and said he'd had a heart attack, a bad one, and had to go to the hospital in Timmins. Trapper was hustled into an ambulance and, with lights flashing and sirens screaming, he was rushed to Timmins. I didn't know if I would ever see him again.

A very heavy snowstorm had hit overnight. I had to get the snowmobile and gear out of the bush.

The following day, another trapper, Ross, and I went down to the foot of Wakami Lake to get the Snowbug and all of Trapper's gear. Counting the number of traps, we knew Trapper had not been able to pick up all the traps before he had his heart attack. The severe storm made it all the more necessary to get all the traps picked up. The heavy snows and brisk winds would have covered many of his tracks, but in the shelter of the bush, we should be able to follow his trail here and there. We each took a machine and headed up to the camp, where we left all the gear on the sleigh and left Ross's little Skidoo with wooden skis. We decided to take only the Snowbug and the big sleigh, as travel would be rough. The Snowbug would handle the weather, the terrain, and the load.

I drove the Snowbug to the head of Wakami Lake, and Ross rode the sleigh with the snowshoes, ice auger, ice chisel, and packs. We had to go all the way up to the head of Wakami Lake and then travel along the remnant of a narrow, old, overgrown ice road that had seen only jumper sleighs of logs drawn by teams of horses in the logging days during the early part of the last century. At this point, Ross drove the Snowbug, and we crossed through to Kebskwasheshi Lake, checking the three small ponds as we backtracked to Wakami. Then we went up into Squaw Lake to check for traps, back out to Wakami, and then followed the remnant of the now century-old ice road through swamps and along the Wakami River, cross-country through a series of six or seven small lakes joined by open creeks, and finally to Nineay Lake. Due to the distance, the recent heavy snows, and the afternoon temperatures rising above freezing, we had to alternate between the Snowbug and the snowshoes. When the darkness of night fell, we had retrieved the last trap, but there was no returning to camp, as the temperatures had opened air holes in the ice and the lakes had opened at the mouth of the creeks. Somewhere—I don't remember precisely where—along the trail between Nineay Lake and Wakami Lake, we had to stop and camp for the night. Even though there was a full moon and it turned cold, it was not safe to travel by dark.

We spent the night huddled around a campfire warding off a pack of wolves that wanted the beaver on the sleigh. We hadn't taken a rifle, as the trapping season was over, and with two of us travelling together with one machine, and our doing a pickup, we had to be aware of the weight factor. To ward off the pack, we pulled firebrands from the fire and threw them at the wolves. Now and then, you could see their brassy eyes glowing in the firelight. In the darkness, just beyond vision, we could hear their snorts and low growls. At times they were together and at other times they would separate, some being on each side of us in the dark. They were using the divide and conquer tactic. They weren't interested in us; they just wanted the beaver on the sleigh. If they had decided to make a real stand to get that meat, someone could have been seriously hurt. To say the least, it was a very long and unnerving night.

The next morning, the wolves seemed to have left, but there was a well-trampled trail completely encircling the site where we had spent the night. We were ready at daybreak to depart and spend another hard day on the trail on what appeared would be a brilliant, sunny day. Cloudy and cold would have been our preference at that time. We left early to travel on the frost. The cloud cover did close in and freezing rain was the order of the day. We got cold and wet, and everything was a struggle. We had to stop several times to chop ice off the snowmobile and the sleigh. The snowshoes were constantly packed with heavy, wet snow. I had to remove them every fifteen or twenty minutes to bang them off and clear the *babiche*.

When we crossed one lake, we had to climb a very steep rock to get up off the ice. As we started up the ice-covered rock, the snowmobile started to spin out and slid backward. The sleigh broke through and got caught under the ice. I pushed on the snowmobile, and Ross lifted and pulled on the sleigh, but he kept breaking through on the ice. The harder he lifted, the more the ice kept breaking off and making the water hole bigger. Eventually, he managed to get the sleigh levelled out enough that he was able to pull the tow pin from the hitch. Somehow, we mustered sufficient strength to wrestle the snowmobile up the rock, and then the sleigh, which we had to unload and drain, rearrange all the gear, traps, and beaver, and then tie everything down again. The Lord had been with us; it just wasn't our time. We settled our nerves and carried on.

Travel conditions were far worse than on the way in, and I snowshoed most of the way out, following the snowmobile. Tremendous strength was required to handle the snowmobile in those conditions. Walking was equally difficult. Even following the snowmobile, the snowshoes were necessary. Even then, the snow would hold you for several steps, and then, with no warning, one foot would drop through, and you'd go down. We were both soaked, not only from the freezing rain, but also with perspiration. By the time we got out to Wakami Lake, it was late in the afternoon. At that point, Ross suggested I could handle the snow machine out on Wakami Lake and he'd jump on the sleigh. We chopped over an inch and a half of ice off of everything, and I jumped into the Snowbug. We travelled as fast as we could to get down to Brown's Bay before dark. The blowing snow and freezing rain made it nearly impossible to see. When we passed by the sandbanks on Wakami Lake, I knew there were only a few miles to go. Minutes later, the snowmobile came to a sudden stop at the shore, nearly throwing us both off the machine.

"Whoa, whoa, whoa, what are you trying to do? Great, you made it okay. We were beginning to get concerned about you."

"Who's there?" I asked.

"What do you mean, 'who's there'? It's me, Tim—you know, your friend, the young, really handsome conservation officer."

"I can't see. I'm blind. I can't see, Tim, I'm blind."

He took my face into his soft, warm hands and told me, "Open your eyes."

"They are open."

"No, they're not. Open your eyes."

"I can't." He laid his warm hands over my eyes and held them there for a few minutes.

"There you go, open them now." I tried again, and they opened.

"You're okay. Your eyelashes were frozen. Can you see okay now?"

Everything seemed to be working.

"Okay, girl, get off that machine, and let's get this stuff loaded and get back to town before it's black dark . . . Well, are you going to get off?"

I couldn't get off the machine. I'd been hanging on to the handle bars so long that my moosehide mitts had become encased in thick ice and my hands had frozen solid about the grips. I couldn't remove them. I couldn't move my fingers to pull my hands out of the mitts. In time, Tim got my hands freed from the handlebars and flexed my fingers for me. We had retrieved all the traps; we had all the gear and, though not comfortable, we were safe; we were alive. We had been gone for thirty-four hours with nothing to eat or drink and we figured I had snowshoed twenty-two miles. All I wanted was something hot to eat and drink; a good night's sleep; and of course to see Trapper.

The following day, another friend drove me to the hospital in Timmins, where I was met by the cardiologist. Yes, Trapper had had a heart attack, a bad one, a big one. It had probably killed 40 percent of his heart. It wasn't good. He would possibly live, but if he did, he wouldn't be going back to the bush anymore. His bush days were done. The next forty-eight hours would be very crucial.

I was allowed to spend only ten minutes of each hour with Trapper. While I waited in the waiting room, one of the ambulance drivers asked me how he was doing. He commented on the trip to Timmins, said Trapper was a tough old gent. Apparently, on the way to Timmins in the middle of the night, the ambulance broke down in the middle of nowhere. There were no communications back then. They had to get a vehicle travelling to Chapleau to get the hospital to phone Timmins to send another ambulance out for Trapper and a tow truck to get their ambulance. Meanwhile, Trapper ranted and raved in the back, tellin' them young christers to quit sittin' up there with their thumb in their bum and their mind in neutral while he was layin' back there freezin' his nuts off. Trapper suggested if they didn't know anything about the mechanics of a vehicle they shouldn't be drivin' one. He said if someone told them to let the clutch out they'd probably open the goddamn door.

"The pump's overheated!" he yelled. "Put some snow on it and let's get this show on the road."

Apparently he was right. They put some snow on the pump, and in a few minutes, the ambulance started up, and they were on their way to Timmins.

Trapper spent several weeks in the Timmins hospital and several more in the Chapleau hospital. I had worked hard and had all of the fur prepared, packed up, put on the bus in Chapleau and shipped to the Ontario Trappers Association in North Bay. I left the bus station and went over to the hospital to see Trapper. When I walked into the room he visibly perked up. He had been down in the dumps when the doctor told him he would never go back to the bush again.

While Trapper was in the hospital, he spent a great deal of his time thinking back to his childhood in the logging camps in Algonquin Park and his years and life spent trapping in Algonquin Park.

He seemed so preoccupied with times gone by and with the

old family history that I worried. Were his ancestors calling to him? Would he be taking a different trail, a trail he would take only one way, a trail he would traverse only once? I felt so privileged to have shared his life, to have shared his experiences and incredible knowledge and lifestyle. He said, "If only I could write, I could tell the story. It is not only my story it is the story of so many." I promised him then that if he told me the story, I would not let it die with him.

When Trapper was released from the hospital, it was into May. The ice had just let go from the edge of the lakes, the creeks were open and flowing fast, the pike were spawning, and the muskrat season was open until the twenty-eighth of the month. I would drive the truck along the old back road and we'd stop by the little creeks and he would stagger out with the smallest Conibear trap and a piece of parsnip and make a set in the creek by the side of the road.

We would stop by Spring Creek or the Little Wenebegon, and he could fish for pike right from the seat of the truck. Trapper was an incredible bushman. I don't know if I ever saw him miss a duck or a goose. It was one thing to shoot partridge. They just sat still and looked at you. It's pretty hard to miss a partridge even with a .22. But Trapper just knew exactly how to lead a duck or a goose. When you are shooting flying birds you have to be able to figure out how fast they are flying. You also have to figure out how fast your shot will travel and then figure out where that bird will be when the shot gets there. If you aim right at a bird in flight, you'll never get it because by the time the shot gets there, the bird has moved. Trapper knew exactly how to lead a bird when shooting.

He was also a fantastic shot with a rifle. When you're not sport hunting but actually living off the land, sometimes circumstance, not the law, dictates your actions. One time, late in the spring when the ice had just gone out and the northern pike were spawning, he saw a huge pike resting on the bottom of the river. It was in about five feet of water.

"We could sure use that pike for the larder. I'm goin' to have that pike," said Trapper.

"Guess not," I commented. "We don't have any fishing gear with us."

He gave me that defiant look of his, leaned forward, and picked up the rifle from the bottom of the canoe. Raising the butt to his shoulder he took careful aim, held his breath, and squeezed the trigger. When that gun cracked, the water literally exploded, and a twenty-pound pike soared like a missile into the air. We hadn't seen *that* one. The one he shot at was floating dead upon the water. That was an almost impossible shot. When you look into the water and see something on the bottom, it isn't where you think it is. It is actually some distance away from where you think it is. Somehow, this never-been-to-school bushman was aware of the refraction of light and could figure it out. He was an amazing man. My father often commented on what this man could have done for the world had he had the opportunity.

We went to all the old campsites where the hunters had camped the previous fall and we picked up beer bottles and cans by the bag full. That kept us in food and gas. We picked wild strawberries, raspberries, and blueberries and sold some fresh ones and preserved the rest for ourselves. We picked Jack pine cones in all of the cuts where the loggers were working. We got a permit from the MNR and each day we would pack up a good lunch and drive out to the cut areas. We would just take our time and pick from the tops that were on the ground. We didn't have to climb any trees. We knew all of the loggers well, and if Trapper were to have any difficulties, they were ready to assist. We had to battle our way through the jungle of all the pine tops and branches to pick the cones. Each day, we were able to pick a bag before lunch and a second bag before dinner. It was slow picking, due to Trapper's health, but also because we picked clean so we wouldn't have to dump and clean the cones at home. We were paid ninety-five dollars a bag, so we were making $190 a day when we could pick. Picking cones was hot work in the summertime, but you were getting exercise and were out in the sunshine and fresh air (AND the flies). You were well paid but you definitely earned your pay.

One time when we were out picking cones, I had worked for an hour or two and filled a fifty-pound lard pail. I was just about ready to quit and go and dump my pail of cones into the big burlap sack when I saw some huge, really good cones. I took my pail and walked along the trunk of the top until I reached the good cones. I was probably about five feet off the ground as I walked along the trunk. All of the cones grow on the ends of the branches, so I reached out to grab the end of a branch and bend it in toward myself so I could pick all of the big cones and fill my pail right to the very top.

As I pulled the branch toward me, I could see through to an opening—and there, not five feet from my face, was the muzzle of a huge black bear. I was so startled that I fell off the trunk and lost my pail of cones, which emptied out onto the ground. You might as well try to pick up a pail of spilt blueberries as pick up a pail of spilt cones in a cutover. I screamed and ran a marathon across the cut through and over and under all of the tops. I was both angry and afraid at what had happened. When I got over to Trapper, I was puffing and cursing and tried to tell him what had just happened. He was having a grand old laugh at my expense.

"Jeez, I ran right into a big black bear. I could have reached out and touched it. It was right there!"

"By Jeez, I've never seen a black bear with a long tail."

"What?"

"Didn't you see the long tail on it?"

"Christ, I didn't hang around long enough to see what kind of a tail it had. It was a bear. I was looking it right in the eye."

"Oh, you didn't have to worry about it. If you were afraid it would grab you, you'd just have to reach into its mouth and reach way back and grab it by the tail, turn it inside out, and it'll run the opposite way."

"Yah, right!"

"It would never catch you anyway. It would be slippin' in what you were leavin'."

"You just go ahead and laugh. I didn't think it was at all funny."

"The mill boss is here on the cut. He's got Kormack with him; he just ran over to see you."

"I should shoot that bastard. I lost a whole bucket of cones and damned near had a heart attack because that damn idiot brought his Newfoundland dog out here in the cut!"

Well, once I had settled down, we did all have a good laugh about it, and I shared my lunch with Kormack.

We fished all summer, ate some, and smoked and salted the rest for the winter. We patrolled the shores of Wakami in early October, and Trapper shot a dry cow moose. The moose was down, but neither of us could handle it alone; we couldn't even handle it together. We gutted it and got some logs under it so the meat would cool, not rot. Now what? We'd split the meat with anyone who would help us. We drove back to town to find someone to help. It was a weekday, and all of the men were at work in the bush or at the mill or on the rails.

There was only one hope: our best friend, the young conservation officer. If we were lucky, he might be at home. We drove over to his home, and he said, "Sure, I'd be glad to help. My mother taught me manners; she told me never to talk when my mouth was full." We all had a laugh over that. He spent all weekend helping us to cut and wrap the meat for freezing. The larder would be in good shape for the winter. What a trio: the young anti, the old poacher, and the conservation officer.

That young conservation officer and his family were wonderful friends. With his daily visits and encouragement, Trapper actually started to talk and make plans for the next trapping season. We spent a lot of time with the conservation officer and his wife, Lorraine, and their little girl. I remember one summer day when we went to visit them, his wife answered the door and called to the little girl, who was next door helping the neighbour plant strawberry plants in the garden. "You aren't bothering Jenny over there, are you?" Rachel called back, "No, Mommy, Jenny and I are just planting Jell-O."

During his spring and summer of recuperating, Trapper wasn't able to be as active as he normally would have been, but we'd go for slow walks and we'd eventually go canoeing. He would greatly enjoy playing with the animals and talking with them. In the evenings, we'd go out and sit and listen for wolf packs. He was a wonderful howler. He'd stand in the dark and give a howl or two and then wait maybe ten minutes and give another howl. Soon you'd hear a wolf howl back to him, and then another; and some evenings you'd hear a second pack. We would just enjoy sitting quietly in the dark and listening to the packs call back and forth to one another.

He loved to get down into a swamp and hoot at the owls. If

he could get a pair of owls going, they'd move closer and closer to each other, and then there would be a big hoo-faraw down in the swamp when the owls had it out with each other.

Loons were another of his favourites. Trapper could call loons from the other side of the lake. There were several different loon calls, and he could mimic them all and bring a loon to within a few feet. It was absolutely wondrous. Similarly, he could talk to the beavers, too, and draw them right out of their houses. One time, we were canoeing at the head of Wakami with another couple who was visiting with us. We stopped and rested quietly outside a big beaver house. Trapper started to moan and call the beavers. The big she-beaver came out with three little ones. The three kits, being curious as all young, wanted to come and see us. The she-beaver kept calling to them and slapping her tail on the water. Eventually, two of the kits returned to the mother, but the third little one stayed with us and kept talking with Trapper. It swam back and forth between the two canoes looking at all of us and finally it came right to the side of our canoe. Trapper just carefully floated his paddle in the water and slipped it underneath the baby beaver then with the blade he lifted the baby beaver out of the water and into the canoe.

The beavers will often change territory in the spring if they are flooded out by the high waters. One spring day, when we were driving back from Chapleau, we saw an adult beaver shuffling its way along the side of the Sultan Road. It was at least three miles from any water. Nothing would have it but Trapper had to stop the truck, open the door, and start talking to the beaver. That beaver sat up on its haunches and looked at us. After Trapper kept moaning to it the beaver started answering him. Eventually that beaver waddled its way across the gravel road and sat right up and put its two front feet on the floor of the truck. Trapper assured me he could talk that beaver right into the truck. I was very sure he could but suggested he not, because if the animal suddenly felt trapped, someone could get hurt badly. It was a very special moment that we enjoyed, and then we and the beaver each went our own ways.

He always had animals as friends: wolves, bears, 'coons, foxes, beavers; you name it, he could talk to them. I called him "Dr. Doo-little" because he could talk to the animals. He kept busy with his animal friends and picking berries and bottles. He loved to whittle and carve, too. He was always making me cooking utensils, or boards for my fishing line, or paddles and whistles.

One morning when we were in camp, Trapper woke up and called to me, "I've got a problem. There's something going on here." I flew out of my cot and across to his. "Is it your heart? Are you in pain?"

"No, no, no. It's nothing like that. I was just thinking about you this morning and I pitched a little tent right here."

"Oh, my God, you're confused. You didn't pitch any tent this morning. You are still in bed."

"No, I'm telling you, I pitched a little tent right here. I woke up with three legs and only socks for two."

I didn't know what was up! (No kidding.)

He rose from the cot and got dressed and opened the camp door and looked across the lake to the far side of Wakami.

"I think there might be a wedding this summer."

"Oh," I exclaimed. "Who is getting married? Did you hear about it in town?"

"Nope!"

"Well, how do you know someone is getting married?"

"I don't know for sure."

"I'm mixed up. Something must have gone right over my head. Who is getting married?"

He slowly turned from the door, walked across to me, took my shoulders firmly in his hands, looked straight into my eyes, and said, "I thought maybe we would."

I was struck dumb. Silence virtually hung in the air forever, caught it seemed, in time. Was this the stuff of "Once upon a Time"? Finally, I stammered, "If this is a proposal, the answer is yes."

I absolutely adored the ground that man walked on. He was indeed "THE KING."

36

The New Shack

Log camp in the early winter.
(Photo by Paton Lodge Lindsay)

Living off the land required few necessities: a roof over our heads, a canoe, paddles, snowshoes, and a firearm for protection and for hunting. In the coming year, I would learn to make all but the firearm—which I would learn to use.

In the spring, just after the snows were gone and the ice was out, we ventured up to the head of Wakami Lake to find a suitable spot to build a new camp, because it would give us access to the lake areas on the other side of Wakami. We beached the canoe on the east shore in a bay just north of the little creek and started to blaze our way up into the bush.

We were in need of a site with fairly level land, a wood supply, a clean water supply for cooking and washing, a sufficient supply of trees of large enough diameter to build the camp, a supply of sphagnum moss to chink the camp, and mud or clay to plaster over the sphagnum moss.

The easiest way to meet the main requirement—proximity to a clean water supply—was to follow the creek up into the bush.

As we walked along the banks of the creek, we made our way through blueberry brush that was just leafing and some water willow brush in the wet areas; and, of course, the ever-present, shoulder-high alders. In the lower areas along the wetland or swamp, we passed through tamarack, cedar, and black spruce. What we really needed was a stand of about ten-inch Jack pine or spruce. As we made our way along the creek, we reached a spot where we could hear running water up ahead. That meant there was a beaver dam or a small natural falls.

The beaver pond would not be a suitable water supply. If there were beaver living in the pond, there would be the danger of beaver fever or tularemia organisms being in the water. As we broke over a small ridge, a breeze rippled the calm waters of a lovely, small lake set in a stand of Jack pines with some poplar and white birch.

"Now, that looks really promising," said Trapper.

We sat on a flat outcropping of granite, munched on some dried pepperoni sticks, and silently surveyed the country. A short walk of about 300 feet from the shoreline, we came upon a flat area where the ground was covered with deep, soft, sphagnum moss. This was it. At this spot, we had level ground to build on, trees suitable for the logs, sphagnum moss for chinking between the logs, mud for plastering, a firewood supply, and a fresh water supply.

Trapper hiked back down to the canoe for the chainsaw. Within minutes of his return, the roar of the chainsaw rattled the branches of the pine. He didn't really bother to check the lean of the trees or anything else. In this pine stand, all the trees stood erect. He paced off an area of about sixty feet by sixty feet. He then began felling the trees in a systematic way such that the outside trees fell to the outside. He made his way about the square until he had dropped a row of trees on all four sides. Then he methodically began to cut another round of trees, and then another. After some six rounds were dropped, he had the area where the footprint of the camp would stand all cleared.

The next step in the process was to lop off all of the branches so that no knots were left sticking out. He did this, working one side at a time; starting from the bottom of each trunk, he worked his way to the top. As Trapper lopped off the branches, I threw them into a pile at the outer edge of that side. This would keep the work area clear and safe, and the boughs neatly piled, ready to decay or to be disposed of later. When all four sides were done, there was a scattering of clean tree trunks just waiting to be cut into logs. That was it for today. We had chosen the site, and the trees were dropped and scattered like a bunch of "pick-up-sticks" so they were off the ground. The boughs were piled off to the four sides, and we were ready to start the next process in the morning.

We returned to the canoe to get our kit and tent to pitch camp before the night set in. Trapper tossed the .22 to me.

"Go get dinner."

"What?"

"Go get dinner. I could eat a horse and chase the rider. I'm sure you are hungry, too. Go get a couple of partridge; you can pull up some bulrushes at the swamp, and we'll have partridge and 'swamp spuds' for dinner."

I headed off to the "grocery store" of the wilderness and came back with both. I cleaned the partridge, peeled and cleaned the rush roots, and we cooked it all on a spit over an open fire.

The night was cold, as it was still only June. A million billion stars twinkled in the deep, blue sky and the wolf packs called back and forth to one another through the night. They were at a considerable distance from us, and we fell asleep listening to their serenade.

In the morning, after a quick bite of scones with jam and tea, Trapper started to measure the logs off into lengths and cut the trees up. That didn't take too long, as he got one long and two short logs out of each tree. The camp would be sixteen feet by twenty feet. We started the job of peeling the logs. Using tools known as a spud and a draw knife, we removed the bark from the logs. It was still a little tight. In July, when the peeling is really good, the bark comes off very easily. Often the bark will peel off in eight- or ten-foot lengths; other times, you might get a strip a few inches wide, but the whole length of the log; and there are the best of times when the whole log just slips right out of the bark. This was a very sticky and slippery, messy job; and the flies were so thick, if you slapped two pieces of bread together, you'd have a sandwich.

When the logs were peeled, they were flawless and golden white and smooth. By removing the bark, the logs were clean to build the camp and there would not be any bugs or borers from the bark. In a few weeks, the logs would dry out and be much lighter to work with. It took us about three days to peel the logs and trim any long knots. Then we piled the logs with the long ones on the two sides and the short ones on the two ends. They were all up off the ground on stringers and would stay clean and air-dry for a few weeks. We would then return to begin building the camp.

Upon our return several weeks later, the spring runoff was gone, the ground had dried up, and the blackflies were for the most part gone. But the mosquitoes were so big they'd take a chunk out of you and get up in a tree to eat it. The logs were bleached white and dry, very much lighter in weight, and we were ready to start building if we could cut our way through the mosquitoes.

Trapper had a preconceived pattern or jig in his brain for the notches to be cut at the ends of the logs. Since the Jack pine logs were all about the same size and straight, he was able to cut the notches in all of the logs before we started to build. As each log was notched, we moved it to the final spot from which it would be lifted into place. I will not say they were light in weight, but with our combined power, we were able to lift them.

We gathered some stones from the creek area and constructed four platforms where the four corners of the camp would rest. The stones would keep the logs up off the ground and they would not rot. We were able to lift the four bottom logs into place and, with some fiddling around on the corners, got the first round squared and completed. There was very little work to fit each notch tightly, but we would use an axe to just shave off small irregularities and set the corners squarely so they were tight. We were able to manage the weight of the logs and lift them into place up to about waist height. After that, it became too dangerous to handle them. Trapper then rigged up a log pole with a large forked piece he had lashed onto the top. He called that a "gin pole." He passed a large rope through the fork and then stood that pole upright and firmly attached it with crossers at the centre of the camp. We could then tie a rope to each end of a log and haul on the gin pole rope to lift the log to the height we needed and move it into position.

Once we had all nine rounds in place, we had a seven-foot wall, and it was really beginning to look like it just might become a habitable little abode. I was very pleased with us. Behind me, I heard the chainsaw roar into action. Trapper walked up to a really big red pine and dropped it. It came crashing down right on top of the camp. Trapper never had anything happen that wasn't a deliberate plan.

"What the hell did you do that for?" I asked.

"It's a quick and easy way to settle all the logs and make sure the corners are all tight. Nothing will settle or shift now. Damn mosquitoes . . . hand me that old motor oil and I'll slap some more on." Oil was sticky and the insects wouldn't land on it.

We discussed where we wanted the door and where we wanted a window or two. Trapper cut some lumber out of the big red pine, and we spiked it along the inside of the logs where the windows and the door would be cut out. These pieces of eight-inch-by-two-inch lumber had to be spiked into each log. They would be left in place and become the window frames; but also, when the logs were cut out, the logs in the camp wall would be held tight and not be able to kick out or move. Without these spiked supports, there would be nothing to hold the walls together once the logs were cut. Trapper, with decades of experience and great expertise, took the chainsaw and cut out the door and the two windows. The log pieces fell free and rolled out of place. Voila! We had a door and two windows.

Trapper cut all of the joists and the lumber for the floor out of logs. He just used the chainsaw—no mill, as do people of today. Those boards were so smooth, you'd have thought they had been planed. The floor supports or stringers he made by flattening two sides of a log and tapering the ends. Then he mortised or notched them into the top side of the bottom logs. Then the lumber was laid into place. With an old hand borer, he made holes and pegged the floor with handmade, hardwood dowels to hold the planking in place.

Getting the superstructure of logs that would support the roof into place was another tough job. We cut two log pieces each about five feet long. Trapper took the axe and shaved a perfect little cradle or bowl at each end. When they were lifted into place, they stood upright, one at the centre of each end wall. The bottom cradle fit perfectly over the top log. The top cradle was ready to support the ridgepole when it was set in place. Then two other pieces were cut on an angle and mortised at a forty-five-degree angle to the top of the centre upright and to the top log of the end wall. There was one of these supports on each side of the centre upright. These had to be very exact so that a log could fit along them from the peak to the eave and make a perfect angle for the pitch of the roof. We did this at both ends. Then we had to place a log right through the centre line and on top of the five-foot uprights for the ridgepole. We both expelled our fair share of methane setting that log into place and into the cradles on top of the five-foot uprights. When you are standing on the ground and looking up twelve feet, it doesn't seem very far. However, when you are balancing on a round log twelve feet up in the air and looking down, it seems a considerable distance.

The roof would be a totally new experience for me. This was a really remote site. Trapper said he couldn't make a board roof because it would leak like a sieve. We would have to cover it with tarpaper or shingles or tin or something. Tarpaper would be no good, as branches falling would puncture it and the bears would make short work of it, too. It was too far and too difficult to haul shingles or tin into this site. Trapper decided to build the roof the way the old-timers did. He would build a trough roof. We spent several days preparing small cedar log troughs for the roof. We would have to go to the cedar swamp and cut the small logs about twelve feet long. Then with an adze we would hollow them out rather like the natives of the world made a dugout canoe. They were then peeled. Hauling them all back to camp was an arduous job. He showed me how to lay these hollowed logs all along the roof so they lay from the ridge to the eave with the hollowed side facing toward the sky like a bunch of little gutters. Then we put a second row of hollowed cedar logs over top of the first. The second layer of hollowed logs we placed with the hollow down and the rounded side up. The edges of the second layer sat in the troughs of the first layer. Any rain that fell upon the roof would run off the rounded top logs down into the trough-up logs below and then run down the troughs to the eave and fall to the ground. The roof would be watertight and strong enough to handle a heavy snow load. It took us two weeks to get the walls up and the roof on.

To finish off the camp, we took the axe and went all around the camp and scored or scarred the logs between each round. Trapper spent several days picking sphagnum moss and filling his No. 1 Woods Special packsack and packing the moss back to camp. That moss was so heavy, the pack was virtually immoveable. With a small wedge he had whittled for me, I spent several days chinking or stuffing the moss in between all of the logs. The scarring on the logs helped hold the chinking in place. I had to chink between all of the logs, around the door, around the window frames, along the eaves, very carefully in the notched corners, and along the gables where the roof met the logs. Once I had completed the chinking, he brought mud from the swamp and we plastered it over top of the sphagnum moss so the walls were weathertight.

Trapper cut some two-inch lumber from the red pine and made a door for the camp. He used some heavy leather to make the hinges and found a gnarled and chiselled beaver stick to make the door handle. In the centre of the camp, he built a wooden box and filled it with stones for the fireplace. Above it, he cut a hole in the roof and then built a wooden funnel or chimney that hung from the roof. When the fire was lit in the open fireplace, the smoke rose up and was sucked through the funnel and out the hole in the roof. He made a couple of pole bunks and with rope he wove a rope spring for each. I stitched some canvas bags, which we filled with dried grasses from the marsh. These were our mattresses. Trapper called them palisades.

The camp was virtually completed but for the required "wee" station yet to be constructed out back. As we would be staying for a couple more days to finish up all little things needed and to clean up, I asked Trapper if he might consider rigging up some type of a temporary facility for me. I really wasn't too keen on the kitty-in-the-sandbox type of sanitation. I'd had enough of that over the past several weeks. Trapper thought it rather unnecessary. I should be able to scratch, squat, and cover like a cat for a few more days. Not happening.

Grudgingly, he went down the trail to prepare the temporary little loo for me and, upon returning, he advised me it was ready.

When the time came to use the facility, I trekked down the trail to find a trench dug in the dimensions of about three feet long, a foot wide, and about two feet deep. THAT was it; a trench with the shovel standing upright in the loose soil he had removed from the hole.

I stomped my way back to the camp. "Couldn't you have at least lashed a couple of poles across between the two trees so there'd be something to sit on?"

"Well, Jeeesssuuusss, what's wrong with that? Can't you just straddle the trench for a couple of days?"

"NO. It would be nice to have a seat to sit on."

He muttered and cursed his way back down the trail for about five minutes and returned to sarcastically advise me that my "throne" was ready. Now in total desperation, I returned to my wilderness relief station. I couldn't believe my eyes: one pole, one pole lashed between two trees. That was it. One might balance there precariously, but there was nothing to even hang onto and no backrest. Now cross-legged, I wiggled my way back to the camp.

"What the hell is wrong with you? I just want a seat I can sit on to have a pee and a dump. Is that too much to ask for?"

"There are two kinds of dogs in the bush, girl: the 'setters' and the 'pointers.' Guess you're a 'setter.'"

Going back a third time, he lashed a second pole to the other side of the two trees and about a foot higher than the first pole. Now finally it had the appearance that it might possibly be functional. I told him to get lost and I dropped my drawers and sat down on the lower pole with my arms reaching backwards and upward to try and hang onto the upper pole. In this contortion I must have resembled a pretzel, and not the "fully dressed" variety. As I let go with my right hand to reach for the roll of toilet paper stuck on a knot, my heart stopped as the pole gave a resounding crack like that of a large-calibre rifle. I dropped butt first into the trench. My hands were wedged into the sides of the trench and my feet were sticking straight up into the air. My bare butt was wedged very firmly into the trench, and I couldn't move.

A considerable length of time passed when I eventually heard sticks snapping and cracking on the trail. Oh, shit! Trapper was coming down the trail, calling me. "Are you okay? Do you need some help?"

"NO! You stay right there. Don't come any further."

"Well, what are you doing?" he asked as he continued to approach.

"You stay there! Go away, get outta here! No, wait—don't go. I need help. Your goddamned pole broke, and I'm stuck in the hole."

"You're what?"

"Just shut up! Shut your eyes and shut your mouth and get me out of here."

Short of renting a Cooper crane or using a stick of dynamite, he somehow managed to get my butt out of the hole, all the while preserving my dignity, what little I had left.

We used that cabin for many years and were very comfortable. It offered us access to the back country and to several small lakes and ponds. Everything for the cabin came from the wilderness but for the two windows and the spikes we found at an abandoned logging camp. Trapper said the Lord put everything on the earth that mankind would ever need. Again, it seemed He really had.

Nature's Cornucopia

Silver fox with a wild edible it caught for dinner.
(Photo by Paton Lodge Lindsay)

The forest was a cornucopia of wild edibles. When it came to bush groceries and keeping the larder full and food on the table, we had tried most of it. I had eaten moose, venison, bear, and beaver. I had also sampled grouse, duck, and goose, as well as pike, pickerel, whitefish, and smoked sucker. The moose was very much like beef and very enjoyable. The venison I found to be a lot like lamb in that it seemed to line your mouth with tallow and stick like paraffin. I couldn't even make myself swallow it. The bear was much like pork, but psychologically I felt like I was eating from a garbage can (though Trapper said that bears in the bush don't eat garbage; they are predominantly vegetarian but they will eat meat). The beaver in the early fall was always delicious whether we stewed it or roasted it. Trapper loved the beaver tails roasted over an open flame on a stick, but I'm afraid I refrained from that sumptuous fare.

I always found the goose to be greasy, and sometimes the duck was as well. Ruffed grouse, with its tender white meat, was wonderful; the spruce grouse with its dark red meat less so to me, but most men, it seemed, preferred it. Rabbit—the snowshoe hare—provided a ready meat supply almost all year.

Trapper ate the meat of all of them, as well as that of racoon, porcupine, squirrel, and lynx. Trapper enjoyed it all, but I have to admit that I definitely refrained from all the latter and distinctly leaned toward being a vegetarian at those meals. Fish were very plentiful and there was always a fresh supply. One only needed to go to the waterhole in front of the camp to return with fresh fish. The pickerel was my favourite, then the smoked whitefish and sucker, and lastly the pike because of its "Y" bones.

We used a lot of wild vegetation. We would pull up cattails and water lilies when available and get the roots from the bottom. In the spring, the stems of the young cattails were good either raw or cooked. In spring we also made maple syrup and syrup from the sap of the yellow birch. The yellow birch syrup had a strong, sweet, peppermint flavour. Trapper always had a yellow birch toothpick in his shirt pocket. The young, pale green shoots on the tips of the white spruce made a lovely spring tea. In the summer, we made raspberry and blueberry tea; and in the fall, we had cranberry tea and the dried, crushed leaves of the goldenrod and purple fireweed. Rosehips from the wild rose bushes made wonderful autumn tea and a great jelly.

Of course, we always had a supply of raspberry, blueberry, cranberry, and rosehip jams. Occasionally we would come across a solitary apple tree growing way back in the bush, the seed having been dropped by a logger or his horse back in the early timber days. Now, nearly one hundred years later, we could enjoy a fresh apple or an apple pie, apple jelly, or apple butter. Sometimes, in the fall, we could pick and roast hazelnuts to use in cooking.

Fungi and mushrooms were a succulent delight to Trapper in the spring and fall. He had a few very simple but strict rules to be followed. If it grew in wetlands or swamps, don't eat it. If it grew where there had been a forest fire, don't eat it. If it grew on dead trees or stumps feeding on dead or dying cells like maggots, don't eat it. If it grew in open grasslands or fields, or if it grew on the forest floor beneath the trees, you had a three-in-five chance of its being safe but you still had to be extremely careful and know what you were picking. If careless, you could become extremely sick or even die. I had a simpler, better rule that beat his all to heck! Just don't eat any of them at all, and I didn't. If he picked them I would cook them for him, but such delectable fare did not reach my plate.

We used several plants for medicinal care. According to the only wilderness doctor available, cranberry juice was good for a urinary infection. The boiled roots of pink lady slipper would relieve muscle pain. Trapper would chew on the leaves of a yarrow plant to relieve a toothache. He would roll the dried leaf of a mullein plant and smoke it to relieve the congestion of a heavy cold. He would take balsam gum from the trunk of a balsam tree, melt it with a little fat, and cover an open sore or cut with it. It kept the wound clean, healed quickly, and usually left no scar. He would chop up beaver castors and leave them in a bottle of gin until they dissolved and the gin was amber brown. Then he would take a tablespoon a day and said it did wonders for the pain and stiffness of arthritis. (That was an absolute "no way" on my list. I'd suffer from the arthritis first.)

The shopping cart when we went to the store would include flour, baking powder, baking soda, salt, coffee, oatmeal, brown sugar, buckwheat honey, and toilet paper, though Trapper said that in season there was no reason one couldn't use burdock leaves.

The forest was indeed a cornucopia of delectable meats, fruits, and vegetables. The Lord had indeed put all the supplies required for sustenance on earth. One just had to learn how to use them. In fact, Trapper started many a fire by rubbing two sticks together, but give me my matches, please.

"I DO"

Ready for the big day. "O Joy, O Rapture."
(Photo by Suzanne Lindsay)

The following June, we had a wonderful wedding day. My mother, my sister, and my bridesmaids all made sure that everything would be perfect. My father had passed away, and I had asked my brother if he would consider walking me down the aisle—if he would give me away. He laughed right out loud, said, "I've waited a lifetime to give you away."

Trapper promised he would do anything to make my day perfect, to make my life perfect. I had only two requests, that he make sure all his bush buddies behave themselves and that he wear a kilt.

"You want me to wear a skirt in front of all my buddies? A skirt? Ho-leee-y yy sheee-it!"

The night before the wedding, several friends had decided to have a rehearsal night dinner for all of the wedding party. Everyone was from out of town, so the group was all billeted with various friends. Trapper and I were staying with the best man and his wife, who were very busy taking care of the last-minute decorating at the reception hall, where we would all gather for dinner.

Trapper and I of course had to get cleaned up and dressed in readiness for the rehearsal and dinner to follow. As I started up the stairs to go and have a shower, Trapper said, "What're the chances of havin' a shower together?"

"Don't think so," I replied with a laugh.

"Are you sure?"

"Quite."

"Just thought I'd ask," said he.

I carried on up the stairs, gathered together all of my toiletries and clean clothes, and headed into the bathroom. Having made use of the "fish bowl" and brushed my teeth, etc., I turned the water on and adjusted the water temperature until it was just comfortable and stepped into the tub, pulling the shower curtain across behind me.

The warm water was very comforting and relaxing. I stood and enjoyed it for several minutes. A little chuckle escaped my mouth. I leaned out through the shower curtain and called out to Trapper, "Hey, are you coming up for a shower?"

"What?"

"Are you coming up for a shower?"

"I'll be up in a few minutes."

"Oh, I thought you wanted to have a shower together?"

"What?"

"You asked about having a shower together. Are you coming up or not?"

"Yah, Yah, I'll be right up."

I could hear Trapper coming up the stairs, and then he reached the landing and carried on up to the second floor. I could hear the floor boards squeaking as he made his way down the hall toward the bathroom. I heard the bathroom door open, then close. Above the sound of the water in the shower running down the walls and bouncing off the floor, I heard one shoe hit the floor and then the second. A striped woollen sock came over the shower curtain rod, and then the second one landed in the tub. I heard the zipper on his jeans zzzzip down and then heard the thud of his heavy western belt buckle as it hit the floor. The snaps popping on his western shirt spoke volumes as he just grabbed it and pulled the front apart.

The bathroom was all hot and steamy, and so was I, just anticipating the coming moment. Trapper reached to the shower curtain and yanked it open with considerable force. There he stood in all his manliness: tall, lean, muscular, sinewy, gorgeous, and totally naked. His jaw dropped leaving his mouth gaping. His eyes glazed in total disbelief as he stood totally naked and totally stunned and looked at me standing in the tub, the hot water from the shower pouring down over me . . . and I was standing in the tub fully clothed.

"About time you got here! What took you so long?"

We were a little late for the rehearsal dinner. The reception hall looked just fantastic. The dinner was wonderful, and we all relaxed and had a great evening.

Nothing but a formal Scottish wedding would do with my paternal Scottish lineage. I didn't sleep all night. My mind just raced thinking about the wedding I had dreamed of all my life. The guest list had included Scottish aristocracy and royalty and a couple of hundred friends. The pipers and the dancers would be there, and my prince had agreed to arrive in full dress attire befitting a Scottish lord.

The following day, the church was a bounty of swags and garlands of white roses and 'mums. Baskets of flowers stood at each pew and along the chancel rail and upon the altar. As the trumpets sounded "Trumpet Voluntare," the Royal Standard of Scotland, the Lindsay Standard and Coat of Arms, and the ancestral family paten and chalice were carried down the military red-carpeted aisle to the chancel rail.

The groom, in full dress kilt of Royal Stewart, complete with silk shirt and lace jabot; black waistcoat; antique sporran; and with a magnificent antique gold, ebony, and topaz dirk at his side, advanced slow march down the aisle to the "Prince of Denmark" march. He looked splendidly regal in his attire, complete with the gold, ebony, and topaz *sgian dubh* tucked into his sock at one

"I DO."

(Photo by Suzanne Lindsay)

knee and his old stag horn Henry Boker belt knife slipped into the sock by his other knee. Three groomsmen in formal evening attire awaited him at the chancel steps.

The bridal attendants wore exquisite scarlet-coloured gowns trimmed in black to complement the groom's highland attire. The flower girl's gown, also scarlet-coloured, was hand-smocked in white. All of the bridal attendants carried beautiful trailing bouquets of white and red roses hung with baby's breath.

The bride (me) wore a very regal gown of white French *peau de soie*. The bodice, adorned with pearls and crystal droplets, was styled with puffed gauntlet sleeves and sweetheart neckline. The Basque waistline dipped to a Viennese lace-appliquéd full skirt with full cathedral train. The bride wore about her neck the magnificent antique Lady Jane Stewart pearl necklace and wore a veiled headpiece with white flowers and pearl droplets beneath the Lindsay crowned tiara with silver coat of arms. In a gloved hand, she carried a white Bible, a heart padlock necklace carved from moose antler, and two white roses and a red rose, symbolic of the Holy Trinity.

Several hundred guests were invited, among them British royalty and aristocracy. It was said the church had never seated more.

So . . . I had my magnificent formal Scottish wedding, and Trapper's old cronies did indeed have their fun as well. When we knelt at the altar rail for the final blessing, the entire church erupted in peals of laughter. As Trapper knelt and the soles of his black patent leather shoes faced the congregation, there for all to see painted on the bottom of his shoes were two words: "HELP ME." As the pipes skirled and we were piped into the reception hall, Trapper's bush buddies had seen fit to make sure all of the ladies were armed with little silver hand mirrors, which they held out beneath Trapper's kilt, seeking the answer to that proverbial old question, "Just what does a highlander wear beneath his kilt?"

There was an extensive display of highland dancing, a grand feast, much music from the live orchestra, and wonderful friendship throughout the evening. Hours later, as we were piped from the reception, a friend handed me a salt shaker as I passed by. Questioningly, I accepted it, figuring it was for good luck—you know, to throw salt over my shoulder. However, a while later, as we shook the popcorn out of the short-sheeted bed, we realized what the salt was for. When we crawled very pleasantly but completely exhausted into bed for the very first time together, Trapper wrapped his arms around me and pulled me toward him.

"M-M-M, well, there is enough of you I don't have to shake the sheets out to find you. I like that."

"Oh, yah, I'm just like a beached whale in bed."

"You females 'av got a big problem. It's not what you have or what you don't have that matters. It's what you DO with what you have that counts."

I said to Trapper, "Wasn't that just the most wonderful day of your life? We should do that again on our tenth anniversary and renew our vows."

As to the answer to the proverbial old question Trapper responded in a Scottish accent, "Aye, Lass, but if we do that again on our tenth anniversary, I'll no' be wearin' a kilt again in blackfly season."

The Little Stripper

Trapper always feeds the ducks and geese in the early spring.
(Photo by Paton Lodge Lindsay)

I might have been born in the city, but I spent every summer until well into my teens in a canoe at my grandfather's cottage. My great-grandfather was the Crown Lands agent for the Muskoka/Parry Sound district at the time Algonquin Park was set aside. As a great-granddaughter of Jon Sampson Scarlett's, I was in a canoe before I could walk. Through my Hanes and Fetterly family, Harold Hanes, at one time chief ranger of Algonquin Park; Dr. John Harkness, chief of the Fish and Wildlife Department for the Ontario Department of Lands and Forests; and my great-uncle, George Lindsay, an Algonquin Park ranger, I indeed had the very genes of Algonquin's gunwale grabbers in my veins right from birth. Now, I was keeping court with the King of the Gunwale Grabbers, The King of the Long Runners, and, verily I say unto you, The King of Algonquin Park.

My ancestors were canoe men. I knew well the feel of a good hardwood paddle and the feel of a good cedar and canvas canoe. I knew what I wanted and it could only be wood. I already had a wooden canoe, handmade a hundred years ago. It is a real heritage classic: a thirteen-foot cedar and canvas with white ash and black cherry gunwales, ash and *babiche* seats, a black cherry thwart and decks. I christened it "Little Beaver." I also had a sixteen-foot fibreglass canoe that I had christened "The Bathtub." Now, if I was going to build my own canoe, it would be wood . . . it would be a classic . . . it would be a little stripper, a little cedar strip canoe.

We couldn't build the canoe until I knew exactly what I wanted. It would be of white cedar, knot-free, and straight of grain so that the strips ran the full length of the canoe, no short strips spliced together. It would be an overall sixteen feet in length and have a thirty-two inch beam. I would design it to have a long, slender, fine bow that would slice through the water. There is a sensuous symmetry to a rounded bow as opposed to a vertical or straight bow. It would be longer in the front portion with a rise from the centre to the bow to lift the bow from the water and provide ease of paddling. It would be shorter and snubbed off more quickly toward the stern to provide better stability and ease of steering. I would of course insert between the gunwales the little pieces of wood that simulate the ends of the ribs between the gunwales. I knew what I wanted. Trapper knew how to help me get it.

The first step in completing this project was to get the design drawn out on paper. That was my responsibility. Once we had established our measurements, Trapper went to work to build what he called a "strong-back." That was a series of moulds that represented cross-sections of the canoe at various points along its length. There were ten of them all cut out of lumber he had cut from logs. Once the ten of them were built, they were set up in order according to size to form the skeleton of the canoe. They were like the bones of the canoe, and the strips would be the tissue. These sections were all held upright and in position by tacking a thin strip of wood down the keel line and along each side at the gunwale edges. With this form erect, we checked and rechecked all our measurements, moving the third bow form back a bit to make the canoe slimmer and longer in front. We stood at both the bow and the stern to eye the length of the canoe form to check its lines and symmetry. We made a slight adjustment to give a little more lift to the bow. When we were totally satisfied with our design, it was time to gather together our needed supplies. We would need a white cedar log straight of grain and knot-free for seventeen feet. Trapper knew where there was a dead old dry cedar standing at the head of the lake. We would cut a seventeen-foot log out of it and then rip one-inch boards from the log. We would then cut that board into strips seventeen feet long by about a quarter of an inch thick. These strips of cedar were so light that we could easily portage them out to the boat and down to camp.

Trapper showed such expertise with the chainsaw that not only could he rip lumber but he was also able to rip the strips that were no thicker than the bar on the saw itself. He cut them so perfectly that they could not have been better had they been planed at a mill. Once back at the camp, we air-dried the strips for a couple of days. We built the canoe in an up-side-down position. The seventeen-foot cedar strips went onto the frame commencing at the gunwales and extended past the end of the canoe on one side and were trimmed on the other side. We worked our way up around the sides of the canoe toward the belly. When we reached the belly of the canoe, the strips got shorter and shorter as we neared the keel or centre line to fill in the oval opening that was left. At this stage, each strip had to be individually fitted and shaped, trimming each piece on an angle with a knife so they met and merged perfectly. The lines of the canoe were really beginning to take shape. We finished the hull with his old antique chisels, hand planes, spoke shaves, and blocks of wood covered with sandpaper . . . and more elbow grease than anything else.

On one of our trips to town, we picked up seventeen feet of fibreglass material and a large container of epoxy, some hardener, squeegees, scrapers, naval brass screws, carriage bolts of different lengths, and marine spar varnish. I had never used fibreglass or epoxy before, and we had to be very careful and quick to get the canoe covered without any wrinkles or drips and just enough epoxy to fill the fibreglass but not so much as to add too much weight to the canoe. Once that was done, we let it dry for a day then sanded it, washed it down, and added another coat of epoxy and the oak keel.

Trapper had made the gunwales and seats from rock ash and the thwart and decks and trim from black cherry. The gunwales were put on with an inner and an outward gunwale, and the little wood spacers placed between them were all screwed together with brass screws. There were two brass screws to each spacer, one screwed from the inside, the other screwed from the outside, and they alternated along the full length of the gunwale. The gunwales looked beautiful and they really added substance, style, and elegance to the lines of the canoe. The symmetry and grace of our design was really beginning to show.

Trapper added the decks to the bow and stern. We were nearly finished. He had cut and mortised the seat frames, but it was summer, and we didn't have any *babiche* left to lace them. Trapper never ceased to amaze me. He had gone for a "wee walk" to the outhouse and came back with an old pair of beaver tail snowshoes. He laid them across the gunwales, one by the bow, the other by the stern. Lifting a leg up level with the gunwale, he adjusted the bow snowshoe to where it would rest and support your backside. He then adjusted the stern snowshoe. Marking each at the gunwales, he cut off the toe and the heel of the snowshoes, drilled them, and hung them from the gunwales with long carriage bolts. They made great canoe seats. Even the old trapper reused and recycled.

The last item to be placed was the thwart. Trapper would never use a neck yoke, as he had known two people who died portaging canoes with neck yokes. One tripped on a root and fell, breaking his neck. The other died when the wind caught the canoe and reefed it around, breaking the man's neck.

Balance is extremely important if you hope to portage a canoe with any comfort. He had readied the thwart and slid it into position so that it caught beneath the inner gunwales. He then stretched out an arm and lifted the canoe up several inches, allowing it to move like a teeter-totter until it came to rest perfectly horizontal. He adjusted the position of the thwart until the stern was slightly heavier and then hung the thwart from beneath the gunwales with carriage bolts. We covered all the wood with seven coats of spar varnish.

She was done and, in my opinion, she was indeed a real beauty—something to be proud of.

Trapper told me to take it for a walk. I took hold of the gunwale about the centre and drew the belly of the canoe up against my thighs. Then I lifted my right knee, which in turn lifted the canoe up, and I turned and flipped it up and over so the thwart rested on the back of my neck, put my hands to the gunwales, and walked about the camp.

"Weight and balance are good," I told him.

"Good," said Trapper. "Now let's see if she's as good on the water as she would be on the trail."

I drop-rolled the canoe down onto a raised knee and then lowered it down onto the water.

"Now you are a real gunwale grabber," said Trapper. "There's only one more thing to do."

I looked inquiringly.

"Make a couple of your own paddles."

And we did, but that is yet another story.

Trail of
the Long Runners

The years and the decades went by, and Trapper always got itchy feet when the leaves began to turn colour in the autumn and when the streams began to give up their ice to the warmth of the coming spring. Well into his seventies, he was lean, strong, sinewy, agile, and able. He could still cut and split with an axe twenty-four cords of firewood a year. He still trapped, not only with his own trapline, but made sure there were no nuisance beavers to cause problems with roads, bridges, highways, railroads, provincial parks, forested lands, or agricultural lands anywhere in the province. He never gave up trapping the beaver on the lands his family had been granted by the king of France. As each year and each decade passed, the seasonal itch of trapper's foot, the gnawing need to make that one last trip along the Trail of the Long Runners, to travel undetected on foot with gun in hand and trap right across Algonquin Park, cross the Ottawa River, and sell the green pelts to a waiting buyer in the land of Nouvelle France just seem to fester and gnaw at his innards.

One spring morning in 1989, as the sun danced on the rippling waters of the marsh, and Trapper listened to the red-winged blackbirds singing in the swamp and the chickadees calling "spring-time, spring-time," he knew that time had come. If he didn't make that last run, he might never be able to do it again. Carefully, as he had done for the past sixty-three years, he readied his pack and firearm and the bare necessities of life. On this morning, prior to departure, he spread an old map of Algonquin Provincial Park out on the kitchen table. With pen in hand, he leaned across the table and put pen to paper. He sat in silence putting the tip of the pen to the map a couple of times never making a mark. He tapped the pen on the map seeming to play an old tune. He leaned back against the chair,

"When you trapped in the park you didn't actually trap, because if you set a trap to catch beaver, then you had to go back to the trap the next day to get the beaver and pick up the trap. If you had been careless and left any kind of mark, the rangers would be on to you. It was too dangerous to backtrack. And you could only carry so much. Every trap you carried was a beaver pelt you couldn't carry. No, no, you never trapped, you never backtracked.

"Trapping in the park was always done in the late fall before the winter snows, or in the late spring when the swamps and marshes started to melt and the ice began to part from the shore. The beaver pelts were prime then; that was when they had their greatest value.

"When you travelled the park, you removed everything from your pockets and your pack that could identify you. You even made sure there were no labels on your clothes or your pack. If there was no way they could identify you, there was no way they could prove who it belonged to. There's no way in hell you'd ever let them catch you, NONE, and you'd give up life before you'd give up that pack o' pelts."

Finally, he leaned forward, put pen to paper, and said, "This is the 'Trail of the Long Runners,' just in case I don't make it back, in case I become bear bait or something, you'll know where I went."

Slowly and deliberately, he moved the pen up along Opeongo Creek to Victoria Lake. From that point, he travelled eastward and northward to Alsever Lake then followed the creek, crossed the hydro line, and made his way on over to the west corner of West Bonnechere Lake.

"When you walked your way through the 150 miles of heavy forest, stony crags, and rocky canyons; creeks and rivers; rapids and waterfalls; marshes and swamps; beaver ponds and loon shit potholes, you had to travel undetected in total silence. You had to sneak through the bush as silently as the shadow of a ghost wolf walking on dew-moistened moss on a foggy morning in a marsh. If you had a partner with you, you'd never ever call out to one another. You communicated with one another using the call of the wild. You'd call out using a wolf howl and your partner would answer with the hoot of a great horned owl. You were careful never to make a sound, never snap a twig or branch; never make a splash; never

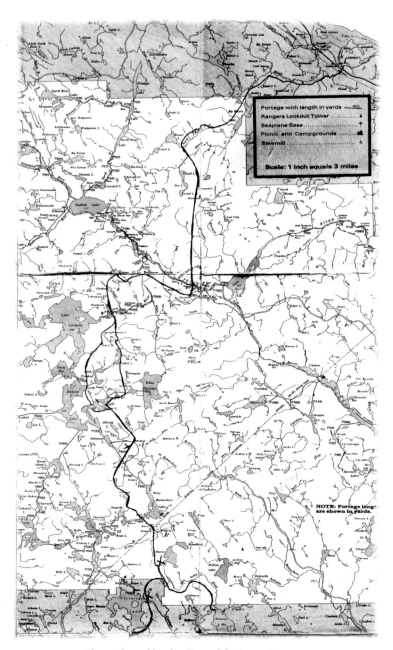

The trail used by the King of the Long Runners
as he crossed Algonquin Park on foot to hunt beaver.

(Map of Algonquin Provincial Park:
By licence, Ontario Ministry of Natural Resources; copyright: Queen's Printer for Ontario, 1961)

Surveying the Kingdom.
(Photo courtesy of the Chartrand family)

stop the flow of water when crossing a beaver dam. The park rangers were not only tuned in to hearing sounds that shouldn't be there but they'd also hear when a sound wasn't there that should be there."

The "Trail of the Long Runners" led him northward from West Bonnechere Lake along the east side of Alluring Lake, thence northerly by the east side of Dickson Lake, on past Hardy Bay, and along the shore of Petite Lake.

"You had to be careful never to walk out in the open. You even had to be careful the light of the sun never flashed off your axe head or your knife blade. When you walked you never stepped on grasses or mosses 'cause that could leave a footprint. You never ever left garbage or even a sign that you had camped and spent a night unless it was a deliberate sign left to throw them off your track. You would step from rock to rock or walk along a fallen log or even walk in the water, making sure you left neither a footprint on the creek bottom nor a wet boot track on a rock."

The "Trail of the Long Runners" led from Petite Lake northeast by way of Lake Lavieille, along Okahan Creek to Little Woodcock Lake, and from there the trail swung east and passed between

Moon Lake and Kawean Lake, crossed a couple of creeks to Wagtail Lake, and on to Eustache Lake.

"When it was really cold and you had to cross an opening, you hung close to the treeline and watched and listened really carefully. You constantly had to keep in mind the angle of the sun to your position so that even the silent stealth of your shadow didn't reveal your presence. You'd just pray to God you didn't have to sneeze or cough or fart; you even controlled your breathing. You always kept your nose and mouth covered so even the steam from your breath wouldn't give you away to the ever-waiting and searching enemy. You really had to know what you were doing and where you were doing it and where you were going and be ready to jump at any given second to change direction at every single step.

"I always carried a take-down model of rifle that you could take apart and put in your pack. Each and every day was spent walking from one wetland to another, because wetlands were where you found beaver. Sometimes they'd be out in the daytime but mostly they would be out and about at daybreak or at dusk. Then you'd sit by the dam and wait for them. You'd never shoot them by the house 'cause if you only wounded them and they got into the house, you might never get them. Beaver in a winter pelt of really late fall or very early spring will float. Their guard hairs are hollow then and the undercoat of wool is light and fluffy and traps air. In the summer they shed out and they will sink."

The next big move was to cross the Petawawa River north of Lake Traverse Station, over to Otterpaw Creek, and on up to Otterpaw Lake. The trail passed east of Reed Lake and crossed over to Bissett Creek and along the west side of Bissett Creek up to Mud Lake.

"It was easy to shoot beaver, but there was no point in shooting them if you couldn't get them. You always tried to shoot beaver close to shore or close to the dam. If it was a good shot, the beaver would die right away. You could always take a long pole from the bush to hook a beaver and pull it to shore. You never cut a pole or whittled anything to leave any sign of a fresh cut or chips to signal you were in the area. A bad shot, and you had a floating beaver or red blood in the snow and either was a dead giveaway.

Beaver boards with pelts stretched to dry.
(Photo courtesy Chartrand family)

Whatever beaver you did shoot, you tied together and sunk them in the water. You only kept out one at a time to skin. If you kept beaver out overnight, you could soon have wolves or a spring bear ready to take them from you, and if hungry enough, they'd kill you for the beaver. Your night was then spent huddled by a small, smokeless fire skinning beaver all night. Once you sat at the edge of the water at dusk, you could be pretty sure the rangers, wherever they were, would be settled for the night. If I had to make a dash I could go. You can travel in the dark when you are on the run, 'cause you can run anywhere. You can't track someone very well in the dark. Once you had fired several shots at night, you knew you had to clear out early in the morning, because the rangers had probably heard those shots for several miles. You can hear a rifle shot a long way on a clear, cold night.

"Regardless of the weather, you had to try and stay dry. If you got wet, you could freeze; you could die. More than once I stripped down to my bare hide and crossed a creek or river with my clothes, my gun, and my pack lashed to a pole that I held high over my head. When I got to the other side, I'll tell you, you didn't waste any time dryin' off—you just got dressed. You had to be a man them times, and a goddamned good one if you were to survive. Mind you, there were lots of times you were so damn cold you had to feel your crotch to see if you were Agnes or Angus."

The trail moved north from Mud Lake, crossed the park boundary, then followed down Bissett Creek to Adelard and thence up the creek to the settlement of Bissett Creek, where arrangements had been made to go to a house where for a fee you'd get a ride across the Ottawa River into the Province of Quebec to sell the green pelts.

"The life of a park trapper wasn't easy. The dirtier the weather, the colder the temperature, the tougher the terrain, the more it rained or snowed, that was the best time, place, and conditions to travel. The ranger could stay in his cabin. I didn't have a roof over my head or a stove or a bunk. I didn't have food to eat but for maybe a bit of flour, some sugar, tea, and whatever beaver tails I'd shoved into my back pockets to cook over the skinning fire at night. If I got injured or killed, nobody was coming to find me. Nobody would admit I was in the park. I was on my own . . . totally on my own . . . just me and my Maker; and my Maker looked after me.

"I trapped the park for sixty years and I never got caught. I lived the best way I knew how. The king gave the beaver to my ancestors, and like I said, I got my share.

"The park rangers ran my ass off for taking a few beaver. I harvested beaver in the park for sixty years and you'd never know I was there. By the time they got done runnin' ya, Jesus, you'd be so damn thin, if you stuck your tongue out you'd look like a zipper.

"That was only half the trip. After a week's rest, you'd head back through the park and trap your way home. The reverse trip was pretty much the same route but for a stopover at the root house on White Partridge Creek. Once you made your way back through the park to Highway 60, you'd get picked up and get a drive to Parry Sound to sell your beaver pelts in a small upstairs room over a store on the main street. That was the end of the trail. When the money was in your pocket, you knew you had reached the end of the trail."

Once upon a Time

The spring and summer, the autumn and winter had come and gone for several decades. I had travelled north seeking answers to the question, "What went ye out into the wilderness to see?" I had lived the life; I had walked the mile; I had learned the way. Life with Trapper truly had been a "Once upon a time" story. Each year, there was a lifetime of love for the beauty and the beast; the princess and the pauper who lived in the magical log castle in the mystical kingdom of the forest.

The season was autumn. More than four decades had passed. I had spent twenty-one years with the King of Algonquin Park and twenty-one more with another. I used to always laugh and say the first time around was spent with a trapper who wanted to be a ranger and the second time around was spent with a ranger who wanted to be a trapper. My life had become a story of contrasts. It was the story of the past and of the future; it was the story of the young and of the old; it was the story of the rich and of the poor; it was the story of those who existed on the urban planet and those who thrived in the wilderness wonderland. My life had become the story of contrasting times; of competing attitudes and life-styles. This was a tale of two lives; of two worlds. It was at times the worst of times, it was at times the best of times; it was the age of my foolishness, it was the age of his wisdom; it was the time of absolute incredulity, it was the time of new-found belief; there was indeed a season of darkness, and there was indeed a season of light; every winter I survived despair, every spring I searched for hope; there were definitely times in life when there was nothing before us, and there were definitely times in life when we had everything before us.

Life had been exciting and adventuresome. I had been a partner in full, and yes, life had indeed been fulfilling. Together we had built four log cabins, several canoes, crafted our own paddles and snowshoes and not only lived off the land but lived well and enjoyed living. Trapper had shown me everything the Lord had put on the earth for mankind and he had shown me how to use it and how not to abuse it. Trapper had taught me to have respect for the environment, to stand up and fight for the wilderness domain that is the home to so many creatures that have no voice. He told me, "Go ye out into the wilderness and seek the truth." He taught me not to run away from those "management conspirators," those "honourable men" who would manipulate the truth and attempt to deceive us, but rather to turn and run right at them. Trapper had taught me much of everything I know. I went out into the wilderness to seek the truth. I had lived the very best of times; I had lived the very worst of times. I had survived it all. I would remember. I would try to make a difference.

Trapper had in his lifetime become one of the most notorious and infamous poachers of Algonquin Park. He was known to be one of the most capable and exceptional wilderness survivors ever known to the Ontario Forestry Branch and the Ontario Department of Lands and Forests.

Trapper had a wonderful voice and sang nearly everywhere he went. During the 1940s or 1950s he sang on a live radio show every Friday night from the radio station in North Bay or Sudbury. In the 1960s, he did the segment, *A Day in the Life of a Trapper* for the CBC series, *A Day in the Life Of*. He was also the trapper in the film documentary, *The Beaver Man*. The MNR said he did such a beautiful job in those two documentaries that in the early 1970s he was approached by the Ontario Ministry of Natural Resources to narrate a proposed new documentary they were about to film on moose. For whatever his reason, Trapper declined.

Trapper had for years been the historian at Algonquin Park's Pioneer Logging Museum.

He was a highly sought-after guide in Algonquin Park, having guided tourists from all over the world. He had also guided biologists, geologists, and several ministers of natural resources. A Canadian prime minister and an American president had sat in Trapper's canoe, as had several famous movie stars. John and Janet Foster, well known for their filmed nature documentaries, and even the infamous "Water Walker" had travelled Algonquin Park with Trapper.

Trapper knew the terrain of Algonquin Park as well as he knew the back of his own hand. He had travelled it in every season and had walked or paddled every inch of it. Sitting about a campfire with Trapper, he would relate the tales of canoe trips that took him down the North Branch of the Petawawa River through the Big Thompson and Little Thompson Rapids; the Grillade and Crooked Chute, down the Rollaway and through the Natch; the Schooner Rapids, the Five Mile Rapids, and Crooked Rapids; the Racehorse and White Horse and the Half Mile. He had run the north branch hundreds of times. He had paddled the south branch from Lake Traverse to Black Bay many hundred times. He had crossed the park from Kiosk to Petawawa and from the Oxtongue to the Bissett. During his travels, his pack had become filled with knowledge that he was only too happy to share with schoolchildren, Boy Scouts, Girl Guides, and Junior Rangers; and with university and college students who would in the future manage the environment, as well as with the new young generation of trappers who would humanely manage wildlife populations.

Trapper was idealistic, compassionate, and honourable. He had a rather peculiar sense of honour. He'd take the shirt off your back if you weren't wearing it and give it to someone who needed it. At the same time, he'd take the shirt off his own back and give it to you if you needed it. He was, to say the least, a man among men. There were those who loved him and those who hated him but everyone had a healthy respect for him.

I had returned to Wakami to revisit my life, to revisit the beautiful pristine wilderness that was now only a memory. I had driven through the clear-cuts that now surrounded Wakami Provincial Park. Everything is clear-cut right to the park boundaries. Having driven through the raped forest that was now a mere slash and tangle of logging debris and blowdown, I found myself sitting alone on the shore of Wakami Lake, looking across the silent waters; looking back in time; looking deep into my heart.

The princess, sleeping beauty, was in a deep slumber, curled within the folds of the arctic sleeping bag on a round pole bunk in the magical log castle. From some distant time sector, a lonely, plaintive cry filtered through the depths of sleep to announce the

Emmett Chartrand at pioneer logging exhibit, Algonquin Park, ca. 1967.
(Photo courtesy Chartrand family)

dawn of a new day. My eyelids struggled against some unknown force that dared to hold them shut tight. I stretched the full length of the sleeping bag until cold nipped at my toes. Quickly they recoiled to my warm body and in protest I drew the folds of the sleeping bag back about my neck. My eyes once more gave way to that involuntary force and I sighed, "Just ten minutes more?"

Again, that eerie call from afar lured me from the peaceful depths. Nature surely seemed to be laughing at my comfort. She beckoned again and again, calling,

"Come on, get up! Come on, get up!"

From mist-enshrouded ponds she laughed, ushering in the cheer of the new morn. Mother Nature, too, must have heard the call, as morning flickered a golden light up over the eastern hills, bringing life to the day. Her children, all in green finery, lined the shore and bade good morning by nodding their heads in a whispered breeze that was escort to a milky film hanging as drapery over this mural painted by God alone. As Mother Nature exhaled, the mists drifted, the masterpiece was unveiled, black, quiet waters mirrored lacy hemlock and tamarack, fluorescent poplar and birch, and maples hot with fire from a sun dripping flames to the waking earth.

"Come on, get up! Come on, get up!"

I sat where the cabin door had once been and I looked out across Wakami Lake to the far pine shores. A sense of pride and longing welled up in my heart. I stared out to the far shores, looking for the flash of a paddle blade, for any sign of my prince who would not return. A vision emerged from the depths of the clear waters. It was as a vision in a crystal ball. He was there, the pauper become king. Slipping a foot beneath the gunwale of the canoe, he flipped it upright. The canoe slipped into the water until just the tip hung onto the shore. He lifted the canoe out into the water and, stepping into it, he remained erect and paddled slowly, almost motionlessly, across the bay, around the point, and out of sight.

He noticed a tiny school of diving ducks frolicking off the island in the bay. They would glide along the surface with their heads bobbing back and forth like a child's wind-up toy. Suddenly they would upend in a maze of bubbles and flying water to disappear below the surface. Scanning the water, he made a game of trying to predict just where they would emerge but they never ceased to amaze him by turning up in the most unexpected places, puncturing the watery reflection to look directly at him. In an unexpected but urgent upheaval they took to the water on foot and, like a team of miniature sprinters on a hurdle track, they raced along the water, took to the air, circled once, and were gone.

He sat motionlessly in the canoe and watched a beaver swim along the shore until it came to a hemlock hanging out over the water. He propelled the canoe forward, never removing the paddle from the water and not making so much as a ripple in the water or a drip to stir the air.

The bay through which he paddled was mainly flooded land. Stumps, deadheads, and roots all came close to the surface and at times touched the belly of the canoe. There was a multitude of black stubs standing upright in the water. Not a ripple disturbed the water. The hills to the west were reflected in greens and yellows, a vision of exquisite skill created by the great Architect of the universe.

Movement caught his eye. One of those black stubs was bobbing up and down in the water like a floating pop bottle — a coughing, spitting, bobbing, floating pop bottle. Two other stubs bobbed and swam away. The largest of the three remained and sat erect in the water. It was long of neck, had a wide, flat head, with grey bristles about the mouth and seal-like whiskers. It looked for all the world like a miniature sea monster. It was a she-otter with her two young.

He sat and studied the bottom of the bay. It was sandy and covered in sticks and bark. Long-leafed weeds grew in clumps here and there among the deadheads and sunken logs that were all a tangle beneath the canoe. As he approached, there was a loud slap on the water, and a long, yellow poplar branch slipped beneath the surface.

The beaver house was built against the side of the bank supported by the trunk of a long fallen hemlock. It was massively constructed of sticks all cleaned of their bark and well-packed in layer after layer of mud. The current layer was not yet complete, and a trail was visible up each side of the house, where the beaver had been busily portaging this new layer of plaster. In front of the house, there was the beginning of a new supply of fresh feed. Poplar and birch branches pierced through the surface; the wilted leaves twisting and turning in the breeze reminded me of cocoons. As they twirled about, and the sun glistened from the undersides, they resembled the shiny glass balls that adorn the Christmas tree. The noon sun danced on the rippling waters, and the aroma of pine permeated the air. Quiet ruled supreme.

The days were cold and clear, the ponds and bays were frozen, and the geese were on the wing. He looked skyward to the undulating "V" and listened to the mellow honk, honk of the flying wedge. He stopped for lunch at the head of the lake. The small clearing had at one time been the entrance to an old portage road. Now spruce and balsam lined the jagged edges of its treeline. Snow covered the two deep ruts that had been cut into the soil by horse-drawn wagons decades ago. The creek wound about between rock outcroppings and into alder swamps. There was the whisper of pine, the laughter of poplar, the hinting rustle of a marten sneaking among tamarack, the thud of a pine cone hitting the ground, and the cursory chatter of a red squirrel from above. In the beaver hay of the swamp, he could hear ducks splashing and the humming of beaver cutting feed up the trail. The meandering footprints left by a fox trotted through the black spruce. The arrowhead trail of a partridge darted from pine to spruce to balsam and along a fallen log. A mink ran its humpbacked way along the entangled flood wood at the mouth of the creek. A muskrat dragged a snake-like tail up onto a floating log to chew on an alder twig, and deep troughs in the snow scooped their way from the water's edge and along the portage where otters had made their way. All of his friends were here, as though it were a preplanned rendezvous. He tossed a crust to the grey jay sitting just above his head.

As he thought back over the more than seventy years he had been in the forest, he paddled and continued to search the hanging banks and rocky islands for sign of beaver. Dusk settled down over the lake, darkness closed in, and the wind died down. A long, lonesome howl prowled the hilltops, calling all the night life together. There was no song of the birds, no hum of the pines, and no lap of water in the flood wood. It was as if the very earth had stopped breathing.

Three spruce spires were silhouetted in the full white face of God as He lovingly looked down on His darkened world. The howl of wolves filled the air with music. The cold winds had blown, and the deep snows had come yet again, bringing with them the time for the long sleep. A cloud passed over his face, the moonlight dimmed from his eyes and rain trickled from the crow's feet at the corners of his eyes and down his weathered cheeks. Falling frost touched his cheek as God kissed him goodnight and called,

"Come on, get up.

"Come on,

"Come home."

Journey's End

Trapper setting a beaver trap under the ice.
(Photo by Paton Lodge Lindsay)

The brilliant hardwood colours had given way to the cooling temperatures of approaching autumn in September of 2000. The mallards quacked in the swamp; the Canada geese honked from high above on their southbound journey. It was that time of year: the time for the fall beaver run in Algonquin Park.

The day he had thought about for so many years had finally come. The Last Voyageur, the King of the Long Runners, the King of Algonquin Park, was about to make the final traverse through his kingdom of Algonquin Park. At the spot where the Petawawa River empties into Lake Traverse, in the hush of this wilderness where the only sound to be heard was the rushing of water flowing over the rocks on its way to its final destination, in the silence of this now sacred moment, the little wooden canoe that contained his ashes was set into the waters of the Petawawa River. The king had begun his final journey through Algonquin Park.

The miniature canoe carrying his ashes was carried on the wind down Lake Traverse past the island, through the narrows of the Petawawa River. It picked up speed as it was drawn into the waters coursing through where the old logging dam had been, then down the Big Thompson Rapids and the Little Thompson Rapids, onward through the Grillade Rapids and Crooked Chute, down through the Rollaway Rapids. The little canoe coursed through the Natch, then the Schooner Rapids and Five Mile Rapids. It slowed as it drifted through the calmer waters of Whitson Lake and Smith Lake, McManus and Montgomery lakes, thence on through the Crooked Rapids, and floated on the current down past Forks Island where the forks of the North Branch and the South Branch of the Petawawa River meet. The little wooden canoe then made its way across the Petawawa River to Black Bay, where it came to rest on the sandy shore in front of the old log house of his Voyageur grandfather, Michel Chartrand.

Will the circle be unbroken? Life had brought him full circle. He had made his last run through Algonquin Park. No one knew he was there. He had travelled undetected as a ghost wolf meandering through the fog on a misty moonlit morning in Algonquin Park. Our Father had called him: "Come on, get up; come on, come home."

Nearly four hundred years ago, his ancestors had set out on a journey that would carry the genes of King Charlemagne to the shores of Nouvelle France. The royal blood of kings is carried in succeeding generations. A paternal fourth-great-grandmother, Charlotte Bayard, had passed the royal genes to him, and his children would pass those royal genes on to the next generation of Canadienne. The Fleur-de-lis, the symbol of the living king, would continue to fly over the lands of his ancestors, the lands of Nouvelle France.

"Though I walk among you, you know not who I am."

Journey's End

I'm going on a journey; my pack's outside the door,
I'm not taking a lot with me; I won't need it anymore.
The fall is now upon us; what better time to go?
I'll get to where I'm going before the winter snow.
So think of me in kindness; have a laugh or two,
I'm picking up my pack; my journey here is through.
If your heart is heavy, go to Lake Traverse,
Look into the mists and the moonlight,
my memories are resting there.[18]

Goin' on a Journey.
(Painting by Paton Lodge Lindsay)

This is my Father's world,
The battle is not done.
Jesus who died
Shall be satisfied,
And Earth and heaven be one.[19]

Endnotes

1   Rev. Maltbie D. Babcock , 1901.

2   G. Tersteegen (1779); translated by Bishop F.W. Foster, Rev. J. Miller, (1789), and Rev. W. Mercer (1854).

3   Rev. Maltbie D. Babcock.

4   Trapper is referring to the fact that you could find the same item in several different stores, and all at different prices.

5   This translates to $50,000 today.

6   Margaret Embers McGee, 1918.

7   Rev. Maltbie D. Babcock.

8   Genesis 7:9.

9   Author unknown.

10   Composer anonymous; *http://www.lib.utk.edu/music/songdb*

11   A green stick or branch.

12   In 1988, that two-and-a-half bushels was worth ninety-five dollars.

13   A type of "crap fish."

14   The beaver castors (perineal sacs) provide a fluid called castoreum, which is used in making some medicine and perfumes, and it is approved by the U.S. Food and Drug Administration for use in some artificial fruit flavours, candy, iced tea, yogurt, and ice cream.

15   Origin unknown; sung since the 1930s.

16   Psalm 65: 7.

17   Rev. Maltbie D. Babcock

18   Jane Ann Chartrand, only daughter of the King.

19   Rev. Maltbie D. Babcock

Sources and Permissions

Prologue:

Map of Nouvelle France: Licenced under the Commons:
GNU Free Documentation Licence Version 1.2

Chapter 2:

Leneuf family history: John DuLong, PhD; *http://habitant.org/leneuf*

Capel Pioneers:
   http://genforum.genealogy.com/capel/messages/137.html

Voyageur ancestors: Centre du patrimoine **shsb@shsb.mb.ca**
   (Gilles Lesage)

Value of 1200 livres 1805: Gerry Lalonde; freepages.genealogy.
   http://rootsweb.ancestry.com

Hunault/Radisson/Groseilliers: *http://voyageurs.shsb.mb.ca*

Chartrand Genealogies:

   Thomas I Chartrand:
   http://www.nosorigines.qc.ca/GenealogieQuebec.
   aspx?genealogy=Thomas_Chartrand&pid=886&lng=en&partID=887

   Thomas II Chartrand:
   http://www.nosorigines.qc.ca/GenealogieQuebec.
   aspx?genealogy=Chartrand_Thomas&pid=888&lng=en

   Charles-Jean Chartand: *http://www.nosorigines.qc.ca/*
   GenealogieQuebec.aspx?genealogy=Chartrand_Charles-
   Jean&pid=891&lng=en

Organization of fur trade; Canadian Museum of Civilization;
   The Fur Trade.
   http://www.civilization.ca/cmc/exhibitions/hist/canp1/ca12eng.shtml

Chapter 42:

Charlotte Bayard, royal descent from King Charlemagne:
   http://www.royalblood.co.uk/D329/I329248.html

Charlotte Bayard,
   marriage 12 November 1731 to Charles-Francois-Jacques Labelle:
   http://www.nosorigines.qc.ca/GenealogieQuebec.
   aspx?genealogy=Charlotte_Bayard&pid=330366&Ing=en

Francoise-Marie-Marguerite Labelle,
   marriage on 27 February 1786 to Jean-Baptiste-Marie Chartrand:
   http://www.nosorigines.qc.ca/GenealogieQuebec.
   aspx?genealogy=Labelle_Marie-Francoise&pid=102281&lng=en

About the Author

Paton Lodge Lindsay
(Photo by Keith Harlen Hoback)

Paton Lodge Lindsay was born in Toronto, Ontario, Canada. Her interests have always been in the out-of-doors. She attributes her very early introduction to nature to the days spent with her grandfather in his canoe, and her lifetime love and respect for nature to Trapper. She always travels with camera or palette in hand and has won several photography awards. Paton's photography credits include several magazine covers and a fire poster for the Ontario Ministry of Natural Resources and Ontario Forestry Association. It has been said of her wilderness painting that she "captured the soul of the earth." Although shy and pleasingly quiet, both her enthusiasm and knowledge of the bush come to life once in her wilderness domain.

Over the years, Paton has sat on the executive of several trappers' councils and local citizens' forest management advisory committees. She has rescued numerous wild animals, nurturing and even vetting them when required before returning them to the wild. Paton has always been concerned with the well-being of wildlife and habitat and has for decades been a constructive activist opposing the massive clear-cuts that in her opinion leave only the perception of wilderness. Due to her major concerns vis-à-vis the loss of wildlife habitat and the destruction of the environment, due in her opinion to forest management policies, she made several addresses to environmental assessment hearings, including a major presentation to the Class Environmental Assessment for Timber Management on Crown Lands in Ontario (EA87/02, 1990). Paton was the only woman in Canada to sit on the National Firearms Advisory Council to the Solicitor General of Canada at the time of its inception in 1979.

Paton is a published writer with many poems, short stories, and environmental pieces in newspapers and magazines.

King of Algonquin Park is her first book.

TO ORDER MORE COPIES:

GENERAL STORE PUBLISHING HOUSE INC.
499 O'Brien Road, Renfrew, Ontario, Canada K7V 3Z3
Tel 1.800.465.6072 • Fax 1.613.432.7184
www.gsph.com